Anonymous

The Scottish Celtic Review

Vol. 1

Anonymous

The Scottish Celtic Review
Vol. 1

ISBN/EAN: 9783337297855

Printed in Europe, USA, Canada, Australia, Japan

Cover: Foto ©ninafisch / pixelio.de

More available books at **www.hansebooks.com**

THE
SCOTTISH CELTIC
REVIEW.

CONTENTS.   No. 1.   MARCH, 1881.

PAGE

I.—Introductory Remarks: Place of Celtic in the Indo-European Family of Languages   Tests of Etymological Affinity—Grimm's Law—Illustrations of the Application of Grimm's Law, - - 1

II.—Indo-European Roots, with Derivatives and Analysis of some Gaelic Compound Words, - - - - - - - - 21

III.—The Laws of Auslaut in Irish.   First Part, - - - - - 28

IV.—Grammatical and Etymological Analysis of Gen. i. 1-8, - - - 40

V.—Specimen of Old Gaelic: St. Patrick's Hymn, with Translation and Analysis of part of Hymn, - - - - - - - - 49

VI. West Highland Tale: How the Tuairisgeul Mor was put to Death, with Translation, - - - - - - - - - - 61

VII.—Gaelic Song by John Macdonald (Iain Lom), the Keppoch Bard, - 77

VIII.—Notes on Gaelic Grammar and Orthography, - - - - - 78

IX.—Gaelic Air: "Coire-a'-Cheathaich," or "The Corrie of the Mist," - 80

GLASGOW:
PRINTED BY ROBERT MACLEHOSE, 153 WEST NILE ST.
MACLACHLAN & STEWART, EDINBURGH.
TRÜBNER & CO., LONDON.

1881.

Price to Subscribers 10s. for four Numbers.

TO OUR SUBSCRIBERS.

WITHIN a few weeks after the circular announcing our intention of starting, if sufficiently supported, a quarterly periodical specially devoted to subjects connected with the Language, Literature, and Antiquities of the Scottish Highlands, was issued, a large number of subscribers was secured. It became necessary, however, to defer issuing the first number until a considerable amount of material was prepared for publication. That having now been done, we expect to be able to keep up, for a time at least, a quarterly issue with some degree of regularity. Perfect regularity, however, cannot be guaranteed; for the labour connected with the conducting of a publication of this kind is too great, and the time at our disposal for such work is too limited, to justify our giving definite assurances.

In conducting the *Review*, we shall aim at accomplishing the following objects:—

1. To apply to the study of Gaelic those methods of investigation which have been so fruitful in results when applied to other languages, such as German and English. To study a modern language successfully, one must avail himself not only of the direct light thrown upon it by what may be called its former

self, but also of the side light furnished by related languages. To understand aright, for example, many of the forms and idioms of Modern English, it is necessary not only to go back to Middle and Old English, but also to consult Gothic and other languages of the same family. It is by a process precisely similar that we obtain accurate knowledge of many of the forms and idioms of the Gaelic language.

2. To furnish English readers, by means of translations, with an opportunity of forming some estimate of the extent and value of our Gaelic literature.

3. To collect the various fragments of unwritten literature preserved in the memories of the people of the Highlands.

4. To collect the numerous Gaelic words current in the different districts of the Highlands, but which have not hitherto found a place in our vocabularies.

5. To record and to help to interpret our Gaelic names of places.

6. To correct the orthographical and other errors by which written Gaelic has been altered and obscured so as to be, in many cases, no longer recognisable. Correct organic orthography must form the basis of the accurate study of Gaelic. To hold, therefore, as some do, that one mode of writing a Gaelic word is as good as another, is to make short work with scientific Gaelic etymology.

As some may think that Philology has received too much attention in our first number, it may be stated that more space will be devoted in future numbers to Gaelic literature, including translations.

Papers on the following Subjects will appear in early numbers:—

I. GAELIC PHILOLOGY.
   1. Affinity of the Celtic and Teutonic Languages.
   2. Indo-European Roots with Gaelic and other Derivatives.
   3. The letter P in Celtic. First Paper on the loss of P.
   4. The Gaelic Vowels and Vowel-changes.
   5. Etymology of the Irregular Verbs.
   6. Evidence of Etymological Affinity furnished by Comparative Grammar. First Paper on Gradation, or the Degrees of Comparison in Gaelic.
   7. Examples of False Etymology.

II. GAELIC ORTHOGRAPHY AND GRAMMAR.
   1. Orthographical and Grammatical Errors with Corrections, intended as a help to the correct writing of Gaelic.
   2. Grammatical Analysis and Discussion of Idioms.
   3. Ancient Forms retained in modern Gaelic.
   4. Eclipsis of Consonants.

III. TOPOGRAPHY.
   Topographical Jottings.

IV. ARCHÆOLOGY.

V. LITERATURE.
   1. Specimens of ancient Gaelic, with Translations.
   2. Specimens of old Gaelic Ballads, with Translations.
   3. Gaelic Tales, with Translations.
   4. Ossian's Poems correctly written, with literal Translation
   5. Specimens of Gaelic Songs, with Music and Translations.
   6. Gaelic Proverbs, with Translations.
   7. Account of Gaelic Printed Books.

VI. NOTICES OF RECENT PUBLICATIONS.

GLASGOW:
Printed at the University Press,
BY ROBERT MACLEHOSE.
EDINBURGH: MACLACHLAN & STEWART.
LONDON: TRÜBNER & CO.

Scottish Celtic Review,

No. 1.—MARCH, 1881.

CONTENTS.

I. Introductory Remarks: Place of Celtic in the Indo-European Family of Languages Tests of Etymological Affinity—Grimm's Law—Illustrations of the Application of Grimm's Law.

II. Indo-European Roots, with Derivatives and Analysis of some Gaelic Compound Words.

III. The Laws of Auslaut in Irish. First Part.

IV. Grammatical and Etymological Analysis of Gen. i. 1-8.

V. Specimen of Old Gaelic: St. Patrick's Hymn, with Translation and Analysis of part of Hymn.

VI. West Highland Tale: How the Tuairisgeul Mòr was put to Death, with Translation.

VII. Gaelic Song by John Macdonald (Iain Lom), the Keppoch Bard.

VIII. Notes on Gaelic Grammar and Orthography.

IX.- Gaelic Air: "Coire-a'-Cheathaich," or "The Corrie of the Mist."

THE SCOTTISH CELTIC REVIEW.

No. 1.—MARCH, 1881.

INTRODUCTORY REMARKS: PLACE OF CELTIC IN THE INDO-EUROPEAN FAMILY OF LANGUAGES—TESTS OF ETYMOLOGICAL AFFINITY—GRIMM'S LAW—ILLUSTRATIONS OF THE APPLICATION OF GRIMM'S LAW.

The Celtic tongues consist of two main divisions—the Gaedhelic and the British or Kymric. The former comprises the Irish, the Gaelic of the Highlands and Western Islands of Scotland, and Manx, still spoken in the Isle of Man; the latter comprises Welsh, Cornish, now extinct, and Armorican, still spoken in Brittany.

Celtic belongs to the Indo-European or Aryan family of speech. The other members of this family are—1. Sanskrit, the ancient classical or learned language of the Hindus; 2. Zend, the sacred language of the Zoroastrians, and, as most closely allied to it, the old Persian and the Armenian; 3. Greek and Albanian; 4. the Italian languages, including Latin, Umbrian, and Oscan; 5. the Slavonic and Lithuanian languages; and 6. the Teutonic languages, comprising (1) Old, Middle, and New High German, (2) the Low German branch, including Gothic, Anglo-Saxon, Old Dutch, Old Frisian, and Old Saxon, with their modern representatives, English, Low German, Frisian, and Dutch, and (3) the Scandinavian branch, including Icelandic, Swedish, and Danish.

The place of Celtic in this family has been a subject of much controversy among philologists. Schleicher holds[1] that it is most

[1] Cf. *Comp. der Vergl. Gramm. der Indo-German. Spr.* 4th ed., p. 6, and also Kuhn's *Beitr. zur Vergl. Spr.* i. p. 437.

closely allied to the Graeco-Italic division, and more especially to Latin. The following diagram represents his view as to the division of the Indo-European family of speech. The length of the lines indicates "the duration of the periods, their distances from one another, and the degrees of relationship":—

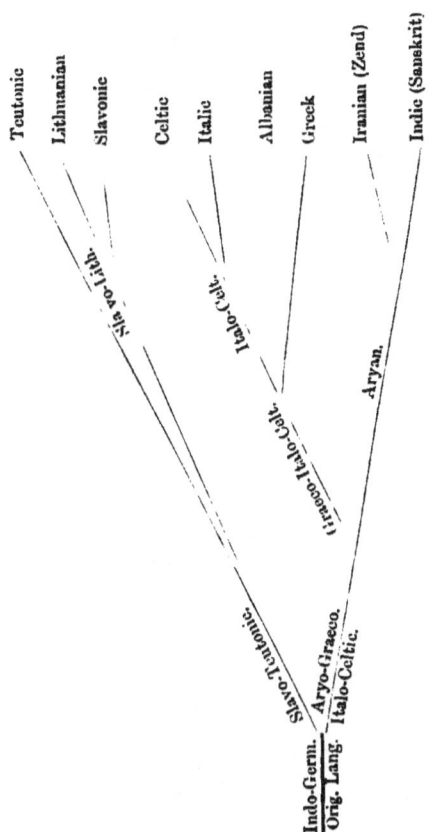

Schleicher's view as to the close affinity of Celtic and Latin is based chiefly on the remarkable agreement of these languages in several of their grammatical inflections; as, for example, in the termination of the dative plural in *b* (cf. *bráithrib* and *fratribus*). The common termination *i* for both the genitive singular and nominative plural of a large class of nouns (cf. *báird* = *bardi

THE SCOTTISH CELTIC REVIEW.

No. 1.—MARCH, 1881.

INTRODUCTORY REMARKS: PLACE OF CELTIC IN THE INDO-EUROPEAN FAMILY OF LANGUAGES—TESTS OF ETYMOLOGICAL AFFINITY—GRIMM'S LAW—ILLUSTRATIONS OF THE APPLICATION OF GRIMM'S LAW.

The Celtic tongues consist of two main divisions—the Gaedhelic and the British or Kymric. The former comprises the Irish, the Gaelic of the Highlands and Western Islands of Scotland, and Manx, still spoken in the Isle of Man; the latter comprises Welsh, Cornish, now extinct, and Armorican, still spoken in Brittany.

Celtic belongs to the Indo-European or Aryan family of speech. The other members of this family are—1. Sanskrit, the ancient classical or learned language of the Hindus; 2. Zend, the sacred language of the Zoroastrians, and, as most closely allied to it, the old Persian and the Armenian; 3. Greek and Albanian; 4. the Italian languages, including Latin, Umbrian, and Oscan; 5. the Slavonic and Lithuanian languages; and 6. the Teutonic languages, comprising (1) Old, Middle, and New High German, (2) the Low German branch, including Gothic, Anglo-Saxon, Old Dutch, Old Frisian, and Old Saxon, with their modern representatives, English, Low German, Frisian, and Dutch, and (3) the Scandinavian branch, including Icelandic, Swedish, and Danish.

The place of Celtic in this family has been a subject of much controversy among philologists. Schleicher holds[1] that it is most

[1] Cf. *Comp. der Vergl. Gramm. der Indo-German. Spr.* 4th ed., p. 6, and also Kuhn's *Beitr. zur Vergl. Spr.* i. p. 437.

closely allied to the Graeco-Italic division, and more especially to Latin. The following diagram represents his view as to the division of the Indo-European family of speech. The length of the lines indicates "the duration of the periods, their distances from one another, and the degrees of relationship":—

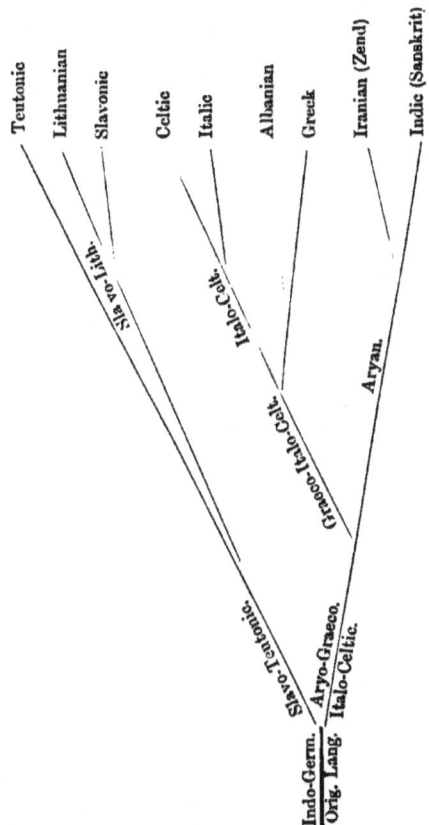

Schleicher's view as to the close affinity of Celtic and Latin is based chiefly on the remarkable agreement of these languages in several of their grammatical inflections; as, for example, in the termination of the dative plural in *b* (cf. *bráithrib* and *fratribus*). The common termination *i* for both the genitive singular and nominative plural of a large class of nouns (cf. *báird* = **bardi*

and *domini*) is another striking instance of this agreement. Ebel, on the other hand, in his papers on the position of Celtic, published in Kuhn's *Beiträge zur Vergleichenden Sprachforschung*, ii. 137, holds that it is most closely allied to the Teutonic languages. This theory is based on the agreement of the Celtic diphthongs, *ai, oi, au, iu*, with the Teutonic diphthongs, *ai, ei, au, iu*, and on other grounds to which it is unnecessary to refer in these introductory remarks. The conclusion to which an examination of the arguments adduced on both sides of this controversy seems to lead is, that, whilst Celtic is undoubtedly closely allied to the Teutonic languages, it stands in the closest relationship to Greek and Latin, but especially to Latin.

In judging of the affinity of languages, grammar furnishes the most reliable criterion. The English language, for example, is derived from many sources, it being estimated that less than one third of its vocabulary is Anglo-Saxon; but, nevertheless, its grammatical inflexions and other features show that it is essentially a Teutonic language.

This remark on the importance of grammar, as a criterion of relationship, applies with special force to the Celtic tongues, in which it is often difficult, and sometimes even impossible, to distinguish between genuine Celtic words and loan-words, which have for centuries borne the stamp and discharged the functions of words of native growth. In judging, therefore, of the affinity of Celtic to the other branches of the Indo-European family, and, more especially, in determining its place in the family, philologists have based their conclusions chiefly on evidence furnished by a comparative examination of the grammatical forms, which Celtic and the other languages of the family possess in common. This evidence will be considered in future papers.

The other principal source from which the evidence of this affinity is derived, is a comparative examination of the vocabularies of the languages, the mutual relationship of which is to be ascertained. This evidence, although less definite and conclusive than that furnished by comparative grammar, is, nevertheless, of great value, when the examination is rightly conducted. A comparison, for example, of the Celtic, Latin, and Gothic vocabularies may be sufficient to establish the fact, that these languages have sprung from a common source, although it may not enable us to ascertain the precise degree of their relationship to one another.

To render this comparative examination, however, of any real value, it is necessary that it should be carried on subject to certain rules and conditions, some of which we shall now state :—

1. It is necessary to distinguish carefully between original and loan-words, since, in judging of etymological affinity, the latter cannot be taken into account. The Latin word *caput*, for example, and the English words *capital*, *chapter*, and *captain*, are evidently connected, but that does not help us to prove that Latin and English are cognate languages; for we know that *capital* is borrowed directly from the Latin, from which also *chapter* and *captain* are derived indirectly through the medium of the Norman French. To prove the affinity of Latin and English from a comparison of their vocabularies, we must find the representatives of Latin words among genuine English words, or words of Anglo-Saxon origin. The English representative of *caput* must, therefore, be sought for among English words of purely Teutonic origin.

To prove, therefore, from a comparison of their vocabularies that Gaelic and English are etymologically related, our examination must be restricted to that portion of the Gaelic vocabulary which is purely Celtic, and to that portion of the English vocabulary which is purely Anglo-Saxon. It is not sufficient for this purpose to prove that such Gaelic words as *mìorbhuil*, *beannachd*, *umhal*, *coisreagadh*, and *aoradh* are connected with such English words as *miracle*, *benediction*, *humble*, *consecration*, and *adoration*; for we know that *mìorbhuil* and *miracle* are derived from Lat. *mirus*, *beannachd* and *benediction* from Lat. *benedictio*, *umhal* and *humble* from Lat. *humilis*, *coisreagadh* and *consecration* from Lat. *consecratio*, and *aoradh* and *adoration* from Lat. *adoratio*. Comparisons like these are of no value in determining relationship; and yet few of our Celtic countrymen are aware of the consequences which would result from a rigid application of this principle. A much larger proportion of our Gaelic vocabulary than is generally supposed, is not genuine Celtic, but consists of loan-words, which, from long existence on Celtic soil, have assumed the form, and become subject to the ordinary rules, of Celtic grammar.

2. The words to be compared must be taken in the simplest and oldest forms in which they are accessible. Words are continually changing both in form and meaning; and, therefore, the older the materials on which the etymologist works, the more likely he is to obtain reliable results. A few examples will

suffice to show the importance of this remark. Few would think of tracing the English word *count* (to reckon) to the Lat. word *putare*, which signifies literally *to lop, to prune*, if we had not the French word *compter* (to reckon) and the Lat. word *computare* (to count, reckon) to supply the connecting links. Gael. *bheil* (is) and Eng. *will* are but distantly connected in meaning, and their resemblance in sound is only fitted to mislead; but, nevertheless, they are derived from the same root. *Bheil* is for *bh-feil*, the substantive verb *feil, fil*, eclipsed by *bh* after words which terminated originally in *n*. *Feil* = **feli-* = *velit or *velti (Windisch) is from the root *var=Skr. *var* (choose), Zend *var* (choose), Gr. βούλομαι, Lat. *volo*, Lith. *vel-yju* (I wish), Goth. *val-jan* (choose), A.S. *willan* (to will), Eng. *will*. We would not suppose, at first sight, that the Gaelic word *aobhar* (cause) is derived from the prolific root *ber*, which is cognate with Lat. *fero*, and Gr. φέρω; but by means of older existing forms of the word, the connection may be easily traced. In Gaelic books, published as late as the beginning of this century, *aobhar* was spelled *adhbhar*, and in ancient Gaelic it was written *adbar*, which shows the prefix *ad* (for *aith*) and the root *ber* (=Indo-Europ. *bhar*). The Gaelic word *cunnart* (danger) would not readily be referred to the same root, but when it is known to be an abbreviated form of *cuntabart*, the connection becomes obvious. That the Gaelic word *cuimhne* (memory) is connected with the Lat. word *memini* (to remember) becomes apparent, only when we know that *cuimhne* is the modern form of *cuman* (cf. Stokes' Ir. Gl., p. 127), which is formed by the prefix *cu-* (Lat. *co-*) from the root *man*, connected with the Skr. root *man* (to think) and with the Lat. root *men*, from which *memini* is derived. Nor is the connection with this root (*man*) of such words as *dearmad* (neglect) and *farmad* (envy) obvious, until we become acquainted with their ancient forms. In Old Gaelic, *dearmad* was *dermet* or *dermat*, formed by the prefix *der-* (=*di-air-*) and *met* or *mat* for *men-t* or *man-t*. Similarly, *farmad* or *formad* was in Old Gaelic *format*, formed by the prefix *for-* from *mat*=*man-t*. In Gaelic, *n* is dropped by rule before the tenues *c, t*. The Gaelic word *aithne* (knowledge) has no resemblance to the English word *note*, but by means of the Old Irish form *aithgne*, we can trace it to the root *gen* (to know), with which *note*, from Lat. *nota* for *gnota*, is also connected. These examples, which might be multiplied indefinitely, show how necessary it is for the etymologist to know the oldest existing forms of the words with which he deals. For the purposes of sound Gaelic etymology, therefore, an acquaintance with the archaic forms of Gaelic words is absolutely indispensable. Of these forms vast stores have been preserved to us in the ancient Irish Glosses and Manuscripts.

3. No value, as evidence of affinity, is to be attached to mere resemblance between words in sound and meaning. Professor Max Müller, in one of his lectures on the science of language, has observed that perfect identity of sound between words of various dialects is always suspicious. "It is only in the present century," he remarks, "that etymology has taken its rank as a science, and it is curious to observe that what Voltaire intended as a sarcasm [1] has now become one of its acknowledged principles. Etymology is indeed a science in which identity, or even similarity, whether of sound or meaning, is of no importance whatever. Sound etymology has nothing to do with sound. We know words to be of the same origin which have not a single letter in common, and which differ in meaning as much as black and white. Mere guesses, however plausible, are completely discarded from the province of scientific etymology."—Lects. ii. 267.

We shall add here a few examples of false Gaelic etymology, which have been based on a resemblance between words in sound and meaning:—

Flaitheanas (heaven) is derived in the Gaelic dictionaries from *flath* (noble) and *innis* (an island), and is explained as the "Isle of the noble." The ancient form of this word, *flaithemnas*, shows that it is simply a derivative from *flaithem* (dominus), which is itself derived from *flaith* (imperium), cognate with Gothic *valdan*, Sclav. *vladiti* (imperare), and German *walten* (to govern). *Flaitheanus*, therefore, has nothing to do with *innis* (an island).

Ifrinn (hell) has sometimes been derived from *I-bhròin* (the isle of sorrow). In Armstrong's Dictionary, it is explained as *I-fhuar-fhonn* (the isle of the cold clime). In Old Gaelic, the word is written *iffern* and *ifurnn*, showing that it is a loan-word from Lat. *infernum*, *n* before *f* being dropped by rule in Gaelic.

Coillinn (a candle) is derived in Armstrong's Dictionary from the Gaelic words *coille* (wood) and *teine* (fire). But *coillinn* is

---

[1] "L'étymologie est une science où les voyelles ne font rien, et les consonnes fort peu de chose."

obviously only another form of *coinneal* (a candle), in Old Gaelic *caindel*, a loan-word from Lat. *candela* (a taper or light).

Lòchran (a light, a lamp) is derived in the Highland Society's Dictionary from *lò* (day) and *crann* (a pole or shaft, lit. a tree). In Old Gaelic, *lòchran* was *lòcharn*, clearly a loan-word from Lat. *lucerna* (a lamp).

Réidhlig (a burying-place) is derived in the same dictionary from *réidh* (a plain) and *leac* (a stone, a flat stone). The old form of this word, *reilic*, shows that it is borrowed from Lat. *reliquiae* (remains, relics).

In Armstrong's Dictionary, *Dìseart*, the name of several ecclesiastical places in Scotland, as Dysart in Fifeshire and *Clachan-dìseirt* in Glenorchy, is explained as a corruption of *Ti 's dirde* (the Highest One). It is obviously a loan-word from Lat. *desertum*.

In the same dictionary, *tighearna* (lord) is identified with Gr. τύραννος (lord, master). The old form of this word, *tigerne*, shows that *g*, which, in consequence of the aspiration, is nearly silent in the modern word, is an organic letter, and that *tighearna* is to be referred to the same root as Gaelic *tigh* and *teach*, Lat. *tego*, Gr. τέγος and στέγος, Skr. *sthag*, *sthag-â-mi* (I cover), Ice. *thak* (roof), Ger. *dach*, Eng. *thatch*. For the suffix *erne* = * *ernia* cf. Zeuss' Gramm. Celt., p. 778.

That no reliance can be placed upon similarity in sound and meaning, as a test of affinity, may be further shown from the fact, that words, which have little or no resemblance to each other in either of these respects, may, nevertheless, be etymologically related. This may be shown by a few examples:—

The Gaelic word *Nollaig* (Christmas) and the English *kind* have no resemblance to each other either in meaning or in form; and yet they have sprung from the same root. *Nollaig*, in Old Gaelic *notlaic*, and in Welsh *nadolig*, is a loan-word from the Lat. *natalicia*, a derivative from *natus* for *gnatus*, (root *gen*). This root, again, is connected with the Indo-European root *gan*, to which may be traced Goth. *keinan* (sprout) and *kuni* (race), O.H.G. *chind* (proles), A.S. *cynd* (kind), and Eng. *kind*.

The Gaelic word *beò* (living) and the English word *quick* (speedy) have not one letter in common, and they differ in meaning; but still they have sprung from a common root. *Bèu* was in Old Gaelic *Bíu*, clearly connected with Gr. Βίος for βιϝος, Lat. *vivus* for * *gvivus*, Skr. *giv, givas* (living), Indo-Europ.

* *giv* (to live), Goth *quius*, from stem **qiva-* or *qviva-*, O.H.G. *quëk*, O. N. *kvikv-*, A. S. *cwic*, Eng. *quick* (living, lively, speedy).

The Gaelic word *bean* (wife, woman) and the English word *queen* are dissimilar in both form and meaning; but, nevertheless, they belong to the same root, *gan*, to which we traced *nollaig* and *kind*. *Bean*, in Old Gaelic *ben*, is cognate with the Bœot. βανά for γυνή = *γFανα, connected with Gr. root γεν, Vedic *gná*, later *gani* (woman), which is related to the Skr. root *gan*, Goth. *qvinô quêns*, A. S. *cwen*, Eng. *queen*.

The Gaelic word *bò* and the English word *cow*, although identical in meaning, are dissimilar in form ; but still they belong to the same root. *Bò*, from which *v* has disappeared leaving only a trace of its existence in the long vowel, is connected with Lat. *bos, bovis*, Gr. βοῦς=βοFος, Skr. *gâus* (stem *gav*), Ch. Slav. *gov-edo* (ox), O.H.G. *chuo*, M.H.G. *kuo*, Ger. *kuh*, A.S. *cu*, Eng. *cow*.

These examples of undoubted relationship between words which have little or no resemblance to each other, suffice to show of how little value is mere identity or similarity in sound and meaning as a test of etymological affinity. Not unfrequently, indeed, identity in sound is positive proof of the absence of affinity. The force of this remark will afterwards appear.

4. To prove that languages are etymologically related, it is not sufficient that we succeed in discovering some genuine but isolated examples of cognate words. To have any scientific value, our conclusions must rest upon a sufficiently large induction of instances. Besides, "what etymology professes to teach is no longer merely that one word is derived from another, but how to prove, step by step, that one word was regularly and necessarily changed into another" (Max Müller's Lects. II., 267). Etymology, like other inductive sciences, is a knowledge, not of facts merely, but also, and especially, of principles or laws, by which the facts are explained, and so connected that they fall into their respective places in one regular system. Nor is scientific etymology satisfied until a general law is discovered, by which the subordinate laws are united into a consistent whole, and by which, at the same time, the apparent anomalies are satisfactorily explained.

We shall now apply the foregoing principles.

To prove by a comparison of their vocabularies, that Latin and English, *e.g.*, are cognate languages, all loan-words must be left out of account, and the representatives of Latin words must be sought for among English words of purely Anglo-

Saxon origin. To return to our former example, the representative of Lat. *caput* must be sought for among genuine English words. The English word for *caput* is *head*: are *caput* and *head* also etymologically related? They have no resemblance to each other in form; but, nevertheless, they may have sprung from a common root, for it has been proved that words derived from a common source may differ so widely in form as not to have one letter in common. To ascertain whether or not these words are cognates, we must first trace them to their oldest existing forms. Thus, *head* can be traced to the Anglo-Saxon forms *heafd*, *heafod*, and even to an older related form, the Gothic *haubith*. By comparing these forms with *caput* we discover that, instead of the tenues or hard mutes, *c, p, t,* of the Latin word, the Teutonic words have the corresponding breaths, *h, f (b), th (d)*. But although one instance may suggest, it does not prove a general law. This must rest upon cases sufficiently numerous to justify us in inferring a rule which will apply universally. If, however, we multiply our instances, similar results will be obtained, as may be seen from the following comparisons:—

Lat. *capio* (I take) and Goth. *hafjan* (to lift), A.S. *hefan*, Eng. *heave*;

Lat. *carpo* (I pick, gather fruits) and A.S. *haerfest*, Eng. *harvest*;

Lat. *celo* (I conceal) and Goth. *huljan* (to veil), A.S. *helan*, Eng. *hele* and *hill* (to conceal);

Lat. *clino, inclino* (I bend, incline) and Goth. *hlains* (a hill), A. S. *hlynian* (to lean), Eng. *(h)lean*;

Lat. *cor* (heart; stem *cord-* = Gr. stem καρδ-, κραδ-) and Goth. *hairto*, A.S. *heorte*, Eng. *heart*;

Lat. *cornu* (horn) and Goth. *haurn*, A.S. and Eng. *horn*;

Lat. *decem* (ten) and Goth. *taihun*, A.S. *tyn*, Eng. *ten*;

Lat. *pater* (father) and Goth. *fadar*, A.S. *faeder*, Eng. *father*;

Lat. *pes* (foot; stem *ped-* = Gr. stem ποδ-) and Goth. *fötus*, A.S. *fot*, Eng. *foot*;

Lat. *dens* (tooth; stem *dent-* = Gr. stem -δοντ-) and Goth. *tunthus*, A.S. *toth*, Eng. *tooth*;

Lat. *tepeo* (to be warm, to glow) and A.S. *thefian* (to rage);

Lat. *tego* (to cover) and A.S. *theccan* (to cover) and *thac* (thatch), Eng. *thack* and *thatch*;

Lat. *frater* (brother) and Goth. *bróthar*, A.S. *bródhor*, Eng. *brother*.

To these examples many more might be added; and, therefore, it may be inferred, as a general rule, that the Latin tenues are represented by the corresponding breaths in Gothic and English.

We also see from the above examples (cf. *cor*, stem *cord-* and *hairto*, &c.; *dens*, stem *dent-* and *tunthus*, &c.; *decem* and *taihun*, &c.; *tego* and *theccan*, &c.), that, when the Latin words show the soft mutes *d, g*, the Gothic and English words show the corresponding hard mutes *t, c*. The same result appears if we compare other instances, as—

Lat. *haedus* (goat) and Goth. *gaitei*, A.S. *gaet* and *gat*, Eng. *goat*;

Lat. *duo* (two) and Goth. *tvai*, A.S. *twa*, Eng. *two*;

Lat. *edo* (I eat) and Goth. *ita*, A.S. *ettan*, Eng. *eat*;

Lat. *sedeo* (to sit) and Goth. *sita*, A.S. *sittan*, Eng. *sit*;

Lat. *fagus* (beech) and Goth. *boka* (a book), A.S. *bóc* (beech and book), Eng. *book*;

Lat. *genu* (knee) and Goth. *kniu*, A.S. *cneo*, Eng. *knee*;

Lat. *genus* (kind) and Goth. *keinan* (sprout) and *kuni* (race), A.S. *cyn*, Eng. *kin* and *kind*;

Lat. *gnosco* (I know) and Goth. *kanu*, A.S. *cnawan*, Eng. *ken* and *know*.

We may conclude, therefore, that the Lat. soft mutes, *d, g* are regularly represented by the corresponding hard mutes, *t, c*, in Gothic and English.

According to the rule now stated, we would expect to find Latin *b* represented by *p* in Gothic and English; but "there seems to be absolutely no instance where the Gothic *p* occurs so as to correspond to a Greek and Latin *b*; almost every word that begins with *p* is borrowed from the Greek, and, therefore, corresponds to Greek π" (Peile's Introduction to Gr. and Lat. Etym., p. 126). From this it has been inferred that, except in some onomatopœetic words, *b* was not in use in the original Indo-European language, at least not at the beginning of a word (Peile's Introduction).

Latin has no aspirates, their place being supplied by the breaths *f, h*, which, in the above examples (cf. *frater* and Goth. *bróthar*, &c.; *fagus* and Goth. *boka*, &c.; *haedus* and Goth. *gaitei*, &c.), are represented by the corresponding soft mutes *b, g*, in Gothic and English. But many other instances, showing the same result, might be added, as—

Lat. *fero* (I bear) and Goth. *bairan* (to bear), A.S. *beran*, Eng. *bear*;

Lat. *foro* (I bore) and A.S. *borian* (to bore), Eng. *bore*;

Lat. *fu-* in *fui* (I have been, &c.) and Goth. *bauan* (to dwell), A.S. *bium* (I am), Eng. *be*;

Lat. *hortus* (garden) and Goth. *gards*, A.S. *geard* (enclosure), Eng. *garden*;

Lat. *humus* (the earth), *homo* (man) and Goth. and A.S. *guma* (a man), Eng. *gom* (a man), *-groom* in *bridegroom* = A.S. *bridguma*;

Lat. *veho* (I carry) and Goth. *gavagja* (to move), *végs* (movement), *vigs* (way), A.S. *waegen*, Eng. *waggon*.

In these examples the Latin breaths *f*, *h* represent the corresponding aspirates φ, χ, in Greek (cf. *frater* and φράτηρ; *fagus* and φηγός; *fero* and φέρω, *foro* and φαρόω, *fu-i* and φύ-ω, *hortus* and χόρτος, *humus* and χαμαί, *veho* and ἐχ- for Fεχ-). But we find also that the Gr. aspirate θ is represented in Latin by *f*, especially at the beginning of words, as, for example, in *foris* (door), *ferus* (wild) and *fera* (a wild animal), *fumus* (smoke), *rufus* (red), compared with Gr. θύρα (a door), θήρ (a wild animal), θύω (I sacrifice, &c.), θύος (a sacrifice), and θύμος (soul, breath), ἐρυθρός (red). This *f*, which represents an Indo-European *dh*, corresponds to *d* in Gothic and English, as may be seen by comparing *foris* and Goth. *daur*, A.S. *duru*, Eng. *door*; *fera* and A.S. *deor*, Eng. *deer*; *fumus* and Goth. *dauns* (odour), A.S. and Eng. *dust*; *rufus* and Goth. *rauds*, A.S. and Eng. *red*.

We thus see that the Latin breaths *f*, *h*, *f* correspond to the Greek aspirates φ, χ, θ, and to the Gothic and English soft mutes *f*, *g*, *d*.

Now, the general results thus obtained from a sufficiently large comparison of instances, prove conclusively not only that *caput* and *head* are etymologically related, but also that Latin and Gothic are but two separate branches sprung from one parent stock—the language spoken by the ancestors of the Latins, Goths, and Anglo-Saxons, before they were broken up into distinct nationalities.

If, now, to the languages above compared we add Sanskrit, Zend, Celtic, Greek, Slavonic, Lithuanian, and Old High German, the following facts in regard to the interchange of the mute consonants in these languages may be ascertained:—

I. The tenues or hard mutes in Sanskrit, Zend, Celtic, Greek, Latin, Slavonic, and Lithuanian are represented by the corresponding breaths in Gothic, and by the corresponding medial or soft mutes in Old High German.

II. The medial or soft mutes in Sanskrit, Zend, Celtic, Greek, Latin, Slavonic, and Lithuanian are represented by the corresponding tenues or hard mutes in Gothic, and by the corresponding breaths in Old High German.

III. The aspirates[1] in Sanskrit and Greek are represented by the corresponding medial or soft mutes in Celtic, Gothic, Slavonic, and Lithuanian, and by the tenues or hard mutes in Old High German.

These statements briefly express the great phonetic law, known as Grimm's Law, and justly regarded as of the highest importance as a test of etymological affinity. This law has been formulated as follows [2]:—

	K	T	P
I. Skr., Celt., Gr., Lat., Slav., and Lith.,	K	T	P
Goth., Anglo-Sax., and Eng.,	Π (G, F)	Th (D)	F (B)
Old High German,	II (G, K)	D	F (B, V)
II. Skr., Celt., Gr., Lat., Slav., and Lith.,	G	D	B
Goth., Anglo-Sax., and Eng.,	K	T	P
Old High German,	Ch	Z	F (Ph)
III. Skr. and Gr.[3],	Kh	Th	Ph
Celt., Slav., Lith., and Goth.,	G	D	B
Old High German,	K	T	P

The letters used in these formulae are mere symbols, and not the real letters of the languages compared. A table of the real letters, taken from Curtius' *Grundz. der Griech. Etym.* (1873), is therefore given on the opposite page, for the purpose of facilitating comparison.

We shall now add some examples of the application of Grimm's Law, taken chiefly from Fick's *Vergl. Wörterbuch* and Curtius' *Grundzüge*.

1. According to the above table, original or Indo-European k is represented in Sanskrit by $k, kh, k', $ or ç; in Zend by $k, kh, c,$ or ç; in Old Irish by c, and sometimes g (in the middle of words); in Greek by $κ$; in Latin by c, q; in Goth. by h and sometimes g; in Old High German by h and sometimes g; in Sclavonic by k, č, c, s; and in Lithuanian by k, sz.

---

[1] Max Müller's Lect., Vol. II., 6th Ed., pp. 216-218.
[2] Cf. Max. Müller's Lectures, Vol. II., pp. 216-218.
[3] The aspirates are not found in Celtic, Latin, Slavonic, Lithuanian, and Old High German. In some of these languages their place is taken up by the breathings h, f.

GRIMM'S LAW OF THE INTERCHANGE OF MUTE CONSONANTS.

	K	G	Gh	T	D	Dh	P	B	Bh
Indo-European, …									
Sanskrit, …	k, kh, k', ç	g, ǧ	gh, h	t, th	d	dh	p, ph	b	bh
Zend, …	k, kh, c, ç	g, gh, j, zh, z	g, gh, j, zh, z	t, th	d, dh	d, dh	p, f	b	b (w)
Old Irish, …	c, ch (g)	g	g	t, th (d)	d	d	lost	b	b
Greek, …	κ	γ	χ	τ	δ	θ	π	β	φ
Latin, …	c, q (Umb.) ç	g	init. h, med. g	t	d	init. f, med. d, b	p	b	init. f, med. b
Gothic,	h (g)	k	g	th (d)	t	d	f		b
Old High German, …	h (g)	k (ch)	g (k)	d	z, sz	t	f, v (b)		b (p)
Slavonic, …	k, č, c, s	g, ž, z	g, ž, z	t	d	d	p	b	b
Lithuanian, …	k, sz	g, ž	g, ž	t	d	d	p	b	b

Examples.—(1) Indo-Europ. root *ḱru (hear), *ḱruta (celebrated, famous), part perf. pass. of *ḱrec, *ḱravas (fame);
Skr. çru (hear), çrutis (reputation), çravas (fame);
O. Ir. clú (fame), cluas (ear), cloor (I hear) for closor;
Gr. κλύω (I hear), κλυτός (renowned), κλέος (fame);
Lat. cluo (I hear), inclutus, also written inclytus (famous);
Goth. hliuma (hearing), A.S. hlud (loud), Eng. loud;
O.H.G. hlut (loud), N.H.G. laut;
Slav. sluti (clarum esse), slovo (word), slava (fame);
Lith. szlové (honour), klausaú (hear);

(2) Indo-Europ. root *ruk, *raukati (to give light, to shine), *rauka (shining);
Skr. ruḱ (to appear, shine), ruḱ (light);
Zend ruc (to give out light);
O. Ir. lóche (lightning);
Gr. ἀμφι-λύκη (twilight), λευκός (white);
Lat. luceo (I shine), lux (light)=lucs, luna (moon)=*lucna;
Goth. liuhath (light), A.S. leoht (light), Eng. light;
O.H.G. lioht (light), N.H.G. licht;
Slav. luča (beam, moon), luči (light);
Lith. laúkas (pale).

2. Indo-European g is represented in Sanskrit by g and ǵ; in Zend by g, gh, j, z, zh; in Old Irish by g; in Greek by γ; in Latin by g; in Gothic by k; in Old High German by k, ch; in Slavonic by g, ž, z; and in Lithuanian by g, ž.

Examples.—(1) Indo-Europ. root, *gan (to beget), *ganatar (begetter), *gand (wife), *ganas (race, species);
Skr. ǵan, ǵan-á-mi (beget), ǵanas (being), ǵanus (race), ǵanitá (genitor; stem ǵanitar), Vedic gná, later ǵani (woman);
Zend zan (beget), ghena (woman);
O. Ir. ro-génair (natus est), gein (child), genemain (birth);
Gr. 2nd Aor. ἐγενόμην of γίγνομαι (I become), γένος (race), γενετήρ (begetter), γυνή (woman);
Lat. gigno (I beget), pf. genui, genus (race), genitor (begettor), genius;
Goth. keinan (a sprout), kuni (race), quéns (female), A.-S. cwen (woman, wife), Eng. queen;
O.H.G. chind (offspring), Old Prus. ganna;
Slav. žena (wife);
Lith. gemù (to be born), gimìnė (origin), gentìs (relation);

(2) Indo-Europ. root, *gan (to know), *ganta (known), *ganti (knowledge);

Skr. gñá, gán-á-mi (know), gñá-na-m (information), gñá-s, gñátis (acquaintance);

O. Ir. ad-gén-sa (I have known), ad-géin (has known);

Gr. ἔγνων 2nd Aor. of γιγνώσκω (I perceive), γνῶσις (perception), γνώμη (opinion), γνωτός (known);

Lat. gnosco and nosco (I know), notus (known), for gnotus, notio (becoming acquainted);

Goth. kunu (perceive), kunths (known), A.S. cunnan (to know), cnáwan (to know); Eng. can, know;

O.H.G. knáu (to recognise), Ger. kennen;

Slav. znati (to perceive); Lith. žinaú (know), part. žīnomas (known).

3. Indo-Europ. gh is represented in Sanskrit by gh or h; in Zend by g, gh, j, zh; in Old Irish by g; in Greek by χ; in Latin by h at the beginning, and by g in the middle of a word; in Gothic by g; in Old High German by g (k); in Slavonic by g, z, z; and in Lithuanian by g, z.

Examples.—(1) Indo-Europ. * ghima (winter), * ghaiman (winter);

Skr. himas (snow), him (cold, frost);

Zend zim, zima (winter);

O. Ir. gam (winter), gaith (wind);

Gr. χεῖμα (storm, winter-weather), χειμών (winter);

Lat. hiems (winter);

Slav. zima (winter);

Lith, žëmá (winter), žëmìnis (wintry).

(2). Indo-Europ. root * righ (to lick);

Skr. rih and lih (lick);

O. Ir. lígim (I lick);

Gr. root λιχ, λείχω (to lick up), λιχμάζω (I lick over);

Lat. lingo (I lick), ligurio (I lick);

Goth. bi- laigôn (to lick), A.S. liccian (to lick), Eng. lick;

O.H.G. lëcchón (to lick), Ger. lecken (to lick);

Slav. lizati (to lick);

Lith. lëžiù (to lick), ližus (fore-finger).

4. Indo-European t is represented in Sanskrit by t or th; in Zend by t or th; in Old Irish by t, and by th or d (when vowel-flanked); in Greek by τ; in Latin by t; in Goth. by th (some-

times by *d* in the middle of words); in Old High German by *d*; in Slavonic by *t*; and in Lithuanian by *t*.

Examples.—(1) Indo-Europ. root *tan, *tanu, *tanuti (to extend, to stretch), *tana (thread, string), *tantu (string, cord);

Skr. root *tan, tan-ó-mi* (stretch oneself), *tánas* (thread), *tantis* (cord), *tanus* (thin), *tanavam* (thinness);

Zend *tan* (stretch out), *tan-ya* (spread out);

O. Ir. *tét* (musical string), Cymbr. *tant* (string, cord), O. Ir. *tana* (thin);

Gr. roots τα, ταν, τεν, whence τάν-υμαι (I stretch myself), τείνω (I stretch), ταναός (extended), τένων (sinew);

Lat. *tendo* (I stretch), *teneo* (I hold), *tentus* (stretched), *tenus* (a cord), *tenon* (sinew);

Goth. *thanja* (I stretch), A.S. *thenian* (to extend), *thyn*, Eng. *thin*.

O.H.G. *dunni* (thin), *dona* (a snare), Ger. *dünn;*

Slav. *tĭn-ĭ-kŭ* (slender, tenuis), *teneto, tonoto* (snare, laqueus) *tetiva* (cord);

Lith. *tempjù* (stretch out), *timpa* (sinew), *temptyva* (bowstring).

(2). Indo-Europ. root * *tars*, * *tarsyati* (to thirst), * *tarsu* (thirsty);

Skr. *tarsh, trshjami* (I thirst), *trsh, tarshas* (thirsty);

Zend *tarshna* (thirst);

O. Ir. *tirme* (dryness), *tirim* (dry), *tart* (thirst);

Gr. root *ters*, from which τέρσομαι (I become dry), τερσαίνω (I make dry), τρασία and ταρσιά (a drying kiln);

Lat. *torreo* (to dry or burn) for *torseo, tostus*, part of *torreo, torris* (torch);

Goth. *ga-thaúrsans* (dry), *thaúrs-ja* (I thirst), *thaúrst-ei* (thirst), A.S. *thyrst* (thirst), Eng. *thirst;*

O.H.G. *derru* (to dry, torreo), Ger. *durst* (thirst);

Ice. *thyrsta* (thirst), A.S. *thyrst*, Eng. *thirst;*

Lith. *tróksztu* (pant, thirst).

5. Indo-European *d* is represented in Sanskrit by *d*, in Zend by *d* and occasionally *dh*, in Old Irish by *d*, in Greek by δ, in Latin by *d*, in Gothic by *t*, in Old High German by *z* (*sz* in the middle of a word), and in Slavonic and Lithuanian by *d*.

Examples.—(1) Indo-Europ. root *div (to shine), *divas (day, *daiva (God);

Skr. root *div* (shine), *divjámi* (shine), *dévas* (God);

Zend *div* (shine), *daêva* (demon);
O. Ir. *Dia* (God), from stem **daiva*, *dia* (day) from stem **diva*
or **divas;* Cymbr. *dyw;*
Gr. root διϝ, δῖος (heavenly) = δiϝος, ἐνδιος (at midday);
Lat. *deus* (God), *divus* (divine), *dies* (day), *biduum* (a period of
two days), *interdiú* (during the day);
A.S. *Tiv* (God of war), gen. *Tives* (cf. *Tives-dǎg*, Tuesday);
Ice. *tívi* (a god, divinity), *tívar* (gods); O.H.G. *zio*, gen. *zures*
(name of a god);
Slav. *dǐnǐ* (day), *dǐnǐsǐ* (to-day);
Lith. *dévas* (God), *déna* (day).

(2) Indo-Europ. root **dant* (tooth) from *da* (to divide);
Skr. *dantas* (tooth);
Zend *dañtan* (tooth);
O. Ir. *dét* (tooth), Cymbr. *dant* (tooth);
Gr. ὀδούς (tooth), gen. ὀδόντος;
Lat. *dens* (tooth) gen. *dentis;*
Goth. *tunthus*, A.S. *toth*, Eng. *tooth;*
O.H.G. *zand* (tooth), Ger. *zahn* (tooth);
Lith. *dantìs* (tooth).

6. Indo-European *dh* is represented in Sanskrit by *dh*, in Zend
by *d* and occasionally *dh*, in Old Irish by *d*, in Greek by θ, in
Latin by *d* (but frequently *f* at the beginning of a word and
sometimes *b* in the middle of a word), in Gothic by *d*, in Old High
German by *t*, and in Slavonic and Lithuanian by *d*.

Examples.—(1) Indo-Europ. root **dhur* (door), **dhvara* (gate,
door), **dhvaria* (belonging to a door);
Skr. *dvārum*, *dvār* (door, gate), Ved. *dur* (fem. door). The
aspirate is lost in Sanskrit. (Cf. Curtius' Grundz., p. 258);
Zend *dvarem* (gate, palace);
O. Ir. *dorus* (door);
Gr. θύρα and θύρετρον (door, gate), θυρίς (door or window);
Lat. *forís*, pl. *fores* (door, gate), Umbr. *vero* (gate);
Goth. *daúr*, A.S. *dor* and *duru*, Eng. *door;*
O.H.G. *tor* (gate), Ger. *thor* (gate), *thür* (door);
Slav. *dvǐrǐ* (door, θύρα), *dvorŭ* (court, fore-court);
Lith. *dùrys* (fores pl.).

2) Indo-Europ. root **rudh* (to be red), **rudhra* (red), **raudha*
(red, copper);
Skr. *rudhiras* (to be red, bloody), *rŏhitas* (red) for *rŏdhitas*.

O. Ir. *ruad* (red), Mod. Gael. *ruiteach* (ruddy);
Gr. root ἐρυθ, ἐρεύθω (to make red), ἐρευθρός (red), ἔρευθος (redness);
Lat. *ruber* (red, ruddy), *rubeo* (to be red or ruddy), *rubor* (redness), *rufus* (red, reddish); Umbr. *rufru*;
Goth. *rauds* (red), *ga-riud-jô* (shame-facedness); A.S. *reod, rude, read, red*, Eng. *red*;
O.H.G. *rôt* (red), *rost* (rust), Germ. *roth* (red);
Ice. *rjódha* (to redden), *rjódhr* (ruddy);
Slav. *rŭdrŭ* (red), *rŭžda* (redness);
Lith. *raudà* (red colour), *rùdas* (reddish brown), *rudìs* (rust).

7. Indo-European *p* is represented in Sanscrit by *p* or *ph*, in Zend by *p* or *f*, in Old Irish it disappears (always when initial) or is replaced by *c* (*ch* when vowel-flanked), in Greek by π, in Latin by *p*, in Gothic by *f*, in Old High German by *f* or *b*, and in Slavonic and Lithuanian by *p*.

Examples (1) Indo-Europ. root *patar (father), from root *pâ (to guard, nourish, defend);
Skr. *pitâ* (father; stem *pitar*);
Zend *pita* (father; stem *patar*);
O. Ir. *athir* (father). gen. *athar*;
Gr. πατήρ (father; stem πατερ);
Lat. *pater*, Umbr. *pater*;
Goth. *fadar*, A.S. *faeder*; Eng. *father*;
O.H.G. *fatar*, Germ. *vater*.

(2). Indo-Europ. root *saptan (seven), *saptama (seventh);
Skr. *saptan* (seven), *saptama* (seventh);
Zend *haptan* (seven), *saptamas* (the seventh);
O. Ir. *secht* (seven), *sechtmad* (seventh);
Gr. ἑπτά (seven), ἕβδομος (seventh);
Lat. *septem* (seven); *septumus* and *septimus* (seventh);
Goth. *sibun* (seven), A.S. *seofon* and *seofan* (seven), Eng. seven, A.S. *seofodha* (seventh), Eng. *seventh*;
Slav. *sedmĭ* (seven), *sedmyj* (seventh);
Lith. *septynì* (seven), *septìntas*, *sékmas* (the seventh).

(3). Indo-Europ. root *svap (to sleep), *svapna (sleep);
Skr. root *svap* (to sleep), *svapnas* (sleep);
Zend *qap* (sleep), *qafna* (sleep);
O. Ir. *suan* (sleep) =* *sopn-*;
Gr. ὕπνος (sleep);

Lat. *somnus* (sleep) *for sopnus, sopor* (sleep), *sopio* (to put to sleep);
Ice. *svefn* (sleep), A.S. *swefen* (sleep), O Eng. *swevene* (dream);
O.H.G. *swebjan* (to put to sleep);
Slav. *sŭnŭ* (sleep) for *sŭpnŭ, sŭpati* (to sleep);
Lith. *sápnas* (dream).

(4). Indo-Europ. root * *par* (to fill), * *paparti* (to fill);
Skr. *par, piparmi* (fill), *prnámi* (fill), *prânas* and *pûrnas* (full);
Zend *par* (fill up), *perena* (full);
O. Ir. root *pal, ro-chomall* (I have filled), *comalnid;* root *pla, lán* (full), *lín* (number), *línmaire* (fulness);
Gr. root πλα, πίμπλημι, infin. πιμπλάναι (to fill), πλήθω (I am full), πλέος (full), πλήρης (full), πλῆθος (crowd);
Lat. *impleo* (I fill up), *plenus* (full), *plebes* or *plebs* (the multitude or many);
Goth. *fulls* (full), A.S. *full* and *folc*, Eng. *full* and *folk*;
O.H.G. *fol* (full), Ger. *voll* (full), O.H.G. *folc* (people), Ger. *volk* (people);
Slav. *plŭnŭ* (full), *plŭkŭ* (crowd), people), *pleme* (tribe);
Lith. *pilti* (fill), *pilnas* (full), *pulkas* (heap, crowd).

8. It has been already remarked that some have held that *b*, at least as an initial sound, did not exist in the original Indo-European language. Schleicher states, generally (cf. *Compendium*, p. 160, 4th ed.) that he "knew of no reliable example of this sound," and adds, in a note, that amongst the examples quoted by Bickell (*Zeitschr.* xiv. 425 ff), he found none which could, with any certainty, be said to belong to the original European language. According to the few examples given by Curtius and Fick, original *b* remains unchanged in Sanskrit, Greek, Latin, and Slavo-Lithuanian.

Examples.—(1) Indo-Europ. *barbar, *barb (to stammer);
Skr. *barbaras* (stuttering, curly, foreign);
Gr. βάρβαρος (strange, foreign), βαρβαρίζω (to speak like a foreigner);
Lat. *balbus* (stuttering), *balbutio* (I stutter);
Ir. *balb* (dumb) is borrowed from Lat. *balbus;*

(2) Indo-Europ. root *bargh (to pluck);
Gr. βραχύς (short), βραχεα (shallows);
Lat. *brevis* (short), *brevia* (shallows);
(?) Slav. *brŭzŭ* (quick). Cf. Peile's Introduction, p. 127.

9. Indo-Europ. *bh* is represented in Sanskrit, Old Irish, Teutonic, Slavonic, and Lithuanian by *b*; in Greek by φ; and in Latin by *f* at the beginning, and *b* in the middle of a word.

Examples.—(1) Indo-Europ. root **bhar*, **bharati* (to bear), **bharti* (to bear), **bhára* (burden);

Skr. root **bhar* (to bear), *bharati*, *bharti* (to bear), *bharas bháras* (burden), *bharma(n)*, maintenance;

Zend *bar* (bear, bring);

O. Ir. *ber-im* (I bear, bring), *as-biur* (I say)=*as-biru*, *tabairt* (giving), *brith* (birth), *bert* (bundle), *bairgen* (bread);

Gr. root φερ, φέρω (I bear), φέρμα (burden, produce);

Lat. *fero* (I bear);

Goth root *bar*, *bairan* (to bear), *baúrthei* (burden), *ga-baúrths* (birth), *barn* (bairn, child), A.S. *beran* (to bear), Eng. *bear*;

O.H.G. *bara* (bier);

Slav. root *ber*, *bera*, *brati* (to bring);

Lith. *bérnas* (child);

(2) Indo-Europ. **bhráktar* (bother), from root **bhrá*=**bhar* (to bear);

Skr. *bhrátá* (brother), stem **bhrátar*;

Zend *brátar* (brother);

O. Ir. *bráthir* (brother), Welsh *brawd* (brother);

Gr. φράτηρ (brother), stem **φράτερ*;

Lat. *frater* (brother), *fraternus* (brotherly);

Goth. *bróthar* (brother), A.S. *bródhor* (brother), Eng. *brother*;

O.H.G. *bruodar* (brother), Ger. *bruder* (brother);

Slav. *bratrŭ*, *bratŭ* (brother);

Lith. *broter-ëlis* (dim.), *brólis* (brother);

(3) Indo-Europ. root **nabh* (to veil, to cover), **nabhas* (cloud, mist, atmosphere);

Skr. *nabhas* (mist, vapour, cloud), *nabhasjas* (misty);

O. Ir. *nél* (a cloud)=**nebl*, *nimb* (drop);

Gr. νέφος, νεφέλη (cloud), νεφόω (to make cloudy);

Lat. *nubes*, *nebula* (cloud);

O.H.G. *nëbal* (cloud);

Ice. *nifl* (mist, fog), *nifl-heimr* (Hades);

Slav. *nebo* (heaven), stem *nebes*;

Lith. *debesis* (cloud), with *d* for *n*;

(4). Indo-Europ. root **bhu*, **bhú* (to be, become), **bhuta* part. pass. of **bhu*, **bhuti*, **bhúti* (being), **bhúman* (being, plant);

Skr. root *bhû, bhavâti (to be, to exist), bhavas (origin), bhavas (rise, condition), bhutis (existence), bhûmis (earth);
Zend bû (to be, to become);
O. Ir. bíu (I am), ro-bá (I have been), buith (to be), =*buti;
Gr. φυ-, φύω (beget), φύομαι (become, grow), φυή (growth), φύσις (nature), φυτός (grown), &c.;
Lat. fu-, fui (I have been), futurus (about to be), futuo (to be to exist);
O. Sax. bium, A.S. beon (to be, exist, become), Eng. be;
Goth. bauan (to dwell);
Slav. byti (to be);
Lith. búti (to be), bútas (house, floor).

The principles stated and illustrated in the preceding pages will be applied, in the next number, to the Celtic and Teutonic languages, and more especially to Gaelic and English, for the purpose of showing their close etymological affinity.

INDO-EUROPEAN ROOTS, WITH DERIVATIVES AND ANALYSIS OF GAELIC COMPOUND WORDS.

We begin these articles with the liquid M, which is preserved in all the languages of the Indo-European family. The references are to the 3rd ed. of Fick's Vergleichendes Wörterbuch der Indogermanischen Sprachen, to the 4th ed. of Curtius' Grundzüge der Griechischen Etymologie, and to the 2nd ed. of Zeuss' Grammatica Celtica.

1. Indo-Europ. root ma, má, man (to measure, build, shape). Cf. Fick's Wört. i. 164.

To the root ma belong tomhas (measure), measarra (temperate), and several other Gaelic words noticed below under expanded forms of this root. Tomhas (= O. Gael. tomus) is referred by Stokes to a base *do-fo-mens-u, the root men-s being an extended form of me = ma. Measarra = O. Gael. mesurda from mens. Cf. Beit. viii. 339.

To the same root belong also Skr. root má (to measure), má-tra-m (measure, measure of time, matter), má-tar (measurer), má-na-m (measure), má-na-s (building); Zend má (measure, make); Gr. με in μέ-τρο-ν (measure), μέτρ-ιο-ς (measured, proper); Lat. metíre (to measure), *meta* (the measuring thing), *mensa* (a table, that which is set on the table, food), *mensura* (measure), &c. Cf. Curt. Gr. Etym., p. 328. Gael. *meidh* (a balance; = *meadh*) is from Lat. *meta*. Gael. *mias* (a dish) = Lat. *mensa*.

2. *Med* (= Europ. root *mad*) is an extended form of the root *ma*. Cf. Fick's Wört. i. 706.

To this root belong O. Gael. *mess* (estimate, judicium, now *meas*) = * *med-tu*, *coimdiu* (lord, dominus, mod. form *coimhdhe*) = *co-midiu, *coimeas* or *coimheas* (equality) = *co-mes* = *co-medtu, *dimeas* or *dimheas* (contempt) = *di-mes* = *di-med-tu, *irmadadar* (intellegit) = *ir-mad-adar*, *conammadarsa* (ut judicem) = *conam-mad-ar-sa*, &c.

To the same root belong Gr. μέδω, μέδομαι (to think on), μέδιμνος (measure); Lat. *modus*, *modius*, *modestus*; Goth. *mita* (I mete), *mitôn* (consider), O.H.G. *mëzan* (to measure), Ger. *messen* (to measure), &c. Gael. *modh* (mode) is a loan from Lat. *modus*. Windish considers an Irish by-form, *mid*, probable. Cf. Curt. Gr. Etym., p. 242.

3 *Mens* = Indo-Europ. *mans* (moon, month). Cf. Fick's Wört. i., 176.

To the stem *mens*, which Curtius refers to the root *ma* (to measure), belongs O. Gael. *mi* (month, now *mios*), Gen. *mis*, acc. pl. *misa*. *N* before *s* is dropped in Gael. by rule.

Other related words are Lat. *mens-i-s* (month), Gr. μήν = *μηνς. Ion. μείς (month), μήνη (moon), Skr. *mâs*, *mâsas* (month), Zend *mâonha* (moon), Goth. *mêna* (moon), *mênôths* (month). Cf. Curt. Gr. Etym., p. 334.

4. Gaelic *mâthair* (mother; = O. Gael. *mâthir*) is to be referred to Indo-Europ. * *mâtar* (mother), a derivative, as shown by the Skr. mas. noun *mâtar* (measurer), from root *ma* (to measure, to shape). To *mâtar* are also to be referred Skr. and Zend *mâtar* (mother), G. μήτηρ, Dor. μάτηρ (mother), Lat. *mater* (mother), O.H.G. *muotar* (mother), Ger. *mutter*, A. S. *moder*. Eng. *mother*, &c. Cf. Curt. Gr. Etym., 335.

5. Indo-Europ. root *man*, *mâ* (to think). Cf. Fick's Wört. i. 165.

To this root belong Gael. *meanma* (courage, spirit, imagination) = O. Gael. *menme* (mens), gen. *menman*, *cuimhne* (remembrance, memory) = O. Gael. *cuman* = *co-man*, *dearmad* (neglect, forgetfulness) = O. Gael. *dermet* = *der-met* of which -*met* = *-*manta*, *farmad* (envy) = O.Gael. *format* = *for-met* = *for-manta.

taithmhead (remembrance, memorial) = O. Gael. *taithmet* = *do-aith-manta, *ermitiu* (perseverance), gen. *ermiten* = *er-mintiu, of which -*mintiu* corresponds to Lat. *mentio*, *toimtiu* (opinion) = *do-fo-mintiu, *ionmhuin* (dear, beloved) = O. Gael. *inmain* = *in-man-i, *domuinur* (I think) = *do-mun-iur* *doménar* (putavi) = *do-mén-ar*, a reduplicated form.

To the same root belong also Skr. root *man* (to think), *manas* (thought, spirit), *matis* (devotion); Zend *man* (think), *manañh*, (thought, spirit); Gr. μένω (I remain), μένος (spirit, courage), μέμνημαι (remember), μνήμων (mindful), &c.; Lat. *maneo* (to remain), *memini* (to remember), *mentio*, *mens*, gen. *mentis*, *moneo*, &c.; Goth. *gamunan* (think, keep in mind), O. H. G. *minnia*, *minna* (love), *meina* (opinion); Lith. *min-iu* (keep in mind). Cf. Curt. Gr. Etym., p. 312.

6. Indo-Europ. *ma* stem of the 1st pers. pron. sing. Cf. Fick's Wört i., 164.

To *ma* belong the first pers. pron. sing. *mi* (I, me) = O. Gael. *mé*, the infixed pron. -*m*-, the suffixed -*m* in *do-m* (to me), now *domh*, and the poss. pron. *mo* (my).

The following are from the same root:—Skr. *ma*, Zend *ma*, Gr. με and ἐμέ (me), ἐμός (mine), Lat. *me* (me) and *meus* (mine), Goth. *mi-s*, *mi-k*, A. S. *me*, Eng. *me*. Cf. Curt. G. Etym., p. 328.

7. Indo-Europ. root *mu*, *mú* (to bind, to fasten, to close). Cf. Ficks's Wört. 179.

To this root belong Skr. *mú* (to bind, tie); Gr. ἀμύνω (to ward off), ἄμυνα (defence), ἀμύντωρ (protector); Lat. *moenia* (that which wards off, walls, inclosure), *munia* (duties, function, official or professional duties), *munus* (office, employment), *com-munis* (common), &c.

With *moenia* = *munia* = *moinia Stokes and Ebel compare O Gael. *moin*, *main*, now *maoin* (wealth). Gael. *comain* (obligation, debt; = *com-main) corresponds to Lat. *communis* for *commoinis*, with which also *comaineachadh* (communicating) is connected, if it be not, like *comunn* (communion), a loan-word. Cf. Curt. Gr. Etym., pp. 324-5, and Stokes' Goid., p. 178.

8. Indo-Europ. root *smar*, *smarati* (to think, keep in mind, remember). Cf. Fick's Wört i. 254.

To this root, which retains *s* only in Sanksrit, belong the Gael. words *mair* (last, remain), O. Gael. *marait* (manent), *meraid* (will remain), *mair* in *ni mair* (lives not), *maireann* and *maireannach* (lasting, everlasting).

To the same root belong Skr. root *smar*, *smar-á-mi* (I remember, I desire), *smr-ti-s* (memoria), *smar-a-s* (love, amor); Zend *mar* (remember, know, mention), *mar-e-ti* (precept); Gr. μέρμηρα and μέριμνα (care), μερμηρίζω (I care), μάρτυρ (witness), &c.; Lat. *memor*, (mindful), *memoria* (memory), *mora* (delay); Goth. *mêrjan* (to proclaim); O. H. G. *mári* (fame), &c.

9. Indo-Europ. root *mar*, *marati* (to die). Cf. Fick's Wört. i. 172.

To this root belong Skr. root *mar* in *marámi* (I die), *mr-ta-s* (dead), *mrt-ja-s* (mortal), *mr-ti-s* (death); Gr. root μερ (μορ, μαρ,) βρο-τό-ς (mortal) = *mor-tó-s* μαρ-αίν-ω (wither); Lat. *mor-i-or*, *mors*, gen. *mortis* (death), *mortuus* (dead), *mor-bu-s* (disease), *marceo* (to wither); Goth. *maur-th-r* (murder), A.S. *mor-dh-or*, Eng. *murder*; Ch.-Slav. *mr-é-ti* (to die), *mor-ŭ* (death), Lith. *mirti* (die), *már-a-s* (plague), *s-mèr-ti-s* (death), &c.

To the same root belong the Gael. words *marbh* (dead = O. Gael. *marb* = *mar-va*), *marbh* (kill) = O. Ir. *marbaim*, *mort* (kill), W. *mar-u* (death).

To the root *mar* may also be referred Gael. *muir* a fem. *i*-stem = *mor-i*, of which the Indo-Europ. base is *mara*, and to which are related Skr. *mîras* (sea), Lat. *mare* (sea), Ch.-Slav. *mor-je* (sea).

10. Europ. root *mal*, *malati* (to grind). Cf. Fick's Wört. i. 719.

To this root belong the Gael. words *mel-im* (I grind), *bleith* (grinding) for *mleith*, *tomil* (to feed, to eat) = *do-fo-mil*, *tomalt*, gen. *tomalte* (edendi) = *do-fo-mal-t*. Cf. Z. 800.

To the same root belong also Gr. μύλη (mill), μύλος (mill), μύλλω (to grind), μυλ-όδοντες (molar teeth, grinders); Lat. *molo* (I grind), *mola* (a mill), *molaris* (of or belonging to a mill), *molendinum* (mill-house); Goth. *mal-v-ja-n* (to rub together), O.H.G. *mul-i* (mill), *mel-o* (meal), *mul-ja-n* (crush), Ger. *mühle*, A. S. *miln*, Eng. *mill*; Ch.-Slav. *mel-ja* (grind), Lith. *mal-ù* (grind). Cf. Curt. Gr. Etym., p. 339. *Muileann* (a mill), in O. Gael. *mulenn*, is from Lat. *molendinum*.

11. Indo-Ger. root *magh* (to be able, to increase), of which *mangh* is a nalised form. Cf. Fick's Wört. i. 168.

To this root belong O. Gael. *cumang* (power, potestas) = *cu-mang*, of which *cu* = *co* = Lat. *co*, and *mang* is a nasalised form of the root *mag* = Indo-Europ. *magh*, *cumaing* (potest) = *cu-maing* = *cu-mangi*, *cumachte* (potestas, now *cumhachd*) = *cu-mach-te*, of which *mach* = *magh*, *cucmais*, for *co-memagsi*, 1st. sing., and *coimsam* for *co-memagsam*, 1st. per. pl. of the reduplicated *s*-fut. of *cumaing*.

To the same root also belong Skr. *mah-as* (power, splendour); Gr. μῆχος and μῆχαρ (means, expedient, remedy), μηχανή (device, design); Goth. *mag* (I am able, possum), *mahts* (power); Ger. *mögen* and *macht*; A. S. *magan* and *meaht*, Eng. *may* and *might*; Ch.-Slav. *moga* (possum), *mostĭ* (power). Cf. Curt. Gr. Etym., p. 335.

12. The root *mag*, which occurs in the following Celtic words, is connected with the Indo-Europ. root *magh* noticed above:—

O. Gael. *do-for-mag-ar* (augetur), *do-for-maig* (auget), *tórmag*, *tórmach* (auctio) = *do-for-mag*, *mó* (more) of which *móo*, *móa*, *má*, *máo* are different forms, for *magius (or *ma-ias) corresponding to Lat. *major* for *magios, Gr. μείζων for *μεγιον, Skr. *mahiyáns*, Goth. *maiza*, O. Gael. super. *mdam*, *méit* = *manti; Corn. *moghya* = *magias, *moycha*. With the Gael. comp. *mó*, *máo*, the W. comp. *mwy* and the Corn. comp. *moy* correspond. To the same root belong also the O. Gael. positives *már*, *mór*, W. *mawr*, Corn. *maur*, which must have early lost the guttural. Cf. Curt. Gr. Etym., pp. 329, 330, and Stokes' Ir. Gl., p. 129.

To the same root with the above belong also Gr. μέγας (great) with the comp. μείζων (noticed above) and superl. μέγιστος, μεγαλύνω (magnify), μέγεθος (greatness); Lat. *magnus* (great) with the comp. *major* (noticed above) and superl. *maximus*, *magis* (in a higher degree), *magister* (master), &c.; Goth. *mik-il-s* (great), *mikiljan* (to magnify), Goth. comp. *mais*, superl. *maist*, A.S. *mare*, *maest*, Eng. *more*, *most*; Ger. *mehr*.

13. From the root *mar* is formed the extended root *mard*, *mardati* (to rub, to soften) and *mardu* (soft, tender). Cf. Fick's Wört. i. 175.

To *mardu are to be referred Skr. *mrd-u-s* (soft, tender), *mrdu-tá* (softness); Gr. βραδ-ύ-ς (slow), βραδύ-τη(τ)ς (slowness); Ch.-Slav. *mlad-ŭ* (tender); Goth. *milds* (mild, soft, tender), Ice. *mild-r* (gracious), Ger. *milde*, A. S. *mild*, Eng. *mild*.

To the same root belongs O. Gael. *meld*, now *meall* (alluring). Cf. *meall-shùil* (soft, winning eye). Cf. Stokes' Goid., p. 18.

14. Root *mer* (to divide). Cf. Curt. Gr. Etym., p. 332.

To this root belong the following words which imply radically the idea of division:—

Gr. μείρ-ο-μαι (obtain a portion), μέρ-ος (portion, part),

μερί-ζ-ω (divide), μόρ-ος (lot, fate), μοῖρ-α (proper portion), μόρ-α (division); Lat. *mer-e-o* and *mer-e-o-r* (to obtain as a portion), *mer-enda* (an afternoon meal).

Gael. *mír* (a piece, part) is connected with μείρομαι in Corm.'s Gloss., p. 118, and with W. *mèr* (a particle) and Gr. μέρος in Stokes' Ir. Glosses, p. 157.

15. With the root *magh*, nasalised form *mangh* (cf. No. 11 above), are connected O. Gael. *mug* (a servant), *mac* (a son), *macamh* (boy, garçon), Corn. *maw*, W. *map* (son), and Gael. *mang* (fawn). *Mug* and Corn. *maw* (= Goth. *magus*) are connected with the form *magh* of the root, and *mac*, *macc*, oghamic *maqo = mac-va*, *mang-va*, also W. *map* and Gael. *mang* belong to the nasalised form *mangh*. Cf. Stokes in Rev. Celt. iii. 38.

16. Indo-Europ. root *mi*, *mî* (to diminish), of which *min* is an extended form. Cf. Fick's Wört. i. 177.

To this root belong Skr. *mi*, *mi-nó-mi* (diminish); Gr. μινύω, μινύθω (diminish, destroy, grow less), μίνυνθα (a little while); Lat. *minuo* (to make small or less), *minutus* (little, small), *minor* (less), *minus*, *minister* (servant, attendant), *minimus*, &c.; Goth. *mins* (less), *minniza* (smaller), *minnists* (smallest); Ch.-Slav. *mĭnij* (minor), Lith. *minù*, *men-ka-s* (little).

To the same root belong Gael. *mean* and *mion* = *min* (small), *mín* (small, tender), *ro-mín* (very meek), W. *mwyn* and *main* (fine, slender, thin), Corn. *muin* (slender, thin), Cf. Curt. Gr. Etym., p. 337, and Stokes in Rev. Celt. iii. 38. Gael. *meanbh* (small, slender) = *menb*, with apparently *b* for *v* as in *marb* = *marv and *fedb* = *fedv, and W. *manu* (to make small), *manw* (of subtile quality), *manwy* (fine, rare, subtile) belong to the same class of words. Cf. Graeco-Ital. stem *minu in Fick's Wört. ii. 190.

17. Indo-Europ. root *mik* (to mix). Cf. Fick's Wört., i. 168.

To this root belong Gael. *measg* (mix, mingle) and *measg* in "am measg" (among). The old form of *measg* was *mesc*, from which are derived O. Gael. *com-mescatar* (miscentur) and *cum-masc* (a mixing, mixtio) = *cum-mesc, *e* of *mesc* having become *a* by rule after *u* of *cum* (cf. Stokes in Beit. viii. 308).

To the same root belong Skr. *miç-ra-s* (intermixed), *miçra-jámi* (mix, intermix), *miksh*, *mi-miksh* (mix); Gr. root μιγ, μίσγ-ω, μίγ-νυ-μι (mix), μίγ-δην (mixedly); Lat. *misceo* (mix), *mixtus*, (mixed), *mixtio*, &c.; O. H. G. *misk-iu* (mix), Ger. *misch-en* (to mix), A. S. *misc-an* (to mix), Eng. *mix*; Ch.-Slav. *měs-i-ti* (to mix), Lith. *misz-ti* (to mix oneself), &c. Cf. Gr. Etym., p. 336.

18. Indo-Europ. *madhu* (honey, mead). Cf. Fick's Wört., i. 170. With *madhu* is connected O. Gael. *med*, gen. *meda* (mead), a *e*-stem = *medu*, W. *medw* (*ebrius*), O. Gael. *mesce* (drunkenness) = *med-ca*, *mescc* (drunk).
The following words are related:—
Skr. *madhu* (something sweet, sweet drink, honey) *madhus* (sweet), Zend *madhu* (honey); Gr. μέθυ (wine), μεθύω (am drunk), μεθύσκω (make drunk), μέθη (drunkenness); O. S. *medo* and O. H. G. *metu* (mead), Ger. *meth* (mead), Dut. *mede*, Eng. *mead;* Ch.-Slav. *medŭ* (honey), Lith. *midŭs* (honey). Cf. Curt. Gr. Etym., p. 260.

19. Indo-Europ. *madhia* (middle). Cf. Fick's Wört. i. 170. With *madhia* are connected O. Gael, *medón* (middle), now *meadhon*, *medonda* (medius).
Connected with the same root are Skr. *madhja-s* and Zend *maidhya* (middle), Skr. *madhja-ma-s* and Zend. *madh-ema* (midmost); Gr. μέσσος for μεθ-jo-ς (middle), μεσσ-ηγύ-[s] (between); Lat. *medius* (middle), *di-midius* (half); Goth. *midji-s* (middle), *mid-uma* (middle), Ger. *mitte*, A. S. *midd*, Eng. *mid* and *middle*; Ch.-Slav. *me:du* (middle), &c. Cf. Curt. Gr. Etym., p. 334.

20. Europ. root *malg* (to milk) = root *marg* (to rub, to stroke). Cf. Fick's Wort. i. 720.
To this root belong O. Gael. *melg* (milk), *do-o-malgg* (mulsi), *bo-mlacht* = *bo-* (cow) and *mlacht* = *mlach-t* (milk), *blighim* (I milk), *bleg-ar* (mulgetur), *blich-t* for *mlich-t*.
To the same root belong Gr. root μελγ, ἀμέλγω (I milk), ἄμελξις (milking), ἀμολγεύς (milk-pail); Lat. *mulgeo* (I milk), *mulctus* (milked), *mulc-tra* (milking-pail); O. H. G. *milchu*, Ger. *milch*, A. S. *melcan* (to milk), *meolc* (milk), Eng. *milk*; Ch. Slav. *mlŭz-a* (mulgeo), Lith. *melžu* (stroke, milk), &c. Cf. Curt. Gr. Etym., 183.

21. Indo-Europ. *sama* (the same, the like). Cf. Fick's Wört. i. 222.
To *sama* belong O. Gael. *samail* (likeness, image, now *samhail*) = *samali*, *amal* (as, like as, now *amhail*) with loss of initial *s*, *samlid* (so), Mod. Gael *samladh* (appearance), O. Gael. *co-smail* (like, similis) = *co-samali*, &c.
To the same root belong Skr. *sama-m*, *samá*, *sama-já* (together), *sama-s* (same, similis), Zend. *hama* (the same, the like); Gr. ἅμα (at the same time), ὁμός (united), ὁμοῦ (together), ὅμοιος (like), &c.; Lat. *similis* (like), *simul* (together, at once), *simultas* (a coming together),*simulo* (I imitate); Goth. *sama* (the same, idem).

O. H. G. *saman, zi-samane* (together), A. S. and Eng. *same*; Ch.-Slav. *samŭ* (ipse, solus), &c. Cf. Curt. Gr. Etym., p. 323.

22. Europ. root *máta* (mowing, Germ. Mahd), from root *má*. Cf. Fick's Wört. i. 706.

With * *máta* are connected O. Gael. *meithel* (a party of reapers) written *meikle* in Highl. Soc. Dict., *meithleoir* (a reaper, messor), Corn. *midil* (reaper). These words are cognate with Lat. *meto* (mow or reap), *messis* (a mowing, reaping, and ingathering of the fruits of the earth), *messor* (mower, reaper); O.H.G. *mádari* (mower), M.H.G. *mát* (mowing). Gr. ἀμάω (mow, gather) and its derivatives ἄμητος (harvest), ἀμητός (time of harvest), and ἄμαλλα (sheaf) seem to be derived from the root *má*. To *má* also belong O.H.G. *má-j-an*, A.S. *máven*, Eng. *mow*. Cf. Curt. Gr. Etym., 323.

23. Indo-Europ. root *áma* (uncooked, raw) from root *am*, *amati* (to befall, to injure).

With **ámu* are connected Skr. *ámas, ama-s* (crude, raw), Gr. ὠμό-ς (raw, undressed; savage, rude, fierce), Lat. *am-áru-s* (bitter). With Gr. ὠμό-ς agrees exactly O. Gael. *óm* (raw), now *amh*. Cf. Curt. Gr. Etym., p. 341.

24. With the Graeco-Ital. stem **melit* (honey), from which are derived Gr. μέλι (honey), gen. μέλιτος, μέλισσα (bee) for **μελιτ-ja*, and Lat. *mel* (honey), gen. *mellis* for **meltis, mulsus* (mixed with honey, sweet) for **melti-us*, are connected Gael. *milis* (sweet) with *s* from *t*, and *mil* (honey), gen. *meala*. The Germanic stem is **melitha*, to which belongs Goth. *melith* (honey). Cf. Curt. Gr. Etym., p. 331, and Fick's Wört. ii. 188 and iii. 235.

THE LAWS OF AUSLAUT IN IRISH.

(Translated from an important paper by Profr. Windisch, of Leipsic, in the Beitr. zur Geschichte der Deutschen Sprache und Literatur, Vol. iv., 1877.)

THE laws of auslaut have the same import in Irish as they have in the Germanic and Slavonic languages: they alone enable us to judge with certainty in regard to every form of inflection. Altogether, I have arrived at the same results as Ebel, who has briefly treated these laws, first in the Beitr. Zur. Verg. Spr. i. 165, 166 (cf. ii. 66), and, afterwards, in the Gramm. Celt., pp. 172–174; but I believe I must differ from our authorities, Ebel and Stokes, in my view of certain forms, on account of the phonetic laws of Irish.

Ebel said in his article on declension in Celtic: "The oldest historical forms of the Irish, in regard to the conservation of the auslaut, are, at most, and even scarcely upon a level with the New High German" (cf., among other places, Beitr., i. 165). Those who do not remember what Ebel has said in other places, may easily misunderstand him here. For, notwithstanding all mutilations, the Irish forms have retained more distinct traces of what they once were than even the Gothic forms; and Ebel himself has done much to clear up the topics that come here under consideration.

The Celtic languages have the peculiarity, that the words in a sentence have the power of mutually influencing each other. The Sandhi rules in Sanskrit admit in this respect of only remote comparison. For, whilst in Sanskrit the words of a sentence, without distinction, are, so to speak, soldered one to another, the words in Celtic influence each other only when they are closely connected in the construction, and constitute, as it were, one grammatical formula.

Such formulæ are:—article and substantive, possessive pronoun and substantive, numeral and substantive, substantive and genitive following, substantive and demonstrative particle therewith connected, substantive and adjective, preposition and the case-form belonging to it, preposition and verbal-form (in composition), verbal particle (including the negative) and verbal-form, pronominal-object (infixed pronoun) and verbal-form, relative pronoun and verbal-form.

That these formulæ were regarded as one united word is evident from this, that in ancient Gaelic MSS. they were frequently written without any separation of the words; as, e.g., *innamban* (of the women; *inna* gen. pl. of the article, *ban* gen. pl. of *ben*, woman, wife), *nimcharat* (non me amant; *ni* the negative, *m* pron. of the first person, *carat* third pl. pres.). Already in prehistoric time, when the ancient auslaut of the word was still preserved unmutilated, these formulæ must have been in use as compound words; since the auslaut of the first and the anlaut of the second part were treated, as we may clearly recognise, according to the phonetic laws applicable to the inlaut of a simple word.

Of the secondary phonetic laws, which apply to the inlaut, two especially come here under consideration:—

1. The tenues *c*, *t* are aspirated after a vowel (*tuath*, people; = Osc. *touto*), and the spirants *s*, *v* are dropped after a vowel (*roi-gu* elegit, root *gus*);

2. The nasal is retained only before a vowel or a medial, whilst it disappears before other consonants (*moinur* puto, Skr. *manye*; but *air-mitiu* honos, cf. Lat. *mentio*).

If, in those grammatical formulæ, the first word-form ended in a vowel, then the anlaut of the second word, if capable of aspiration, was aspirated. The Old Gaulish *ambi carpenton* (circa carpentum) would have corresponded in prehistoric Old Irish to *imbe charpantan*. If the first word ended in a nasal (*n*), this *n* was preserved only when the anlaut of the second was a vowel or a medial. The Old Celtic *decen equi* would have been *dechen equi* in prehistoric Old Irish; but *decen tarvi* in Old Celtic must have been *deche tarvi* in pre-historic Old Irish.

These conditions were preserved in the formula, even after the original last syllables of the words had been suppressed. In this way is explained the form which the examples just mentioned have assumed in historical Old Irish: *imm charpat, deich neich, deich tairb;* apart from the formula they are *carpat, deich, eich*. In the Homeric language it is the verse-formula, in the Celtic it is the grammatical-formula, which preserved the prehistoric condition of the language.

Something similar we observe in the French language, in which throughout, as Ebel has frequently shown, much of the Celtic spirit is preserved. Here the ancient *t* of the third per. sing. has been retained in the grammatical formula *aime-t-il, a-t-il*. Also the drawing forward of *s* to the following word, as in *les ongles*, may be mentioned here.

Terminations, the articulation of which depends upon the anlaut of the following word, are easily drawn towards it. This has happened already in Old Irish to the *n* retained before vowels and medials, since we write, e.g., *deich neich*, sometimes with a dot over an *n* of this kind. In modern printing the mode of writing, *deich n-eich*, is to be recommended.

This nasal is rarely omitted by mistake in the MSS., whilst, on the other hand, the aspirate is less regularly marked, even in good manuscripts. But for the philological examination of a form, it is sufficient if aspiration can be proved after it in a large number of instances.

In the native Irish grammar the subjects here briefly discussed, are known by the name of aspiration and eclipsis. O'Donovan explains the latter, in his Ir. Gramm. (p. 58), in the following manner: "Eclipsis in Irish grammar may be defined the suppression of the sounds of certain radical consonants, by prefixing others of the same organ." In this way, *b* is eclipsed in pronunciation by *m*, *d* by *n*, *g* by guttural *n*; e.g. *ár m-bó* (our cow) is pronounced like *ar mó*, *ár n-doras* (our door) like *ár noras*, and so forth. In the same way, the nasal is assimilated to the following medial. The same law applies also to the inlaut: to the Old Gaulish *ambi* corresponds Ir. *imm*, and the root *gradh* (Lat. *gradior*) has become in Irish, through nasalising, *grann*, *grenn*, e.g. *in-grennat* persequuntur; (cf. K. Slav. *grędą*). The right view of aspiration and eclipsis was first represented by Bopp in his treatise on the Celtic languages (cf. Ebel, Beitr. zur Vergl. Spr. i. 155), although he only knew the facts of the modern language. The subject of aspiration is discussed in the Gramm. Celt., pp. 180 ff. The eclipsis, on the other hand, is (p. 184) only briefly treated, and even Ebel's (at that time) important article, "The so-called prosthetic *n*," does not exhaust the subject. The cases of aspiration and eclipsis, which occur in the Fis Adamnáin, Stokes has collected at pp. 24 and 38 of his (very scarce) edition of that little text.

The comparative philologist, however, must, for practical purposes, keep in mind the three following statements:

1. Words, after which aspiration appears, had originally a vowel in auslaut.

2. Words, after which a nasal appears joined to the beginning of the following word, had originally a nasal in auslaut.

3. Words, after which, when they form the first part of a grammatical formula, neither aspiration nor a nasal appears, had originally one of the remaining consonants in auslaut. Here *r*, *s*, *d*, and *t* come under consideration. Of these only *r* is preserved, the other three having always fallen off.

However, in the application of these statements caution is necessary. Aspiration and eclipsis have become, in Old and Middle Irish, grammatical principles, which have been applied where organically they had no right to be used. Aspiration appears, for instance, as a distinguishing characteristic after the nominative singular of all feminine nouns, although originally it was used only after the feminine nouns in *á*. In the same way, a succeeding *n* has been given, in the nom. and acc. sing., to all neuter nouns, e.g. even to those in *i*, whilst originally it belonged, of course, only to the *a*-stems.

Finally, the phonetic peculiarities of Irish enable us to know what kind of vowel stood at last in the suppressed final syllable. To this point Ebel has already drawn attention in the Beitr. zur Vergl. Spr. i. 164.

The *i* of the dropped last syllable has never been lost so completely that no trace of it has been preserved, for it has always entered into the preceding syllable. The regressive influence of the preserved slender vowel on the preceding syllable is not always expressed in Old Irish writing, for we find, side by side, *fáthi* and *fáithi* (vates), *sude* and *suide* (seat). The slender vowel of a lost end-syllable, on the other hand, always appears in the foregoing syllable, and many forms of inflection are clearly distinguished from others by the regular penetrating of *i* into the stem-syllable. This is effected, in the last syllable, not only by a primative *i*, but also by one originating from weakening of other vowels. In prehistoric time, the *a* of the last syllable was weakened to *e* and further to *i*, in the same case, in which this happened in Latin and Greek (*amice*, πατέρες, *aye, agis, agit, agite,* λέλοιπε). After a syllable of which the vowel is *a, o,* or *u,* one must never infer the loss of a syllable with *e* or *i.*

Though the *a* of an end-syllable has thrown back its influence into the preceding one, yet this is not always clearly seen. Original *i* was always modified into *e*, by the action of *a* of the final syllable, whence *fer* (man) for a prehistoric *vir-as*. In like manner, *a* of the final syllable has caused the broadening of *e* (originating out of *ai*) into *ia*; as, e.g. iu *dia* (god) for prehistoric *dév-as*. The influence of the once existing termination -*as* is remarkable in the genitive singular *máthar* (matris) for *mater-as*, as compared with the dative and nominative singular *máthir*. Cf. Ebel, Beitr. zur Vergl. Spr. i. 179. After a syllable with short *i*, one must never infer the loss of one with *a*. The consonant before a lost *a* does not require the softened pronunciation, even when a long *i* precedes it, e.g. in Old Irish *fír* (verus). Generally the succeeding vowel determines the pronunciation of the preceding consonant. This is shown in the later Irish by the example just mentioned in the way of writing *fíor*. In the same way, every *e*, after which a syllable with *a* has been lost, is written *ea* in he modern language: Old Irish *dliged*, New Irish *dligheadh* (law), for a prehistoric *dliget-an* ; Old Ir. *ech* (horse), New Ir. *each*, for a prehistoric *equ-as*.

The *u* of the final syllable has been preserved with less regularity in the preceding one. In the ancient language this happened always in the infinitive of the 3rd conjugation: *imbrádiud* (cogitare) stands here for *rádia-t-us*. Also, *e.g.*, forms like *fiur*, Lat. *viro*, *eoch*, Lat. *equo*, enable us clearly to see that the dative singular of masculine and neuter *a*-stems ended, in prehistoric time, in *u*, although this is not so evident in all cases.

After these preliminary remarks we turn to the exposition of the laws of auslaut.

A.

Preservation of original end-syllables.

The original end-syllable of polysyllabic words is preserved in Old Irish—(I.) When a double consonant, and (II.) When *r*, *s*, *t*, or *d*, stood in auslaut after a long vowel.

I.

A double consonant stood originally in auslaut. It disappeared when *s* was the last consonant. This loss of consonants we observe also in the original monosyllabic words *mi*, gen. *mis* = Gr. μήν; *rí*, gen. *ríg* = Lat. *réx*; *a* (*ass*) = Lat. *ex*, *é*. Here come under consideration:—

1. The accusative plural of the masculine stems in *a* and *u*, and of the masculine and feminine stems in *i*. Original -*ans*, -*uns*, -*ins* represented by Old Ir. -*u*, -*u*, -*i*. From *mís* (Gr. μηνός) we infer that there must have existed prehistoric middle forms in -*ns* (-*ôs*), -*ús*, -*ís*.

Old Ir. *firu* (nom. sing. *fer*) = Goth. *vairans*, Lat. *virôs* (Z. 277); *mugu* (servos; nom. sing. *mug*) = Goth. *maguns* (Z. 240); *fáthi* (prophetas, nom. sing. *fáith*, masc.), cf. Goth. *balgins* (Z. 237); *súli* (oculos, nom. sing. *súil*, fem.), cf. Goth. *anstins* (Z. 252). The acc. plur. of feminine *i*- stems may have been formed originally in -*is*, as in Sanskrit.

2. The nominative singular of the stems in *ant*, the *n* of which, according to the phonetic laws of Irish, was dropped in prehistoric time (as in *cét* = Lat. *centum*, *dét* = Skr. *dantas*). These are original present participles, which in Irish have become substantives or adjectives (see Stokes in Beitr. zur Vergl. Spr. vii. 66).

Original -*ents*, -*ants* represented by Old Irish -*e*, -*a* (-*o*, -*u*).

Old Ir. *bráge* (gullet, throat, neck), gen. *brágct*,* almost identical with Lat. *gurges*, only that the latter contains the suffix *at*; *lóche* (lightning, gen. *lóchet*), stem *laukant*, whilst Lat. *lúcens* = Skr. *rocayan*; *tee* (contracted *té*), later *teo* (tepidus, nom. plur. *téit*) = Skr. *tapan* (Beitr. zur Vergl. Spr. viii. 13); *care, cara* (friend, gen. *carat*), a participle, like Lat. *amans*; *dínu* (lamb, gen. *dínet*), perhaps a participle of a present-tense-form, like Skr. *dhinoti* (Rt. *dhi*, to satisfy; surely related to the root *dhé, dhá*, to suck) Z. 255.

In the same way is formed the nom. sing. of the multiples of ten from 20 to 90 (Z. 305); e.g., *fiche* (twenty, nom. plur. *tri fichit* = 60), for original *vicents*; *tricha* (thirty) = Old Baktr. *thriçáç-ca*.

3. The nom. sing. of the stems in *at*, the *t* of which, in the remaining cases, has become *th*, generally *d*, according to the phonetic laws of Irish. This suffix was originally the shorter form of the participial suffix mentioned under 2 (cf. Skr. acc. *bharantam*, gen. *bharatas*), but it appears in all Indo-European languages only in adjectives and appellatives.

Original *-ats, -ets* represented by Old Irish *-a, -u, -e, -i*. E.g., *tenga* (tongue, gen. *tengad*) connected with Lat. *tango* (for the transition of meaning cf. Eng. *taste*); *fili, file* (poet, gen. *filed*), as if it were a participle to the Cymbr. *gweled* (to see), cf. Lat. *dives, gurges*; *coimdiu*, gen. *coimded* (Lord, God), probably for *com-mediu*, belonging to the present stem *media-* in *midiur* (cogito, judico); cf., however, Old Saxon and A.S. *metod* (God). In some cases the vowel has disappeared, except in the loan-word *mil* (miles), e.g. in *cing* (bellator, gen. *cinged*) Z. 255.

Atrebas (the Atrebate: Caes. de Bell. Gall. iv. 35) may pass as an Old Gaul. nominative of this kind, nom. plur. *Atrebates* (cf. Gluck, Kelt. Namen, p. 36), connected with Old Ir. *atreba*, i.e. *ad-treba* (possidet, habitat).

4. The nom. sing. of the abstracts in *tát*, which, in the remaining cases, has become *tud* (seldom *tuth*), according to the Irish phonetic laws. Original *-tats* represented by Old Irish *-tu, -thu*. E.g.,

* Beside Ir. *bráge* Stokes (Beitr. zur Verg. Spr. viii. 351) rightly places also Gr. βρόγχος; O.H.G. *chraye* (neck, throat) also belongs here (Rt. *gargh*). The length of the *a* in *bráge* is explained by the metathesis, as in *lám* (hand) = Lat. *palma*. But one must not, referring to the Gr. βρόγχος, assume the loss of a once existing nasal. In Irish the nasal before a tennis or *s* is dropped out without exception, but one cannot regard the loss of the nasal before the medials as a phonetic law in Irish.

beothu, gen. *bethad*, = Gr. βιότης; *dentu*, dat. *dentid*, = Lat. *unitas*, Z. 256.

5. The nom. sing. of some guttural stems.

Original *-aks*, *-eks* represented by Old Ir. *-a*, *-e*. E.g., *aire* (primas, gen. *airech*, *arech*), perhaps connected with Skr. *áryaka*, cf. Gr. φύλαξ; *ruire* (dominus, gen. *rurech*). Sometimes the vowel also disappears, e.g., *ail* (saxum, gen. *ailech*). The nom. *cathir* (city), *nathir* (serpent), &c. (Z. 259), have been formed, according to my opinion, without the secondary suffix *ac*, which, in the most of the remaining cases, has become fixed, e.g., gen. *catrach*, *nathrach* (for *cutarac-as*, *natarac-as*).

6. The nom. sing. of stems in *nn* and of some stems in *n*. See Excursus iii. 2.

7. The conjunctive form of the 3rd pers. plur. active.

In combination with prepositions, and in the enclitic leaning towards certain other particles (*no*, *ro*, *ni*, &c.), an Irish verb takes other forms than it would, standing alone. The distinction between these conjunctive and absolute forms consists, in most cases, according to my view, which I have already stated (Beitr. zur Vergl. Spr. viii. 450), in this, that the first are formed with the secondary, the second with the primary personal endings. Some of the absolute forms seem certainly to have originated through later agglutination of pronominal elements. Stokes, however, would have all absolute forms explained in this way (Beitr. vi. 465).

Original *-ant* represented by Old Ir. *-at*, with loss of the nasal, as in *cét* = *centum*, *dét* (tooth), &c. E.g. *asberat* (dicunt) = Lat. *efferunt* (if it has not lost an *i* in auslaut). Stokes traces *berat* back to *beranti*, but in Irish the *i* of the original auslaut is never lost without a trace remaining, since it always penetrated, ere it was lost, into the preceding syllable (see B. xii.). From an original *beranti* must arise *berait*, *berit*, a form which has actually been preserved as the absolute form of the 3rd plur. active, and has gradually displaced entirely that shorter form. The only thing that can be said against my view, is that, in many places, aspiration has been proved after the 3rd plur. in *-at*, *-et*; e.g. *acht ropat saini* (modo sint diversae), *fodalet chenel* (distinguunt genus), Z. 182, Beitr. zur Vergl. Spr. vi. 464. We would naturally infer from such aspiration that the preceding word ended originally in a vowel. Since an *i*, as we proved above, is not to be thought of, it only remains to try *a* and *u*.

But -*ant-a* would lead to a medial form altogether unusual in the present indicative active, whilst -*ant-u* would lead to an indicative form unheard of in this tense. I believe, therefore, that the aspiration which has been proved in some places after the 3rd person plur. in *at* must be otherwise accounted for. That there may be cases, in which the aspiration could not have been caused by the original auslaut of the preceding word, Stokes has already shown in his tract Fis Adamnáin. Thus, the preposition *co* (ad), when joined with pronominal elements, sometimes in Old Irish, but regularly in the middle and later language, took the form *chuc-* (*chucu* ad eos, *chucum* ad me, &c.). Also, in the before-mentioned *asmbiur frit* (quod dico tibi), the silencing of *f* has probably not been caused by the preceding word, since the preposition *fri* loses its *f* gradually in all other places. Of other words there are especially the particles *thra* and *chena*, which, in early Middle Irish, appear nearly always with aspirated *anlaut*. In *chucu* for *cucu* the aspiration may have been produced by a certain tendency towards phonetic dissimilarity, in other cases through the carelessness with which enclitic and proclitic words were pronounced. But they evidently are cases, in which aspiration has been used in a transferred or figurative manner to denote relationship or dependence, when of two words the succeeding was closely connected with the preceding one, in the construction and pronunciation of a sentence.

To these I add those, which, if the aspiration appears in the relative verbal-forms, follow immediately after their relative words. This usage is not prevalent, but it is found, for example, in *inaní choínte* (eorum qui deplorant, Z. 181), *ni fri biasta chathaigmit-ni* (it is not against beasts that we fight). In New Irish it has become a rule to distinguish the accusative of the pronoun of the second person by the aspirated form *thú* from the nominative *tú* (O'Donovan's Ir. Gramm., p. 127). Of the same kind are probably those cases, in which after the 3rd plur. in -*at*, -*et*, the object immediately following has been aspirated, as in *fodalet chenél*. We may expect this aspiration also after every other verbal-form, and, indeed, we find *ro gab chrine* (cepit marcorem) given in Z. 182. Also, the aspiration of the subject or the predicate immediately after the copula, of which I have given above the example, *act ropat saini* (modi sint diversae), I should like to explain in a similar manner: here the aspiration was originally rightly used only, when the form of the copula, as in the 3rd sing. perf. *bói, bo*, ended originally in a vowel (*ro bói chocad*, fuit bellum), but it was also further introduced where the phonetic cause did not exist. In the modern language this aspiration has been preserved only after that 3rd sing. perfect *ba*, and after no other verbal-form (O'Donovan's Ir. Gramm., p. 386). Like the aspiration, so the *n* also enters in the older language after word-forms, to which it originally did not belong (See B. vi.).

II.

r, s, t, or *d* with a preceding long vowel stood originally in auslaut. The length of the vowel has been shortened. The consonant was retained only, if an *r*. Also, an original short vowel with *r* is preserved as a special syllable. Aspiration never appears after the forms that come under this head. These come under consideration :—

1. The nom. sing. of the names of relationship. The more primative *ár (ér, ór)*, represented by Old Ir. *ir, ur*; e.g. *athir* = Gr. πατήρ, Lat. *pater; mathir* = Dor. μάτηρ, Lat. *mater; bráthir* = Gr. φρατήρ, Lat. *frater; siur* = Lat. *soror* (for *svesor*), Z. 262;

2. The preposition *eter, etir*, for prehistoric *enter* = Lat. *inter*, Skr. *antar*; Z. 656;

3. The nom. and acc. plur. of feminine stems in *á* (Z. 244).*

Original *ás*, represented by Old Ir. *a*, seldom *e*, e.g. *tuatha* = Goth. *thiudos*, Old. Sax. *thiodá; runa* = Goth. *rûnôs; mná* (women), for *bná, bana* (nom. sing. *ben* = Bœot. βανά) = Ved. *gnás*. Ebel has advanced the opinion (Beitr. zur Vergl. Spr. i. 181) that -*a* in the nom. plur. originated out of *ái* ("as in Gr. and Lat."), but as he did not introduce it into the Gramm. Celt. (p. 245), he probably abandoned it. Against this opinion there is to be said (1) that original *ái* would not have been preserved as a special syllable (as proved, for example, by the dat. sing. *tuaith*), and (2) that the nom. plur. fem. of the article *inna* or *na* never causes aspiration (*inna tuatha, inna caillecha*), consequently, it must have ended in a consonant, i.e. in *ás*. For the Gaulish nom. plur. of this declension, see H. D'Arbois de Jubainville's "La Déclinaison Latine en Gaule," p. 23.

The neutral stems in *a* follow, in this case, already in Old Irish the analogy of feminines: *dligeda* (laws, nom. sing. *dliged*, for *dliget-am*, related to Goth. *dulgs*, K. Slav. *dlŭgŭ* debitum, and

* For the gen. sing. of these stems see Excursus II. 12.

connected in the stem-formation with Skr. *rajata-m*, Goth. *liuhath); imneda* (tribulationes, nom. sing. *imned*), Z. 226. H. d'Arbois Jubainville, at p. 56 and other places, has proved that, likewise, in the Lat. of the Merovingian period, the neuters in the nom. plur. were formed most frequently after the analogy of the feminines. For the genuine neuter form of the nom. and acc. plur. *dliged* for *dliged-a* still preserved in the Old Irish, see B. xi. 3. At first the feminine form for the neuter form, as Ebel already saw (Beitr. zur Vergl. Spr. i. 157, 175), was introduced into the article (Z. 215); the neuter *inna*, *na*, is identical in form with the acc. plur. feminine; a genuine neut. form is not to be met with in the oldest sources (according to the analogy of *dliged*, *imned*, it ought to have been *in*, *ind*, with aspiration following). In the acc. plur. there is existing even for the masculine no other form than the feminine *inna*, *na*: already in Old Irish *inna firu* (τοὺς ἄνδρας), instead of *inmu firu*. The nom. plur. masculine has yet in Old Irish the special form *ind* or *in* (*ind fir*, οἱ ἄνδρες); already, however, in Middle Irish this genuine form is suppressed by the *inna*, *na* of the feminine. The adjectives follow the article: instead of Old Irish *in maice* (pueri) one could say *na maice* in Middle Irish, and instead of Old Irish *maice bice* (pueri parvi), *maice becca* in Middle Irish.

The same analogy is, according to my opinion, to be accepted in the consonantal stems (masc. and fem. gen.), which end in *a* in the acc. plural, e.g., *fileda* (poetas), *aithrea* (πατέρας). The Skr. *as* in *bharat-as*, Gr. φέροντ-ας, would not have remained as a full syllable in Old Irish. That a prehistoric πατέρας was attracted by a prehistoric *toutás* is not to be wondered at, especially if we keep in mind that the always unchanging accusative plural of the article could only favour this transition, and that, on the other hand, the same stems agree also in the accusative singular (B. V. 2). The termination *ás* in the acc. plur. of the consonantal stems Ebel has explained also in the Beitr. zur Vergl. Spr. i. 168, from whom, however, I differ in view. For the Gaulish forms of this kind see H. d'Arbois de Jubainville (Rev. Celt. i. p. 320).

4. The 2nd pers. sing. of the present conjunctive of the conjunct flexion may be best observed in the 1st conjugation (= 3rd Lat. conjugation). Also, here the older *-ás* is represented in Irish by *a*, and in further weakening by *e*. E.g., *cia as-bera*, *cia as-bere* (quamvis dicas), Z. 440; *-bera* = Lat. *feras*, cf. Ved. *gacchás* (Delbrück, Alt-Ind. Verb. p. 37). In open contrast to this stands

the corresponding form of the indicative *as-beir* (dicis) for *-beris*. That form can be traced back to *-bharás*, this to *-bharas*.

Conjunctive-flexion is also in the reduplicated future; e.g., *ní béra-so* (non feres tu), Z. 452, 1091. Probably only the forms ending in *a* and *e* belong to the conjunct flexion. On the other hand, I am inclined to add the forms in *ae* and *ai* to the absolute flexion, which here is not sharply distinguished from the conjunct flexion, and, e.g., to trace back *fo-n-didmae-siu* to a more primitive *dedamási* (Rt. *dam*), Z. 452. At any rate, the 3rd sing. conjunctive of the conjunct flexion, which will be treated next, has always an *a*. Such forms as the inferred *dedamási* (from *didmae*) correspond in their formation most closely to Gr. conjunctives, like πέφνῃς.

5. The 3rd sing. conjunctive present of the conjunct flexion. Original *át* represented by Old Irish *a*. E.g., *air-ema* (suscipiat), Z. 441, *-ema* = Lat. *emat*; *cia at-bela* (quamvis pereat, Rt. *bal*, Ger. *qual*). Cf. Skr. *bharát*, *patát*, &c. (Delbrük's Alt-Ind. Verb, p. 57). In direct contrast to this in the corresponding forms of the indicative are *ar-fo-im* (accipit; for *em-it*), *at-bail* (perit; for *bal-it*). Similarly, in the 3rd sing. of the reduplicated future of the conjunct flexion, e.g., *for-cechna* (praecipiet; rt. *can*), to be compared in the formation to the Gr. πέφνῃ, only that the latter had the primary personal ending.

6. The emphatic form of the 2nd sing. imperative. Original *-tád* represented by Old Irish *-te, -ta*, the *t* of which has become, after a vowel, *th* or *d*, according to the Irish phonetic laws. E.g., *cluinte* (audito, Stokes in Beitr. vii 2; Z. 443, 1090), as it were a Ved. *çrnu-tád*, which may have been formed according to the analogy of *krnutád*, quoted in Delbrück's Alt-Ind. Verb., p. 39. In the Italic the ending in *tád* appears in the 2nd and 3rd person sing. imperative, in Old Irish and in the Vedic languages it is limited to the 2nd person, except in that one Vedic example *gachatád*, which Delbrück, at p. 59 and other places, quotes for the 3rd person. I regard *tád* as the ending properly to be inferred, not *tát*, because of the Oscan *estud* (orig. *d* also in the abl. sing. and in the pronominal forms, like Skr. *tad*, Lat *istud*).

7. *cetu, ceta* (primum), Z. 614, a more uncertain case. For Lat. *primus* the Irish has the two words *cét* and *cétne* (Z. 307, 308), the former of which has the stem *cinta*, and the latter the further developed form *cintania*. If the adverb *cetu, ceta* be a petrified

case of *cét* (stem *cinta*), it could originate only as an ablative from the original *cintád*. The shortening of the proper long *é*, which appears especially in the form *cita*, may be attributed to the frequent proclitic use of this adverb. When aspiration appears after *ceta*, as, for example, in *corrop si ceta thé* (that it is she who goes first), then it must occur unorganically, as in the cases mentioned at pp. 31, 36.

Surely with regard to the Latin, the case-form in which the compared subject stands after the comparative (e.g., *lia . . . triur*, *plures . . . quam tres*), and, further, the case-form in which the adjective has become an adverb (e.g., *in biuc paullum*, from *becc parvus*), have, in the Gramm. Celt., been placed along with the Indo-European ablative. I do not think this right; in the masculine and neuter *a*- stems the vowel *a* would have remained at the end from the original *-ád* of the ablative. The just-mentioned forms are rather to be classified with the Indo-European instrumental case, as I have done B. XI. 9.

For the formation of the ablative in *-tas* see under B. I. 8.

(*To be continued.*)

GRAMMATICAL AND ETYMOLOGICAL ANALYSIS OF GENESIS I. 1—8.

1. "'S an toiseach chruthaich Dia na neamhan agus an talamh."

'*S* is for *anns* (in), a prep. governing the dative case. *Anns* was in Old Gaelic *is* and sometimes *iss* for *ins*, the prep. *in* with the suffix *s* which properly belongs to the article in the dat. case. The prep. *in* is cognate with Lat. *in*, Gr. ἐν or ἐνί, Skr. *an*- in *antar* (within), Goth., Ger., A.S., and Eng. *in*. Cf. Zeuss' Gramm. Celt., p. 626.

An (the) is the modern form of the article. The ancient forms were for the mas. sing. *int* and *in*, for the fem. sing. *ind* and *in*, and for the neut. sing. *an* and *a*. The stem is *sind* = *sanda*. Zeuss' G. C., p. 209. The Gaelic article, originally a demonstrative pronoun, is cognate with Skr. dem. pron. *ana*, Lit. *ans*, fem. *ana* (that, that one), Slav. *onu*. The modern article, although agreeing in form with the ancient neuter article now lost, represents the ancient form *in*. Cf. mod. prep. *an* = anc. *in*.

Toiseach (beginning) is dat. of mas. noun *toiseach*, gen. *toisich* in Old Gael. *toiseach* was in nom. *tosach* and *tossach*, and in dat. *tosuch*, *tossuch*, *tosug*, and *tossvg*, all which forms are found in Zeuss. *Toiseach* and its related words *tòiseach* (princeps) and *tùs* (beginning) for *tovus*, are derived from the root *tuv*, which is connected with the Skr. root *tu* (to increase), *tuv-i* (strong), *tav-i-mi* (to be strong), Zend *tu* (to have power), Gr. ταῦς, for ταF-υς (strong), Goth. *thiv-an* (to prevail upon), A.S. *thû-ma* (thumb), O.H.G. *dû-mo* (thumb), Eng. *thu-mb*. Cf. Welsh *twf* (increase, growth), *tyfu* (to grow). See root *tu* in Williams' Skr. Dictionary; cf. also Curtius' Grundzüge, 4th ed., p. 225. The loss of *v* in *tùs* (beginning) is shown by the W. *towysogion*, now *tywysogion*, *tywys*. To the same root belongs Gael. *tuath* (people).

Chruthaich (created, formed), of which the inf. in O. Gael. was *cruthugud*, is the pret. ind. act. of the verb *cruthaich* (create) from *cruth* (form). *Cruth*, a *u*-stem, of which the gen. in O. Gael. is *crotho* (= *crutavas*) seems connected with the Indo-European root *kar* (to do, to make), Skr. root *kar* (to do, to make), *kar-tr* (completer, creator), Gr. root κρα, κραν, whence κραίν-ω (I complete), Lat. *cre-o* (I create), Lith. *kur-iu*, *kur-ti* (to build). Cf. Stokes' Irish Glosses, p. 71, Curtius' Grundz., p. 154, and Fick's Vergl. Wort., p. 520.

Dia (God) is nom. to verb *chruthaich*. The gen. sing. is *Dé* and the nom. plur. *dée* or *diathan*. *Dia* (= *Dé*, for *ia* = *e*), which has dropped an original *v* as may be seen by comparing W. *Dyw*, is connected with Lat. *div-us* (divine) and *deus* (God), Gr. δῖος (= διFιος), Ζεύς, Skr. *dévas* (God) and *divjas* (heavenly), Zend *div* (shine), *daeva* (demon), Old Norse *tivar* (gods, heroes), A.S. *Tives* in *Tives-däg* (Tuesday). For loss of *v* in Gaelic cf. *cliù*, *lì*, *òg*, *ola*, &c.

Na (the), the acc. plur. of the article, in O. Gael. *inna* and *(s)na*.

Nèamhan (heavens), the acc. plur. of *nèamh*, gen. *nèimhe*. *Nèamh* was in O. Gael. *nem*, gen. *nime*, an *as*-stem (**nebhas*) connected by Dr. Stokes and others with Gr. νέφος (clouds), νεφέλη (cloud), Lat. *nebula* (cloud), O.H.G. *nëbal*, N.H.G. *nebel* (mist, fog), Ch. Slav. *nebo* (heaven). These words are all connected with Skr. *nabhas* (heaven), from root *nabh*. To this root belongs also Gael. *neul* (cloud), in O. Gael. *nél* = **nebl*. For other examples of the passing of *b* into *m* cf. *claidheamh* (sword) = O. Gael. *claideb*, *mnà* (gen. sing. of *bean* = *ben*) = *bena*, and *naomh* (holy) = O. Gael.

noib. *Nem* and *nemed* (sanctuary) are referred by Windish to the Skr. root *nam* (s'incliner, vénérer). Cf. Rev. Celt., iii, 330.

Agus (and) is the modern form of the conjunction *acus* or *ocus*, which Ebel regarded, because of its power of aspirating, as a dative locative. Other related Celtic words are W. *ac* (and), Gael. *oc* (at). now *ag* and *aig*, Gael. adj. *acus* or *ocus* (near), now *fagus* or *fogus*, with prosthetic *f*. These and several other words were connected by Ebel (cf. Celtic Studies, p. 109) with Gr. ἄγχι (near), ἐγγύς (near), Lat. *ango* (I draw or press tight, squeeze), *ang-ustus* (narrow), Goth. *aggvus* (narrow), O.H.G. *angi*, N.H.G. *enge*.

Talamh (earth, the earth), O. Gael. *talam*, gen. *talman*, dat. *talmain*, is a fem. *man*-stem (Z. G. C., p. 775), formed by the suffix -*man* from a root connected apparently with Skr. *tala* (flatness, soil, ground), *mahi-tala* (the surface of the earth, the earth itself). Cf. Slav. *tilo* (ground, soil). See *tala* in Williams' Skr. Dictionary and in Bopp's Glossarium. "*Talamh* has nothing to do with Skr. *dhanvan*, which Kuhn (Beitr. I., 368-9) has identified with Lat. *tellus* = *telvûs*." (Stokes' Glosses, p. 48.) Bopp and Williams connect both *talamh* and *tellus* with Skr. *tala*.

2. "Agus bha'n talamh gun dealbh agus falamh; agus bha dorchadas air aghaidh na doimhne; agus bha Spiorad Dè a' gluasad air aghaidh nan uisgeacha."

Bha'n = *bha* (was) and *an* (the). The vowel of the article is elided because *bha* ends with a vowel. *Bha*, in O. Gael. *ba* and *roba* (with verbal prefix *ro*), is the pret. ind. of the verb *bi* (be thou), of which the 1st per. sing. pres. ind. in O. Gael. was *biu* (I am). The aspiration of *bha* is explained by the loss of the particle *ro* in the modern preterite. *Biu* is from the root *bu* cognate with Skr. root *bhû*, Zend *bû* (to be), Gr. φυ in φύω, Lat. *fu* in pret. *fui*, O.H.G. *bim*, Old Sax. *bium*, A. Sax. *beom*, Eng. *be*. The Indo-European root is *bhu*.

Gun (without) is the modern form of the prep. *cen*, which, since it always aspirates, must have ended originally in a vowel, probably *e*. Stokes, in Kuhn's Beitr. (vol. iii, p. 312), connects *cen* or *cene* with Gr. κενεός (empty), Skr. *çûnja* (inanis). Cf. Z. G. C., p. 655. *Cen* is one of the prepositions that governed the acc. in ancient Gaelic. In modern Gaelic *gun* governs either the dat. or acc., as "gun chrìoch," "gun chèill." Cf. Stewart's Gram., p. 161.

Dealbh (form), in O. Gael. *delb* (= W. *delw*), with *b* for *v* as in *tarb* and *marb*, now *tarbh* and *marbh*, is referred by Stokes (Beitr. iv. 410) to the root *dhar*, Skr. *dhara* from *dhri*, with which may be connected Lat. *for-ma*, from which Eng. *form* is derived. Cf. Williams' Skr. Dictionary. The gen. of *delb* is *delbe*, the dat. *deilb*, the acc. *delb*, and the nom. plur. *delbae*. Cf. Nigra's Turin Glosses, p. 41. Other connected forms are *dolbud* (figmentum) and *doilbtheoir* (fictor) from root *dal*. *Delb* is a fem. *a*-stem = *delva*.

Falamh or *folamh* (empty, void), in O. Gael. *folam*. Cf. *folom*, *folomm* = *fo-lomm* (the pref. *fo* and adj. *lom* or *lomm*, bare). See Wind. Ir. Texts, p. 562. Bopp. compares *lonaim* (I shear, make bare), and Skt. *lumpámi* (break, cut, cut off) from rt. *lup* = *rup*.

Dorchadas (darkness) is an abstract noun mas. (nom. to *bha*) from adj. *dorcha* (dark) = O. Gael. *dorchae*. Is *dorcha* = *do-r'ch-a* = *do-ruch-a*, the pref. *do* cognate with Skr. *dus* and Gr. δύς, and the root *ruch* (to shine) with suf. *a*? Cf. Skr. *ruch* (to shine), Gr. λευκὸς (light), Lat. *luceo* (I shine), *lumen* (light) for *lucmen*, and *luna* (moon) for *lucna*, Goth. *liuh-ath* (light), O.H.G. *leoht*, A.S. *leóht*, Eng. *light*. If *dorcha* = *do-r'ch-a*, its opposite, *sorcha* = *so-r'ch-a* = *so-ruch-a*, of which *so* is cognate with Skr. *su* and Gr. εὖ. Cf. Stokes' Ir. Glosses, pp. 46 and 69. With *dorcha* Ebel has connected A.S. *dëorc* and Eng. *dark*, O. H. G. *tarch*, O. N. *döckr*.

Air (on), a prep. governing the dat. and acc., was in O. Gael. *ar* and in Gaul. *are-* (cf. *Aremorici*), the original vowel-ending of this word accounting for its power of aspirating. *Air* is for *ari = *pari (initial *p* being dropped, as usual in Gaelic), cognate with Skr. *pra-* (fore-), Zend *fra-* (fore-), Gr. πρό (before), Lat. *pro* (for) and *prae* (before), Goth. *fru-* in *fruma* (first), Slav. *pra-*, *pro-*, *pre-* (fore-), Lith. *pra-* (fore-). Cf. Curtius' Grundz., p. 285.

Aghaidh (face) = O. Gael. *agaid*, also *agid*, dat. of noun *agu*, which Windisch has connected with Skr. *aksham*, *akslam*, *akshi* (eye), Zend *akhsh* (see), *ashi* (eye), Gr. ὤψ (sight, face), Lat. *oculus* (eye), Goth. *augo* (the eye), *augjan* (show), Lith. *akis* (eye), Slav. *oko* (eye). Cf. Curtius' Grundz., p. 457. In modern Gaelic *aghaidh* is a fem. noun indeclinable in the singular.

Na (the) is the gen. sing. fem. of the article, in O. Gael. *inna* and *na*.

Doimhne (of the deep) is the gen. sing. of the abstract noun *doimhne* = O. Gael. *domnu* from *domun* (deep), now *domhain*. The *m* of *domun* is for *b*, as may be seen by comparing *Damnorix* for *Dubnorix*, *Cogidumnus* for *Cogidubnus*, and *Samnites* for *Sabnites* in Z.G.C., p. 40. *Dubn* is connected by Glück (Kelt. Namen, p. 72) with Goth. *diup* from *dup*, O.H.G. *tiof*, Eng. *deep*.

Spiorad (spirit), in O. Gael. *spirut*, is borrowed from Lat. *spiritus*.

Dé is gen. sing. of *Dia* compared above.

A' = *ag* (at) = O. Gael. *ac*, which is connected with the conjunction *ocus* compared above. *Ag* is contracted into *a'* before infinitives beginning with a consonant. *Ag* governs the dative.

Gluasad (moving) is the inf. dat. after *a'* of the verb *gluais* (move), referred by Nigra to "a root *gval*, Gr., Lat., and Celt. *gvol* (fluere, jacere)." Cf. Rev. Celt., ii., p. 448. Nigra also compares Lat. *volare*, *volucer*, Gr. βόλος, βολή, Skr. *gula*, *glau*, O. Ger. *quella*, *cliuwa*, *chliuwa*, *cliuwi* (glomus).

Nan (of the) gen. plur. of the article, in O. Gael. *innan* and *inna*.

Uisgeacha (waters), gen. plur. of *uisge* (water), a mas. noun indecl. in the sing. *Uisge* was in O. Gael. *uisce* and *usce* = *ud-ce. For change of *d* to *s* before *c*, cf. *mesce* (now *misge*) = *med-ce from root *med* cognate with Gr. μέθυ (wine), Skr. *madhu* (honey), Lith. *medus* (honey), A.S. *medo* (mead), Eng. *mead*, and also Lat. *esca* = *ed-ca. The root *ud* of *usce* is identical with the Skr. root *ud*, from which come *und-ami* (to gush forth), *ud-am* and *uda-kam* (water), *ud-an* (wave, water), Lat. *und-a* (wave), Gr. ὕδ-ωρ (water), ὑδαρός (watery), Goth. *vato* (water), O.H.G. *wazar* (water), O.N. *vatn* (water), Eng. *water*. Cf. Curtius' Grundz., pp. 248, 249.

3. "Agus thubhairt Dia, Biodh solus ann: agus bha solus ann."

Thubhairt (said) is 3rd sing. pret. ind. act. of irreg. verb *abair* (say). *Thubhairt*, like *abair*, is a derivative from the O. Gael. verb *biur* (I say) = *biru. The suf. *tu-* = *do- fo-*. Cf. Z. G. C., p. 883. *Thubhairt*, therefore, if not for *dubhairt* (= *do-ber-t*), the form in Bedel's Translation, is for *do-fo-ber-t*, from the root *ber*, cognate with the Skr. root *bhar*, *bhri*, Gr. φέρω, Lat. *fero*, Eng. *bear*. The root is general in the Indo-European languages.

Biodh (let be), in O. Gael. *bid*, *biid*, *biid*, *biith*, *biith* (cf. Z. G. C., p. 495), is the 3rd sing. imper. of the verb *bi*, from the root *bu*, compared above.

Solus (light) = *svalas-tu, from root *sval* connected with Skr. *svar* (to shine), *sûrjas* (sun) for *svarjas*, Zend *hvare* (sun), Gr. σέλας (brightness), σελήνη (moon), Lat. *serénus*, *sól* (sun), Goth.

sauil (sun), O.N. *sól* (sun), Lith. *sáule* (sun). To the same root belong *soillse* (brightness), *soillsich* (enlighten), *súil* (eye), = **svali* and W. *haul* (sun). Cf. Curtius' Grundz., p. 541, and Kuhn's Ztschr., xxi., 428.

Ann (there)=O. Gael. *and*, an adverbial locative of the article (cf. above), with initial *s* of the stem **sandu* dropped. See Beitr., iii., 272. For loss of initial *s* in Gaelic cf. *amail* = *samail*.

4. " Agus chunnaic Dia an solus gu'n robh e math; agus chuir Dia dealachadh eadar an solus agus an dorchadas."

Chunnaic (saw), is 3rd sing. pret. ind. act. of the irreg. verb *faic* (see). *Chunnaic* = *chonnaic* (cf. O'Don.'s Gramm., p. 223) = *con-faic*, of which *con* = Lat. *con* and *faic* (Ir. *faicim*) = *f-aci* = O. Gael. *aci* = *adci* (videt) = *ad-ci*, the pref. *ad* and the verb *ci*, in 1st sing. pres. ind. *ciu* = **cesiu* (vowel-flanked *s* having dropped out) from the root *cas* (to see) cognate with Skr. root *caksh* (to see) and *cakshus* (eye). From the same root come Ir. *cais* (eye) = **cas-ti*, *imcasti* (consideranda), and *remcaissiu* (providentia). Cf. Kuhn's Ztschr., xxi., 424. The *f* of *faic* and *faca* is prosthetic, as in *fan* (stay), *fás* (grow), and *fáinne* (ring).

Gu'n (conj. that, *ad quod*). This conjunction is the prep. *gu* (to), in O. Gael. *co* = **cot*, cognate with Gr. κατά, and *an* (that) the relat. in the acc. (cf. p. 79), which is identical in form with the neuter article **san*. Cf. Ebel in Kuhn's Beitr. ii., 75, and Trans. of Celtic Studies, p. 89.

Robh (was), pret. rel., with pref. *ro*, of verb *bi*, in O. Gael. *biu* (I am), from root *bu*. Cf. *bha*, above. *Ro* = Lat. *pro*, initial *p* being dropped according to rule. This pref. is, therefore, radically connected with the prep. *air* compared above.

E (he, it) is the 3rd per. pron. sing. mas., in O. Gael. *é* and *hé*. The fem. was *si* and the neut. *ed*. These forms correspond exactly to Goth. mas. *is*, fem. *si*, and neut. *ita*. Cf. also Lat. *is*, *ea*, *id*.

Math (good) is also written *maith* = **mati*, O. Gael. pl. *maithi*. The Gaulish form of this word, *matos* (cf. *Teuto-matus*), shows that it is not connected, directly at any rate, with Lat. *mītis* = **moitis*, of which the regular Gael. representative is ancient *moith* (soft, tender), Mid. Gael. *maeth*, Mod. Gael. *maoth*. For Lat. *ī* = *oi*, cf. *vinum* and Gr. οἶνος = *Foινος* and *vicus* = οἶκος = *Foικος*. Dr. Stokes, in Rev. Celt., iii., 36, gives *maith* as perhaps derived from a stem **mandi* from the root *mand*, but adds that the etymology of this word is "still highly uncertain." For the root *mand* cf. Fick's Wörterbuch, i., 392.

Chuir (set, put, place) the pret. of *cuir*, infin. *cur*, is perhaps connected with the Skr. root *kar* (to do, to make), Lith. *kur-iu* (to build), and the other words compared under *cruth*. Cf. Curtius' Gr. Etymology, p. 154.

Dealachadh (separation) is the inf. or verbal noun, acc. case, of the verb *dealaich* (separate, divide). *Dealachadh* = O. Gael. *deliugud* (Corm.'s Glossary, p. 54) is from the root *dal* (to divide) identical with Skr. root *dal* (to divide, to split), *dala* (a part or portion), Ger. *theilen* (to divide). Goth. *dails* (a part), Ice. *dalr* (a dale), A.S. *dael* (a part) and *daelan* (to divide), Eng. *deal*. To the same root belong Gael. *dail* (a dale), Ger. *thal*, and Eng. *dale*.

Eadar (between) is the modern weakened form of the prep. *eter*, also written *etir* and *itar*, cognate with Lat. *inter* (between), from prep. *in* cognate with the Gaelic prep. *in* compared above. *Eter* has dropped *n* before the tenuis *t* by rule. Cf. Z.G.C., p. 42.

5. "Agus dh'ainmich Dia an solus Là, agus an dorchadas dh'ainmich e Oidhche: agus b'iad am feasgar agus a' mhaduinn an ceud là."

Dh'ainmich (named) = *do ainmich*. *Do* is a verbal particle always used before the pret. ind. of verbs beginning with a vowel or with *f*. It is identical with the prep. *do*, which is etymologically connected with Slav. *do* (to), Goth. *du*, Ger. *zu*, A.S. *to*, Eng. *to*, Lat. *do* in *endo*, Gr. δε (towards), Zend *da*. Cf. Curtius' Grundz., p. 233. *Ainmich* is the pret. act. of *ainmich* (to name) from *ainm* (name) (= *anmi*), plur. *anman*, connected with Skr. *naman*, Gr. ὄνομα, Lat. *nomen* (name) and *cognomen* (surname), Goth. *namo* (name), A.S. *nama*, Eng. *name*. The stem is *gnâman* from root *gna, gan*, cognate with Skr. *jna*. To the same root belong Gr. γιγνώσκω, Lat. *nosco* for *gnosco*, Eng. *know*, Gael. *aithgne* (knowledge), *gnùis* (countenance), *nòs* (custom) for *gnòs*, &c.

Là or *lò* (day) is referred by Nigra to a stem *pratia, cognate with Skr. *pratar* (the morning), but the connection is doubtful. The forms *lá, làa, ló*, must have early lost a *t*. Cf. *làthe, làithe*.

Oidhche (night), in Old Gael. *aidche*, was connected by Pictet (cf. Orig. Indo-Europ., II. 588) with Skr. *andhika* (night), the nasal being suppressed in Gaelic. For suppression of nasal cf. Skr. root *bandh* and O. Gael. *buiden*, now *buidhean* (a troop).

B'iad = *bu* (was or were) and *iad* (they). *Bu* is the regular Gael. representative of Gr. φυ- in φύω, and of Lat. *fu-* in *fui*, compared above under *bha*.

Iad is the modern weakened form of the ancient 3rd per. pron. plur. *iat*, from which, as shown by the absence of aspiration, *n*, preserved in W. *wynt*, has dropped out, as is usual before the tenues. *Iad* is thus shown to correspond to the Skr., Gr., and Lat. suffixes in *nt* of the 3rd per. plur. of the verb. Cf. Bopp's Comp. Grammar. It is worthy of notice that these pron. verb suffixes are preserved as separate words in the Celtic languages.

Feasgar (evening) was in O. Gael. *fescor*, dat. *fescur*, agreeing to, if not, as is more probable, borrowed from Lat. *vesper*, Gr. ἕσπερος. The Corn. *gwespur*, Arm. *gousper*, and W. *gosper* have retained the *p* which Gaelic has changed into *c*, as is usual in loan-words. In W. *ucher p* has become *ch*.

Maduinn (morning) is the modern form of *matin*, connected with, or rather borrowed from, Lat. *matutinus*.

Ceud (first) was in O. Gael. *cét* = W. *kynt* = Gaul. *cintus* (cf. *Cintugenus* = Gael. *Cetgen*).

6. "Agus thubhairt Dia, Biodh athar am meadhon nan uisgeachan, agus cuireadh e dealachadh cadar uisgeachan agus uisgeacha."

Athar (the air, firmament) = Gr. αἰθήρ, Lat. *aether*.

Am meadhon (in midst, amidst) was in O. Gael. *immedon*, the prep. *im* and noun *medon* written together as one word. *Am* (in) = O. Gael. *im* for *in* compared above under *anns*. *N* of the prep. becomes *m* before the labial *m* of *meadhon*. It may be noticed here that *am* is not a contracted word, and that, therefore, it should not be written with an apostrophe before it. Of this prep. there is a reduplicated form *ann am*, as "ann am meadhon" (in midst, amidst). *Meadhon* (middle, midst) in O. Gael. *medon*, is cognate with Skr. *madhjas* (middle, midst), Zend *maidhya* (middle), *maidhema* (the midmost), Gr. μέσσος, Lat. *medius*, Goth. *midjis*, Slav. *mezda*, Ger. *mitte*, A.S. *middle*, Eng. *mid*.

7. "Agus rinn Dia an t-athar, agus chuir e dealachadh cadar na h-uisgeachan a bha fuidh 'n athar, agus na h-uisgeachan a bha os cionn an athair: agus bha e mar sin."

Rinn (made), now used as the pret. of the verb *dean* (do), is for *rinne* (cf. Bedel's Translation) = *-rine* in *dorine* (cf. Stokes' Glosses, p. 125) = *-rigni* (cf. *dorigni* in Z. 463) = *rogéni* (fecit) 3 per. sing. pret. act (with pref. *ro*) of the verb *gniu* (I do) from the root *gen* = Indo-Europ. root *gan*, with which are connected Skr. root *ǵan*, Zend *zan* (beget), Lat. and Gr. *gen* in Lat. *gigno* = *gigeno*, *genus*, *genitor*, *natura* (= *gnatura*), Gr. 'ε-γεν-όμην, γίγνομαι, γένος, Goth. *kein-an* (sprout), *kun-i* (race), O.H.G. *china*, A.S. *cynd*, Eng. *kind*, *kin*. The form *gen* of this root is common to Gr., Lat., and Celt., one of many proofs of the close relationship of these languages.

"*An t-athar*." Both the art. *an* and the noun *athar* have been already considered, but the *t-* inserted between the art. and the noun in certain cases (cf. Stewart's Gramm., pp. 148-9) must be noticed here. The modern *an t-* was in O. Gael. *int*, as, "intathir nemde" (the heavenly father), "intoin ball" (the one member). Cf. Z. 210. We thus see that *t*, which is now written as if it were a euphonic letter, belongs in reality to the article.

"*Na h-uisgeachan*." Unlike *t-*, the *h-*, now regularly inserted between the article and the noun in certain cases (cf. Stewart's Gram., p. 149), is not organic, as is shown by its having been sometimes used and sometimes omitted in the ancient language. Cf. Z. 48. A similar irregular use of *h-* exists in modern Gaelic between certain prepositions and the nouns they govern, as, "le h-uamhas" and "le uamhas," "le h-urram" and "le urram."

A (which) is the nom. of the rel. pron., the two modern forms being *a* for the nom. and acc. and *an* for the gen. and dat. of both numbers. *An* and *a* agree in form with the neut. forms of the art. *an* and *a*, and belong to the same stem.

Fuidh (under) is *faoi* in Bedel's Translation. *Faoi* corresponds to the Gr. prep. ὑπαί, *f* representing an original *v*, and *p* being dropped, as is usual, in Gaelic. *Fo*, the only form of this prep. used in Scottish Gael., is from a base *va*, corresponding (*p* being dropped), to Skr. *upa*, Zend *upa*, Gr. ὑπό, Lat. *sub*, Goth *uf*. Cf. Rev. Celt. ii., 324.

Os (above). The prep. *ós*, of which *uas* is another form (*o* and *ua* being identical), belongs to the same root as Skr. *vaksh-* in *vakshami* (I increase), Gr. αὐξ- in αὔξω and αὐξάνω (I increase), αὔξη (increase), Lith. *auksz-* in *auksztas* (high), Goth. *vahs-* in *vahs-ja* (wax), Ger. *wachsen*, Ice. *vaxa*, A.S. *weixan*, Eng. *wax*. (Cf. Curtius' Grundz., p. 386). To this family of words belongs also Gael. *fás* (to grow) = *f-ás* (with prosthetic *f*) = O. Gael. *ás-aim*.

Cionn = *ciunn*, dat. sing. of *cenn* (head), now *ceann*. For etymology, see p. 57.

Mar (as) corresponds to W. *mor*, Corn. *mar*, connected by Ebel with the conjunction *ma*, from a ground form *sma* identical with the Skr. pron. *sma*, which Williams (cf. Skr. Dict.) regards as for *samā*, an old instrumental case of *sama* (even, same, equal), and meaning "wholly, entirely." To the root of Skr. *sama* belong O. Gael. *samail* (= *samali*), *amal* and *amail*, *cosmail* (= *consamali*), of which the modern forms are *samhail*, *amhail*, *cosmhail*. Cf. Gr. ἅμα and ὁμός, Lat. *similis*, Ch.-Slav. *samu*, Goth. *sama*, O.H.G. *sama*, A.S. and Eng. *same*.

Sin (that) is in O. Gael. *sin*, the locative of the pron. stem *sa*, with the suf. dem. *na*. *Sa* is identical with Skr. *sa*, *sa-s* (he), and connected with Old Lat. acc. *su-m*, *sa-m*, Goth. *sa* (the ; mas.), *si* (she). Cf. Stokes in Beitr. viii. 345, and Curt. Grundz., p. 397.

8. "Agus dh'ainmich Dia an t-athar, Nèamh: agus b'iad am feasgar agus a' mhaduinn an dara là."

An dara (the second) appears to be from the old ordinal num. *indala* (the second, the other, one of two) = *ind-ala*, the art. *ind* and *ala* which frequently occurs without the art. Cf. 309. *Ala* is connected with O. Gael. *aile*, now *eile* (other). *Aile* is cognate with Lat. *alius*, Gr. ἄλλος, Goth. *ali-s* (another), *alja* (beside), *aljar* (elsewhere), O.H.G. *ali-lanti* (foreigner). Cf. Gael. *ailithir* (pilgrim), now *oilear* and *oil-thireach*.

(*To be continued.*)

[SPECIMEN OF OLD GAELIC.]

PATRICK'S HYMN.

Patraicc dorone inuinmunsa. Inainiscir loegaire meic néil doringed. Fád adénma hautem diadídcn conamanchaib arnáimdib inbáis robátar inetarnid arnacleircheib. Ocus isluirech hirse inso fribimdegáil cuirp 7 anma ardemnáib 7 dúinib 7 duálchib. Cech duine nosgéba cechdía coninnithem léir india nfthairisfet demna friagnúis . bid dítin dó arcechneim 7 format . bidcomna dó fridíanbas bidlúrech dianamain iarnaétsécht. Patraicc rochan so intan dorata nahetarnaidi arachinn óloegaire nadigsed dosilad

Patrick's Hymn.

chreitme cotemraig conid annsin atchessa fiadlucht nauctarnade comtis aige alta 7 iarróe inandiaid .i. benen .7 Faeth Fiada ahainm.

Atomriug indíu niurt trén togairm trinoit
cretim treodataid foisi*tin* óendatad indúlemain dail
Atomriug indiu niurt gene Cri*st* conabathius
   niurt crochta conaadnocul
   niurt n-eseirge cofresgabail
   niurt tóniud dobrethemnas bratha

Atomriug indiu niurt grád hiruphin
   inurlataid aingel
   ifrestul nanarchaingel
   hifrescisin escirge arcenn fochraice
   inernaigthib huasalathrach
   itairchetlaib fátha
   hipraiceptaib apstal
   inhiresaib fuismedach
   inendgai nóemingen
   hingnímaib fer fírean

Atomriug indiu niurt nime
   soilse gréne
   etrochta snechtai
   áne thened
   déne lóchet[1]
   luathe gáethe
   fudomna mara
   tairisem talman[2]
   cobsaidecht ailech

Atomriug indiu niurt Dé domluamaracht
   cumachta Dé dómchumgabail
   ciall Dé domminthús
   rosc Dé domreimcise
   cluas Dé doméstecht
   briathar Dé domerlabrai
   lám Dé domminadegail
   intech Dé domremthechtas
   sciath Dé domdítin
   sochraite Dé dommanucul
   arintledaib demna
   araslaigthib dualche
   arirnechtaib aicnid
   arcech n-duine midúthrastar[3] dam

[1] Gl. lassrach.   [2] MS. talmain.   [3] MS. midústhrastar.

fcéin 7 inocus
inuathed 7 hisochaide

Tocuirius etrum thra nabuile nertso
fricechnert n-amnas n-étrócar fristí domchurp ocus domm-
anmain
fritincbetla saibfáthe
fridubrechtu gentliuchta
frisáibrechtu heretecda
fribimcellacht n-idlachta
fribrichta ban 7 goband 7 druad
fricechfiss arachuiliu anman duini

Crist dommimdegail indiu arneim
arloscud arbadud arguin,
conomthair ilar fochraice
Crist lim Crist rium Crist imdegaid
Crist innium Crist issum
Crist úasum Crist dessum
Crist tuathum Crist illius
Crist issius Crist incrus

Crist icridiu cechduine immimrorda
Crist ingin cechóen rodomlabrathar
Crist incechrusc nomdercaedar
Crist incecheluais rodamchloathar

Atomriug indiu niurt trén togairm trinoit
Cretim treodataid f. o. in d.

Domini est salus domini est salus christi est salus
salus tua domine semper nobiscum

Translation.

Patrick made this hymn. In the time of Loegaire son of Nial it was made. The cause of making it, however, was for his protection with his monks against the deadly enemies who were in ambush against the clerics. And this is a corslet of faith for the protection of body and soul against demons, and men, and vices. Every one who shall sing it every day, with pious meditation on God, demons shall not stand before his face: it will be a defence to him against every poison and envy: it will be a safeguard to him against sudden death: it will be a corslet to his soul after his death. Patrick sang this when the ambuscades were set against him by Leogaire [lit., were given against him from Loegarie] that he might not go to Temair to sow the faith, so that then they seemed before the ambuscaders to be wild deer, and a fawn after them, viz., Benén; and "Facth Fiada"[1] is its name.

> I bind myself to-day to the power (a strong invocation)—the Trinity—Belief in threeness — confession of oneness in the Creator of the world.
>
> I bind myself to-day to the power of Christ's birth with his baptism,
> to the power of his crucifixion with his burial,
> to the power of his resurrection with his ascension
> to the power of his coming to judgment of doom.
>
> I bind myself to-day to the power—the order of cherubim,
> In obedience of angels,
> *In attendance of archangels,*
> In hope of resurrection to reward,
> In prayers of patriarchs,
> In predictions of prophets,
> In precepts of apostles,
> In faiths of confessors,
> In innocence of holy virgins,
> In acts of righteous men.
>
> I bind myself to-day to the power of heaven,
> Light of sun,
> Brightness of snow,
> Splendour of fire,
> Speed of lightning,
> Swiftness of wind,
> Depth of sea,
> Stability of earth,
> Firmness of rock.
>
> I bind myself to-day to God's power to pilot me,
> God's might to uphold me,
> God's wisdom to guide me,
> God's eye to see before me,
> God's ear to hear me,
> God's word to speak for me,
> God's hand to protect me,
> God's way to lie before me,
> God's Shield to defend me,
> God's host to preserve me,

---

[1] "Guard's cry."

> Against snares of demons,
> Against allurements of vices,
> Against solicitations of nature,
> Against every one who wishes evil to me
> Afar and near,
> Alone and in company.

I have now invoked all these powers for my protection [lit. between me]

> Against every cruel, merciless power, which may come against my body and my soul—
> Against incantations of false prophets,
> Against black laws of gentiles,
> Against false laws of heretics,
> Against craft of idolatry,
> Against spells of women and smiths and druids,
> Against every knowledge that defiles (?) the soul of man.

Christ to protect me to-day against poison,
> Against burning, against drowning, against wound,
> Until abundance of reward comes to me.

Christ with me, Christ before me, Christ behind me,
Christ in me, Christ below me,
Christ above me, Christ at my right,
Christ at my left, Christ in breadth,
Christ in length, Christ in height.

Christ in the heart of every one who thinks of me,
Christ in the mouth of every one who speaks to me,
Christ in every eye that sees me,
Christ in every ear that hears me.

I bind myself to-day to the power (a strong invocation)—the Trinity—Belief in threeness—confession of oneness in the Creator.

[This hymn forms one of the Irish hymns in the "Liber Hymnorum," a MS. belonging to Trinity College, Dublin, and written, as Dr. Stokes conjectures, about the end of the eleventh, or the beginning of the twelfth century. The hymn itself, however, belongs to a much earlier date.

The text now printed follows that recently published by Prof. Windisch, of Leipzig, in his valuable work, "Irische Texte mit Wörterbuch," to which we take this opportunity of directing the attention of Scottish students of Old Irish.

In preparing the translation, Prof. Windisch's Notes and Dictionary, and Dr. Stokes' "Goidelica" published by the Messrs. Trübner & Co., of London, have been consulted.

We subjoin an analysis of part of the hymn, which it is hoped may be of some assistance to persons desirous to begin the study of Old Gaelic.]

ANALYSIS.

Atomriug (I bind myself, ally myself, *adjungo me*) = *ad-dom-riug* = *adriug* with infixed pron. *dom* (me). *Adriug* is the 1st. per. sing. pres. ind. of comp. formed by the pref. *ad* = Lat. *ad*, from *riug* = *rigu or *regu, cognate with Lith. *riszu* (I bind). The root is *rac* cognate with Skr. root *raç*. Cf. Z., 428, Beit. z, Gesch. Deut. Spr., iv. 234, Kuhn's Zeit., xxiii. 213, and Stokes' Goid., p. 154.

Indiu (to-day) = *in-diu*, of which *in* is the prep. *in*, now *an*, and *diu* the dat. sing. of *dia* (day), from stem *diva, connected with Lat. *dies*. *Diu* is now *di* in *Di-luain* (Monday), &c.

Niurt is the dat. sing. of *nert* (strength), now *neart*. *Nert* (= *ner-t*) is from the root *ner* (cf. *bert* = *ber-t* from *ber*), cognate with Skr. *nar*, *nara-s* (man), Zend *nar*, *nara* (man), Gr. ἀνήρ (man) from stem ανερ, Sabin. *nero-n* (fortis) and *nerio* (fortitudo). Cf. Gaul. *Nertomarus* and *-nertus* in *Cobnertus*. *Nert* is a neut. *o*-stem.

Trén (strong), now *treun*. *Trén* (= *tresn) and the compar. *tressa*, now *treasa*, are connected by Zeuss and Ebel with Gr. θρασύς, although contrary to rule, for θ corresponds to Gael. *d*. Cf. Z., p. 37. *Trén* is more regularly connected with Ved. *dhṛshṇú* (bold, brave, courageous), Skr. *dhṛshta* (insolent, bold). Cf. Kuhn's Zeit., xxiii., p. 209.

Togairm (invocation), a neut. *n*-stem = *do-fo-gar-man (cf. Stokes' Goid., p. 64, and Z., p. 268), from the root *gar*, cognate with Skr. root *gar*, from which *gr-ṇá-mi* (I call), Zend *gar* (sing, extol), Gr. γῆρυς (speech) and γηρύω (I speak), Lat. *garrio* (I chatter) O.H.G. *kirru* (creak), Lith. *gársus* (voice). Cf. Curt. Gr. Etym., p. 177. *Togairm* is probably a shortened dative (for *togarmim*) standing in apposition to *niurt*. Cf. Wind., Ir. Texts, p. 53.

Trinoit, either for *trinóite*, gen. of *trindoit* (= Lat. *trinitas*, gen. *trinitat-is*, trinity), or dative (cf. Wind. Ir. Texts) in apposition to *togairm*.

Cretim, either the 1st per. sing. pres. ind. of *cretim* (I believe), formed by the pronom. suff. *im* from *cret-*, cognate with Skr.

craidtha (trusting), *ṛraddhana* (faith), *ṛraddladhami* (I believe), or the dat. of the noun *cretem* (belief, faith), in apposition to *niurt*. Cf. Rys' Lectures, p. 72, Curt. Gr. Etym., p. 254, and Windisch's Gramm., p. 62, and Ir. Texts, p. 53.

Treodataid, dat. sing. of *treodatu* (threeness), a derivative from *tri* (three), cognate with Skr. root *tri*, *trajas* (three), Zend *thri* (three), Gr. τρεῖς, Lat. *tres*. For suff. *-adatu* cf. Z., p. 804. Instead of the dat.-form *treodataid*, Windisch suggests the gen.-form *treodatad* (of threeness) governed by noun *cretim*.

Foisitin, which Stokes considers the correct word here (cf. "*cretem oenatad cofoisitiu trédatad*, belief of oneness with confession of threeness," in Goid., p. 101), is the dat. sing. of *foisitiu* (confession). Cf. Z., pp. 264, 266, 800. *Foisitiu* (confession), now *faosaid*, is a fem. *n*-stem, gen. *foisiten*, dat. *foisitin*, acc. *foisitin-n*, formed by pref. *fo*, cognate with Gr. ʽυπό, from root *stu*, connected with Skr. root *sthá*, Gr. ἵστημι, Lat. *sisto*, &c. Cf. Wind. Gramm., p. 88.

Oendatad is the gen. sing. of *óendatu* (oneness), formed by the suff. *-datu* from *óin* or *óen* (one), cognate with Gr. οἰνός one, Old Lat. *oinos* (one), Lat. *unus*, etc.

Indúlemain (in Creator) = *in-dúlemain*, the prep. *in* (= Lat. *in*), and *dúlemain* dat. sing. of *dúlem*, gen *duleman*, a mas. *n*-stam from *dúil* (element) = *duli, cognate with Skr. *dhātu* (element), from root *dhā*. Cf. Stokes' Fel. Oeng., p. 254.

Dail is explained by Dr. Stokes (cf. Goid., p. 155) as gen. sing. of *dal*, probably cognate with Gr. δαίδαλος, δαιδάλμα, and signifying the *universe*, κόσμος, but rather, perhaps, to be read as *dúil*, gen. of *dúl*, a by-form of *dúil* (element, creature). Cf. Goid., p. 155, and see *dail* in Wind. Wörterbuch.

Gene (of birth), for *geine*, gen. sing. of *gein* (birth), from root *gen*, common to Gr., Lat., and Celt. Cf. Gr. 2nd aor. ἐγενόμην and Lat. *gigno*, *genui*. The Indo-Europ. root is *gan*.

Crist (Christ) from Gr. Χριστός, Lat. *Christus*.

Conabathius (with his baptism) = *con-a-bathius*, of which the prep. *con* = Lat. *co*, *con*, *a* (his) = Skr. *asya*, and *bathius* is the dat. sing. of the O. Gael. noun *baithis* (baptism), which, together with its related words *baithiu* (I plunge), *bádud* (drowning), *robaded* (were drowned), and W. *boddi* (to drown), is connected with Gr. βαθύς (deep), Skr. *gáh* (dip oneself, bathe), from a common root *gvadh*. Cf. Corm. Gl., p. 18, and Curt. Gr. Etym. p. 467.

Crochta for *crochtho* (crucifixionis), gen of *crochad*, from *croch* = Lat. *crux*. *Crochad* is a *u*-stem.

Conadnocul (with his burial) = *con-a-adnocul*, being the prefix *con*, the poss. pron. *a*, and *adnocul*, dat. sing. of *adnacul* (burial), inf. of *adnacim* (I bury), now *adhlacaim*, from the root *nac*, *nanc* (to deliver up, *tradere*), connected with Skr. root *naç* (to reach, attain), Gr. aor. *'ή-veγκ-a*, Lat. *nanc-iscor* (I get, obtain), Lith. *nesz-u* (carry), *nasz-ta* (burden), Ch-Slav. *nes-a*, *nes-ti* (to bring, carry). Cf. Mod. Gael. *tiodhlaic* (anc. *tidnacim*, from the root of *adnacul*), which signifies both to *give* and to *inter*.

N-eseirge (of resurrection) for *eséirge*, the transported *n* being erroneously inserted after the dat. sing. Cf. Goid., p. 135. *Eséirge* (resurrection) = *ess-éirge*, a deriv. of *éirge* = *ess-rige* the pref. *ess* = Lat *ex* and *rige* from root *rag*, *arg*, cognate with Skr. root *arg*, *arg'-â-mi* (attain to), Gr. ὀρήγ-ω and ὀρεγ-νυ-μι (stretch out), Lat. *rego* and *é-rig-o*. Cf. Beit. viii., 444. *Esseirge* is now *aiseirigh*. *Esséirge* is an *ia*-stem.

Cofresgabail (with ascension) = *co-fres-gab-ail*, the prep. *co* = Lat. *co* (with), *fres* for *fris* = *frith* referred by Stokes to Skr. root *vart* (vertere), Lat. *versus*, and *gabail* (= *gab-ali*) connected by Zeuss and Ebel, although contrary to rule, with Lat. *capio*. Dr. Stokes has given *gab* (Beit. viii., 311) as an example of an abnormal sinking of the tenues in Old Gaelic; but cf. Fel. Oeng. Gloss.

Tóniud for *tóiniuda*, gen. sing. of *tóiniud* (coming), a mas. *u*-stem. Cf Z., p. 802. *Toiniud* is the infin. of *toiniu* = *do-feniu*, cognate with Lat. *venio* (I come), Gr. βαίνω (I walk, step). Cf. Zeit. xxiv., 218.

Dobrethemnas (to judgment) = *do-brethemnas*, the prep. *do* = Lat. -*do* in *en-do*, *in-du*, Gr. δε (towards), Goth. *du*, O. H. G. *zuo*, Eng. *to*, and *brethemnas* (judgment), from *brithem* (= *brithema*) gen. *britheman*, dat. *brithemain*, acc. *brithemain-n*, a mas. *n*-stem from *breth* (judgment). With *brithema* cf. Skr. *brahma*, gen. *brahman-as*. Cf. Z., p. 775, Beit. z. Gesch. Deut. Spr. iv., 322 and Wind. G., p. 34.

Bratha (of doom) gen. sing. of *bráth* (doom), a mas, *u*-stem, etymologically connected with *breth*, *brithem* above.

Grád = Lat. *gradus*. *Grád* is an *a*-stem.

Hiruphin = Lat. *seraphim*, a loan from the Hebrew.

Inurlataid (in obedience of angels) = *in-urlataid*, the prep. *in* and *urlataid* = *aurlatid* (cf. Z. 7), the dat. sing. of *aurlatu*, (obedientia) = *aur-latu*, of which the pref. *aur* = *air* = *are-* = *pari*, cognate with Skr. *pra-*, Zend *fra* (fore), Gr. πρό (before), Lat. *pro* and *prae* (before), and *latu* = *la-tu*, the suf. *tu* (cf. Z. 804) and the root *la* = *las*, cognate with Skr. root *lash*, *las*, Gr. λα in λά-ω (wish), Lat. *las-* in *las-c-ivus*, Goth. *lus-* in *lus-tu-s*, Eng. *lus-t*. To the same root belong the O. Gael. words *airle* (voluntas) = *air-le*, *comairle* (counsel) = *com-air-le*, *irladigur* (oboedio) = *ir-ladigur*, and *airlam* (paratus) = *air-lam*. *Aurlatu*, *treodatu*, and *oendatu* are dent.-stems.

A ingel (of angels), gen. plur. of angel = Lat. *angelus*, Gr. ἄγγελος.

Ifrestul (in attendance) = *i-frestul*, of which *i* = *in* (*n* of the prep. being elided before *f*) and *frestul* the dat. sing. of *frestal* = *fres-tal*, the pref. *fres* = *fris* = *frith* (noticed above) and *tal*, the same, perhaps, with *tal* in *tuarastal* (hire, wages) = *do-fo-ar-as-tal, connected by Stokes with Gr. τέλος (office, duty, tax).

Nanarchaingel (of the Archangels) = *nan-archaingel*, *nan* being the gen. plur. of the art., and *archaingel* = Lat. *archangelos*, Gr. ἀρχάγγελος.

Hifrescisin (in hope) = *hi-frescisin*, the prep. *in* (with *n* elided before *f* as above) and *frescisin*, the dat. sing. of *frescisiu*, gen. *frescisen*, dat. *frescisin*, acc. *frescisin-n*, a fem. *n*-stem compounded of the pref. *fres* already noticed, and *aicsiu* = *acsiu* = *adcastio from root *cas*, cognate with Skr. *caksh* for *cakas*. Cf. Wind. Gramm., pp. 12, 55, and Z. 775, 875.

Arcenn = *ar-cenn*, of which *ar* = prep. *air* = Gaulish *are-* compared above, and *cenn* is the acc. sing. of *cenn* (head), gen. *cinn*, dat. *ciunn*, referred, together with W. *penn* (head), by Windisch to a common base *cvinda-m, from, possibly, an extended form of the Indo-Europ. root *çvi, *çvayati* (to swell), Skr. *çvi*, *çvayati* (to swell). Cf. Beit. viii., 43, 44. *Cenn* is an *a*-stem. Cf. Z. 623.

Fochraice, gen. sing. of *fochraic* or *fochraice* (reward) = *fo-chraic*, the pref. *fo* = W. *gwo*, cognate with Skr. *upa*, and *craic* = *cranci (cf. Z. 812), connected with *crenim* (I buy) and cognate with Skr. krīnāmī (I buy). Cf. Rev. Celt., p. 340.

Inernaigthib (in prayers) = *in-ernaigthib*, the prep. *in* and *ernaigthib* the dat. plur. of *ernaigthe* = *aurnaigthe* = *air-chonig-the*, the prefixes *air* and *con*, suffix *the*, and root *ig*. related to Skr. *ih*, *ihate* (to long for, desire), *ihā* (desire, wish), Hesych. Gr. ἰχανάω (to long for, desire eagerly). Cf. Zeit. xxiv., 206. *Ernaigthe*, now *arnuigh*, is an *ia*-stem.

Huasalathrach, gen. plur. of *uasalathir* (patriarch) = *uasal-athir*. *Uasal* (= *uas-al*, noble) is from the prep. *uas* = *os*, cognate with Skr. *vaksh* in *vakshámi* (cresco), Gr. αὔξ- in αὔξω (I increase), Goth. *vahs-ja* (wax), Lith. *duksz-tas* (high), Ice. *vaxa* (to increase), Eng. *wax*. Cf. Curt. Gr. Etym., 386. *Athir* (father) is cognate with Lat. *pater*, Gr. πατήρ, Skr. *pitar*, Goth. *fadar*, O.H.G. *fatar*, Eng. *father*. Cf. Curt. Gr. Etym., p. 270. *Athir* is an *r*-stem, but is here declined in the plur. like the *c*-stems.

Itairchetlaib (in predictions, prophecies) = *i-tair-chetlaib*, *i* being the prep. *in* (with *n* dropped before the tenuis *t*), and *tairchetlaib* the dat. pl. of *tairceltal*, also *tairchital* (cf. Z. 881), of which *tair* = *do-air* (Z. 880), and *cetal* or *cital* is from the root *can* (*n* being dropped before the tenuis). *Can*, from which *canim* (I sing) is derived, is cognate with Lat. *cano*, *cantus*, Gr. καν in κανάζω (I sound), Skr. *kan-* in *kan-kan-i* (bell), *kvan* (to sound). *Tairceltal* is a neut. *a*-stem.

Fátha for *fáthe*, gen. pl. of *fáith* (prophet), gen. *fatho*, an *i*-stem cognate with Lat. *vates*. Cf. Goid., p. 155.

Hipraiceptaib (in precepts) = *hi-praiceptaib*, the prep. *hi* = *i* = *in* (*n* being dropped before the tenuis *p*), and *praiceptaib*, the dat. pl. of *praicept* = Lat. *praeceptum*.

Abstal (of apostles), gen. pl. of *apstal*, from Lat. *apostolus*.

Inhiresaib (in faiths) = *in-hiresaib*, the prep. *in* and *hiresaib* for *iresaib*, the dat. pl. of *ires* (faith) = *iress* (cf. Z. 10) = *air-ess*, the pref. *air* and *ess* = *sess* (?) from root *sta*, cognate with Skr. *sthá*, Gr. ἵστημι, Lat. *sisto*, Goth. *stam* and *standu*, Eng. *stand*. Cf. O. Gael. *sessam*, now *seasamh* (standing) = *se-stam-a*. Rev. Celt. III. 35. *Iress* is a fem. *a*-stem.

Fuismedach, gen. pl. of *fuismedach* (confessor), connected etymologically with *fóisitiu* (confession) noticed above, both being derivatives, with pref. *fo* cognate with Gr. ὑπό, from root *sta* reduplicated. Cf. *sessam* above.

Inendgai (in innocence) = *in-endgai*, the prep. *in* and *endgai*, for *enncai*, dat. sing. of *enncae*, a derivative from *ennach* = Lat. *innocens*. Cf. Stokes' Ir. Gl., p. 151, Goid., p. 155, and Wind. Gr. p. 7.

Nóemingin (of holy virgins) = *nóem-ingen*. *Nóem* (holy), now *naomh*, was in ancient Gael. *nóib* and *nóeb*, connected in Kuhn's Zeit. xxiv. 210 with Old Pers. *naiba* (beautiful, good), New Pers. *nīw* (beautiful, good).

Ingen = *in-gen*, the pref. *in* and *gen* = Lat. *gen* in *gigno*, *genui*

Gr. γεν in ἐγενόμην, Skr. ján in gan-á-mi, Goth. keinan, O.H.G. chind. The Indo-Europ. root is gan. Cf. Curt. Gr. Etym., p. 174, and Z. 877. *Ingen* is a fem. a-stem.

Ilingnímaib (in acts, deed) = *hin-gnímaib*, the prep. *hin* for *in* and *gnímaib* the dat. pl. of *gním* (act, deed), now *gníomh*, a mas u-stem from the root *gen* noticed above.

Fer, now *fear*, is the gen. pl. of *fer* (man), gen. *fir*, dat. *fiur*, acc. *fer-n*, a mas a-stem cognate with Lat. *vir*, Goth. *vair*. The W. is *gwr*, gen. *gwir*.

Fírean for *fírían* (righteous) from *fír* (true), now *fíor* = W. *gwîr*, cognate with Lat. *verus* (true).

Nime (of heaven), gen. sing. of *ném*, now *nèamh* (heaven), from stem **namas*, which, along with *nemed* (sanctuary), Windisch connects with Skr. *namas, namati* (to bow oneself), *namasyati* (to honour, to venerate). *Ném* is connected by Ebel and others with Skr. *nabhas* (heaven) and the related words previously noticed. Cf. p. 41.

Soilse (light), nom. form of fem. ia-stem = **svalastia* (cf. Kuhn's Zeit., xxi. 428) from the root *sval* = Skr. *svar* (to lighten), and cognate with Lat. *sol* (sun), Gr. σέλας (light).

Gréne, gen. sing. of *grian* (sun) = **grena*, a fem a-stem, perhaps connected with Skr. *ghrini* (sun), *ghar-ma* (heat), Gr. θερμός (heat), Lat. *fervere* (to be hot), Eng. *warm*. With the same root is connected Gael. *garaim*. Cf. Stokes' Ir. Gl., p. 113.

Etrochta (brightness), an ia-stem, from *étrocht* (bright).

Snechtai, gen. sing. of *snecta* (snow) from the root *snag* or *snig*, from which come *snige* (dropping), *snigester* (has dropped, stillavit), and the reduplicated perf. *senaich* (stillavit) for *sesnaig*. These words are cognate with Lith. *snig-ti* and *sningti* (to snow), *snëg-as* (snow), Ch.-Slav. *snëg-ŭ*, Goth. *snaivs* (snow), O.H.G. *snéo*, N.H.G. *schnee*, A. S. *snaw*, Eng. *snow*, Lat. *ninguis*, and *nix* (snow), Gr. νιφα (snow, acc.). Cf. Curt. Gr. Etym., p. 318.

Ane (splendour) = **agne*, a fem. ia-stem cognate with Gr. αἴγλη (the light of the sun, radiance) for **ἄγνιη, Lat. *ignis* (fire), Skr. *agni* (fire). The loss of *g* in Gael. before *n* is common. Cf. *sén, fén, óen* now *uan*. See Goid. p. 155.

Thened (of fire), gen. sing. of *tene* a dental-stem (Z. 254), from root *tep* cognate with Skr. root *tap-* in *tapas* (heat). The root *tep* appears in Lat. *tepeo*. Cf. Rev. Celt. ii. 324. To the same root belong *tess* (heat; now *teas*) = **tepest-us*, and *té* (hot; now *teath*) = **tepent-, teit*, corresponding to Lat. *tepens*, gen. *tepent-is*.

Gaelic regularly drops Indo-Germ. *p*. On *tene*, W. *tan*, cf. also Beit. viii. 438.

Déne (swiftness, speed), a fem. *ia*-stem from *dian* (swift), cognate with Skr. *dî*, from which comes *dî-já-mi* (hurry, fly), Gr. root δι in δί-εσθαι (hasten), δει-νό-ς (frightful), Lat. *di* in *dirus*. Cf. Curt. Gr. Etym., p. 234.

Lóchet (of lightning), gen. sing. of *lóche* (lightning), an *nt*-stem (= *laukant), cognate with Gr. λευκός (white), Lat. *lux* (light) and *luceo* (I shine), Goth. *liuhath* (light), O.H.G. *lioht* (light), Eng. *light*. The Skr. root is *ruk* (shine), Zend *ruk* (to give out light). Cf. Curt. Gr. Etym., p. 160.

Lassrach, by which *lóchet* is glossed, is gen. sing. of *lassair* (flame), a fem. *c*-stem from *lassim*, now *lasaim*, related to Skr. *laksh* (to perceive, to mark). Cf. Kukn's Zeit., xxi. 427, and Williams' Skr. Dictionary.

Luathe (swiftness), a fem *ia*-stem from *luath* (swift) = *plauta related to Ice. *fljótr* (swift), Lith. *pláu-ju* (wash; infin. *pláu-ti*), Lat. *plu-* in *pluvia*, Gr. πλέ- in πλέ-ω, Skr. *plu*. Cf. Curt. Gr. Etym., p. 280, and Kuhn's Zeit., p. 431.

Gáethe, gen. sing. of *gáeth* = *gáith* (wind; now *gaoth*) from root *ghi*, cognate with Skr. root *hi-* in *himas* (snow), Gr. χι- in χιών (snow), χειμών (winter), Lat. *hiems* (winter). O. Gael. *gam* (winter), from which *geamhradh* is derived, is connected.

Fudomna (depth), is from *fudomain* (deep) = *fu-domain*, the pref. *fu* for *fo*, and *domain* (deep), with *m* for *b* as shown by comparing *Dumnorix* and *Dubnoreix*, *Cogidumnus* and *Cogidubnus*. *Dubn* is connected by Glück, as noticed at p. 44, with Goth. *diup* from *dup*, O.H.G. *tiof*, Eng. *deep*. Cf. Kelt. Namen, p. 72.

Mara, gen. sing. of *muir* = *mori, a neut *i*-stem, cognate with Lat. *mare* (sea) from root *mar*.

Tairisem (stability) = *tairissem*, a fem. *a*-stem = *do-airissem*, the prefixes *do* and *air*, and *issem* = *issem* = *ess-ma for *sess-ma (?). Cf. *iress* above.

Talman, the gen. sing. of *talam* (earth), a fem. *n*-stem = *talma, gen. *talman*, dat. *talmain*, "reminding one as to the rt. syllable of Lat. *tellus*, as to the stem formation of Skr. *stariman, stariman* (couch), from rt. *star* (to spread out)." Cf. Beitr. z. Gesch. Deut. Spr. iv. 232. Cf. p. 42 above. *Talmain* in MS., which Dr. Stokes construes as a locative case.

Cobsaidecht (firmness, solidity, compactness), a derivative from *cobsaid* = *con-fos-ud* (cf. Goid., p. 22) from root *fos* = *foss* (cf. Z., 42), cognate with Skr. root *vas, vastu* (place, house), Gr. ἄστυ for Fάστυ (city), O.H.G. *wist* (mansion). To this root belong Gael. *fois*, in O. Gael. *foss* (rest, and *àros* (an abode) = *ar-foss*.

Ailech (of rock), the gen. sing. of *ail* (rock, cliff), a *c*-stem. Cf. *Ail-Cluade*, now Dumbarton.

Dé, gen. sing. of *Dia* (God), = **deva*, a mas. *a*-stem, cognate with Skr. *dévas* (God), Lith. *dëvas* (God), Lat. *deus* and *divus*, Gr. δῖος (heavenly).

Domluamaracht (for my piloting, to pilot me) = *do-m-luam-ar-acht*, the pref. *do*, the infixed pron. *m*, the suffixes *ar* and *acht*, and *luam* (pilot) = **plauman* from the root *plu* noticed above under *luathe*. Cf. Beit. viii., 9.

Cumachta for *cumachte* (power), a neut. *ia*-stem = *cu-mach-te* from root *mag*, of which *mang* is a nasalised form, cognate with Skr. *mah* in *mah-as* (power), Gr. μῆχ-ος, μῆχ-αν (means), Goth. *mag* (I am able, possum), *mahts* (power), Ch.-Slav. *mog-a* (possum), A.S. *moeg, magan* (to be able), *meahte* (power), Eng. *may, might*. Cf. Curt. Gr. Etym., p. 335.

Domchumgabail (for my keeping, to keep me) = *do-m-cum-gab-ail*, the prep. *do*, the infixed pron. *m*, the pref. *cum* = *con*, the root *gab*, and the suff. *ail* (= **ali*). The root *gab* was noticed above under *fresgabail*. *Cumgabail*, with *m* for *n* in pref. before *g*, is now *cumail*.

Ciall (wisdom, sense) = W. *pwyll*, a fem. *a*-stem, connected (cf. Beit. viii. 39) with Skr., root *ći* (to observe, perceive).

(To be continued.)

MAR A CHAIDH AN TUAIRISGEUL MOR A CHUR GU BÀS.

For the following West Highland Tale and translation, we are indebted to the Rev. Mr. Campbell, Tiree.—ED.

[THE following tale was written down some years ago, in Gaelic, from the dictation of John Campbell, Hianish, Island of Tiree. It has the chief or necessary recommendation of whatever is gathered from oral sources, that it is given exactly as it came to hand, and that it is as free to the reader to draw his own conclusions from the language, or any other part of it, as to the person who committed it to writing. The tale was at one time well known. Many old people have heard its title, but it required a search to find any one who could go through its incidents. Of these there were various versions. The attention is kept alive by the name; it is only at the end that the listener becomes aware that the "Great Tuairisgeul" was a giant of the kind called *Lamhanaich*—that is, one who lived in a cave by the sea-shore, the strongest and coarsest of any. The translation is literal in the proper sense of the word—that is, each clause is rendered by the English expression which conveys to the English reader the same idea and the same phase of thought that the Gaelic conveys to the Gaelic reader. When there is anything noticeable in the difference of idiom, it is pointed out.]

'S e mac rìgh Eirinn a bh' ann, agus bha e dol do'n bheinn-sheilg; agus bhiodh uaislean òga 'g a choinneachadh an sin. Bha e an sin a'tighinn dachaidh oidhche bial an anmoich, agus chunnaic e fras a'tighinn air as an àird'-an-iar; agus thàinig òlach mòr as an fhrois, agus steud bhriagh aige, agus an t-aon bhoirionnach 'bu bhriagha 'chunnaic e riamh aige air an steud air a chùlaobh. "An tu so, a mhic rìgh Eirinn?" thuirt e. "Is mi," thuirt mac rìgh Eirinn. "An iomair thu cluich riumsa?" "Iomairidh," thuirt mac rìgh Eirinn; "cha b'ann ri m' dhaoine féin a rachainn mur iomairinn cluich riutsa. Thòisich iad air a' chluich, 's chaidh a' chluich le mac rìgh Eirinn. "Tog brìgh do chluiche," thuirt an t-òlach. "Is e brìgh mo chluiche-sa, am boirionnach briagh so bhi leam a' dol dachaidh." Dh'fholbh e, 's thug e leis i, agus ràinig e 'n tigh.

Co moch a 's 'g an d'thàinig an latha màireach, rinn e deas air son dol do 'n bheinn-sheilg; agus thuirt am boirionnach ris, "Tha thu air son falbh an diu, agus coinnichidh am fear ud thu an nochd fhathasd. Théid e dh'iomairt cluiche leat, agus théid a' chluich leatsa, agus na gabh ni ach an steud a tha aige fodha." Dh'fholbh e, 's thug e a' bhoinn-sheilg air; agus anmoch dar a bha e a' tighinn dachaidh, chunnaic e fras a' tighinn air as an àird-an-iar, mar a rinn e roimhe; agus thàinig an t-òlach sin air làr, agus an steud aige. "An tu so, a mhic rìgh Eirinn?" "Is mi," thuirt mac rìgh Eirinn?" "An iomair thu cluich rium an nochd, a mhic rìgh Eirinn?" "Iomairidh," thuirt mac rìgh Eirinn; "cha b'ann ri m' dhaoine féin a rachainn mur iomairinn cluich riutsa." Chaidh a' chluich le mac rìgh Éirinn. "Tog brìgh do chluiche." "Is e sin," thuirt mac rìgh Eirinn, "an steud so bhi agam." Dh'fholbh e dhachaidh, 's ràinig e 'n tigh.

An là 'r na mhàireach chuir e air gu dol do'n bheinn-sheilg a choinneachadh uaislean òga eile. Thuirt am boirionneach ris, "Tha thu falbh an diu a rìs air t' ais; ach coinnichidh am fear ud thu, agus théid a' chluich ortsa an diu; agus cuiridh e mar gheasan ort gun thu dheanamh stad, tàmh, no fois, agus gun uisge dhol as do bhròig, gus am faigh thu mach ciamar a chaidh an Tuairisgeul Mòr a chur gu bàs; agus cuir thusa mar gheasan air-san gun e dh'fhàgail na tulaich ud gus an till thusa. Their esan an sin, 'Sìos is suas do gheasan ort;' 's their thusa, 'Cha sìos 's cha suas ach mar sud.' Their esan an sin, 'Fuasgail orm, agus fuasglaidh mi ort.' Their thusa an sin, 'Cha 'n fhuasgail thu orm, 's cha 'n fhuasgail mi ort.'"

Dh'fholbh e 'n bheinn; 's dar a bha e a' tighinn dachaidh. choinnich an t-òlach mòr-sa e, gun each, gun steud, gun ni aige. "An tu so, a mhic rìgh Eirinn?" "Is mi," thuirt mac rìgh Eirinn. "An téid thu a chluich riumsa," ars' esan? "Cha b'ann ri m' dhaoine féin a rachainn, mur iomairinn cluich riutsa." Thòisich iad air a' chluich, agus chaidh a' chluich air mac rìgh Eirinn, 'Tha mise cur mar chroisean 's mar gheasan ortsa, gun uisge dhol as do bhròig, gus am faigh thu amach ciamar a chaidh an Tuairisgeul Mòr a chur gu bàs." "Tha mise a' cur nan geasan ciadna ortsa," ars' mac rìgh Eirinn, "gun thu dh'fhàgail na tulaich so gus an till mise." "Sìos is suas do gheasan ort," thuirt esan. "Cha sìos 's cha suas ach mar sid," thuirt mac rìgh Eirinn. "Fuasgail orm agus fuasglaidh mi ort." "Cha 'n fhuasgail mi ort," thuirt mac rìgh Eirinn, "'s cha'n fhuasgail thu orm."

Dhealaich iad, 's chaidh mac rìgh Éirinn dachaidh; 's thuirt am boirionnach ris, "Seadh, thàinig thu." "Thàinig mi," ars' esan. "Tha thu nis a' dol a dh'fheuchainn ciamar a chaidh an Tuairisgeul Mòr a chur gu bàs." "Tha," ars' esan. "Is ioma mac rìgh agus ridire," ars' ise, 'chaidh air an t-saothair sin nach do thill; ach cha 'n iad sin 'bheir ceann saoghail dhuit-sa, air son sin." Chuir e mu dhéigh'nn falbh anns a'mhaduinn; "Agus bheir thu leat an steudsa fodhad," ars' ise. "Tha triùir bhràithrean agamsa, agus is e 'n Ridir Dubh a th' air fear dhiubh, agus an Ridir Bàn air fear eile, agus an Ridir Donn air fear eile; agus tha fear dhiubh a' cur cuairt air an treas cuid de'n t-saoghal, agus tha fear eile cur cuairt air leth an t-saoghail, agus tha 'm fear eile cur cuairt air an t-saoghal air fad. Mur faigh thu fios aca sin, feudaidh tu tilleadh dhachaidh ; agus tha astar là agus bliadhna eadar tigh a h-uile fir dhiubh ; agus mur deachaidh an steud air a h-ais, o 'n bha i aig mo bhràthair-sa bithidh i ann an tigh a' chiad fhir dhiubh mu 'n téid a' ghrian fodha : agus 'n uair a ruigeas tu, iarraidh tu stàbull do d' steud air a' ghille-stàbuill; agus their an gille-stàbuill riut, "Dé 'n stàbull a bhiodh tusa 'g iarraidh ach an stàbull a th' aig ar cuid each fhéin. Bheir thusa sin breab da, agus gabhaidh tu stigh, agus bheir thu leat an steud do 'n t-seòmar am bi thu fhéin ; agus bithidh an darna gréim agad fhéin agus an gréim eile aig an steud. Thig mo bhràthair far am bi thu, agus their e riut, 'C'àit,' 'ille mhaith, an d'fhuair thu 'n steud-sa ?' Their thu ris, ' Fhuair mis' an steud-sa air greigh each a bha aig m' athair fhéin ; ach c' àit' air bith an d'fhuair mi i, b'fheàrr leam gu'n robh na fhuair mi leatha agam an so nochd.' Their esan an sin, ' Tha mi 'g ad chreidsinn.' Theirig a nis air muin an steud, agus aithnichidh mis' an téid do thurus leat."

Chaidh e an so air muin an steud, agus e dol a dh'fholbh. Thug an steud an crathadh sin oirre, 's thilg i sìos air a tulchainn e ; agus thug i 'n ath-chrathadh oirre, 's thilg i sìos air a gath-muing e ; agus air an treas crathadh, dh'fhan e 'n a àite fhéin. "O!" ars' ise, "théid do thurus leat—biodh misneach mhath agad."

Thog esan ri 'astar 's ri sìor-imeachd ; agus bha e aig tigh an Ridire Dhuibh mu 'n deachaidh a' ghrian fodha. Ràinig e an gille-stàbuill : " Bheir dhomhsa stàbull anns an cuir mi an steud so." " Ciod an stàbull," ars' esan, " a bhiodh tusa 'g iarraidh, ach an stàbull a tha aig ar cuid each fhéin ? " Thug e breab dha, 's ghabh e stigh, agus thug e leis an steud far an deachaidh e fhéin. Bha 'n darna gréim aige fhéin, agus an gréim eil' aig an steud. Thàinig an Ridir Dubh far an robh e. " C' àit', 'ille mhaith, an d'fhuair thu an steud-sa?" "Fhuair mis' an steud-sa air greigh each a bha aig m'athair fhéin ; ach c'àit air bith an d'fhuair mi i, b' fheàrr leam gu'n robh na fhuair mi còmhla rithe agam an so an nochd.' " Tha mise 'g ad chreidsinn," ars' esan ; " agus is maith a's aithne dhomhsa ceann do shaoid agus do shiubhail. Tha thu dol a dh'fhaotainn amach ciamar a chaidh an Tuairisgeul Mòr a chur gu bàs ; agus is ioma mac rìgh agus ridire 'chaidh air an turus sin nach do thill ; ach cha 'n iad sin a bheir ceann saoghail dhuitse. Tha mise cur cuairt air an treas cuid de 'n t-saoghal, agus cha 'n eil fios 's am bith agam mu dhéigh'nn ; ach tha mo bhràthair eile, a tha cur cuairt air leth an t-saoghail, astar là agus bliadhna as a so—an Ridir Bàn; agus mur deachaidh an steud dad air a h-ais o'n bha i aig mo bhràthair, bithidh tu an sin mu'n téid a' ghrian fodha."

Dh'fholbh e 's a' mhaduinn, 's thug e gu 'astar, 's bha e ann mu 'n deachaidh a' ghrian fodha. Ràinig e an gille-stàbuill. "Bheir dhomhsa stàbull anns an cuir mi an steud so." "Ciod e'n stàbull," ars' esan "a bhiodh tusa 'g iarraidh ach an stàbull a tha aig ar cuid each fhéin?" Thug e breab da, agus ghabh e stigh; agus thug e leis an steud, far an deachaidh e fhéin. Bha'n darna gréim aige fhéin, 's an gréim eil' aig an steud. Thàinig an Ridir Bàn far an robh e. "C' àit', 'ille mhaith, an d'fhuair thu'n steud-sa?" " Fhuair mis' an steud-sa air greigh each a bha aig m' athair fhéin; ach c'àit' air bith an d'fhuair mi i, b' fhèarr leam gu 'n robh na fhuair mi còmhla rithe agam an so an nochd." "Tha mise 'g ad chreidsinn," ars' esan; "agus is maith a's aithne dhomhsa ceann do shaoid agus do shiubhail. Tha thu dol a dh'fhaotainn amach ciamar a chaidh an Tuairisgeul Mòr a chur gu bàs; agus is ioma mac rìgh agus ridire 'chaidh air an turus sin nach do thill; ach cha'n iad sin a bheir ceann saoghail dhuitse. "Tha mise cur cuairt air leth an t-saoghail, agus cha'n'eil fios 's am bith agam mu dhéighinn; ach tha mo bhràthair eile, a tha cur cuairt air an t-saoghal air fad, astar là agus bliadhna as a so—an Ridir Donn, —agus mur deachaidh an steud dad air a h-ais o'n bha i aig mo bhràthair, bithidh tu an sin mu 'n téid a' ghrian fodha."

Dh'fholbh e 'sa' mhaduinn, agus thug e gu 'astar, 's bha e ann mu'n deachaidh a' ghrian fodha. Ràinig e an gille-stàbuill. "Bheir dhomhsa stàbull anns an cuir mi an steud so." "Ciod e 'n stàbull," ars' esan, "a bhiodh tusa 'g iarraidh ach an stàbull a tha aig ar cuid each fhéin?" Thug e breab dha, agus ghabh e stigh, 's thug e leis an steud, far an deachaidh e fhéin. Bha'n darna gréim aige fhéin, agus an gréim eile aig an steud. Thàinig an Ridir Donn far an robh e. "C' ait', 'ille mhaith, an d'fhuair thu an steud-sa?" "Fhuair mis' an steud-sa air greigh each a bha aig m'athair fhéin; ach c' àit' air bith an d'fhuair mi i, b'fheàrr leam gu'n robh na fhuair mi còmhla rithe agam an so an nochd." "Tha mise 'g ad chreidsinn," ars' esan; "agus is maith a's aithne dhomhsa ceann do shaoid agus do shiubhail. Tha dol a dh'fhaotainn a mach ciamar a chaidh an Tuairisgeul Mòr a chur gu bàs; agus is ioma mac rìgh agus ridire 'chaidh air an turus sin nach do thill; ach cha 'n iad sin a bheir ceann saoghail dhuitse. Tha mise cur cuairt air an t-saoghal air fad, agus cha 'n 'eil fios 's am bith agam mu dhéigh 'nn ; ach dh'fhaoiteadh gu'n seòlainn thu air an dòigh air am faigheadh tu mach ciamar a chaidh a chur gu bàs. 'N uair a dh'fholbhas tu am màireach, bheir thu leat seachd botuill fhìona ; agus tha loch romhad, agus leth an rathaid suathaidh tu trì botuill ris an steud an aghaidh an fhionnaidh agus leis an fhionnadh, agus dar a ruigeas tu taobh an locha suathaidh tu na ceithir botuill eile rithe ; agus mur deachaidh an steud air a h-ais o 'n bha i agam-sa, gearraidh i 'n loch ; agus dar a théid thu bhàrr an locha, coinnichidh òganach thu, agus farraidìdh e dhìot, ciod a ghabhas tu air an steud, agus their thusa, nach gabh thu dad oirre ; agus tairgidh e dhuit a cudthrom do airgiod oirre, agus cha ghabh thusa sin. Tairgidh e a cudthrom do òr oirre, 's cha ghabh thusa sin. Tairgidh e dhuit leth a rìoghachd oirre, agus cha ghabh thusa sin ; ach abair gu'n gabh thu 'n seann duine liath a tha aige stigh air a son : agus 'n uair a bheir thu dha i, thoir an t-srian as a ceann, agus gleidh i ; agus dar a bhios an steud a dhìth ort, crath an t-srian, agus bithidh i agad." Thug e dha an seann duine liath an so. "Nis, ni 's am bith a dh'iarras an seann duine liath ort, dean thusa an ni an aghaidh sin."

Dh'fholbh e, agus an seann duine liath aige mu chnàimh amhcha. Thuirt an so an seann duine liath ris, "Am faic thu dà rathad an sin ?" "Chì," thuirt mac rìgh Eirinn. "Rathad a' dol an àird'-an-iar, 's rathad a' dol an àird'-an-ear ?" "Seadh," thuirt mac rìgh Eirinn. "Gabh, matà, an rathad a tha dol do'n àird'-an-iar." Ghabh mac rìgh Eirinn an rathad a bha dol do 'n àird'-an-ear. "O ! cha 'n 'eil dùil leam fhìn gur h-e 'n rathad ceart a ghabh thu ; ach tha sin a' toirt barrachd saoghail dhuitse, agus giorraid saoghail dhomhsa. "Am faic thu tigh an sin ?" thuirt an seann duine liath. "Chì," thuirt mac rìgh Eirinn. "Dà dhorus air ?" thuirt an seann duine liath ; "gabh thusa stigh air dorus na h-àird'-an-iar, agus seachainn dorus na h-àird'-an-ear." Chaidh esan stigh air dorus na h-àird'-n-ear. "Cha b'ann air an dorus cheart a chaidh thu stigh ; ach tha sin a' toirt barrachd saoghail dhuitse, agus giorraid saoghail domhsa." Chaidh iad a stigh do'n tigh. "A bheil dà chathair an sin ?" thuirt an seann duine liath. "Tha," thuirt mac rìgh Eirinn. Shuidh e 's an dara cathair, 's an seann duine liath 's a' chathair eile. "Am faic thu coire an sin ?" "Chì," thuirt mac rìgh Eirinn. "Cuir air e. Is maith a 's aithne dhomhsa ceann do shaoid agus do shiubhail. 'S ann a dh'fhaotainn amach ciamar a chaidh an Tuairisgeul Mòr a chur gu bàs a shaothraich thu gus a so ; agus is ioma mac rìgh agus ridire 'chaidh gu bàs 'g a fhaighinn amach, ma gheibh thus' amach e. Is e mac rìgh 'tha annam-sa mi fhìn ; agus shiubhail mo mhàthair, agus dh'fhàg i triùir mhac, mise agus dithis eile ; agus phòs m'athair ban-righinn eile, agus thàinig an Eachrais-ùrlair gu tigh m'athar. Thuirt i ri m' mhuime, gur beag a gheibheadh a cuid cloinne-sa do mhath o aon ni 'bh' aig an athair, ach gu 'm biodh a mhath uile aig a' chloinn eile. Agus ghabh i duais o m' mhuime air son sinne chur fo gheasaibh ; agus bhuail i 'n slacan draoidheachd a bh' aice oirnn, agus rinn i tri madacha-galla[1] dhinn. Chaidh sinne air folbh, agus ghabh sinn amach ris na beanntan 'n ar trì madacha-galla ;[1] agus bhitheamaid a' tighinn rathad a' bhaile, agus a' marbhadh nan cearc oirre-sa. Cha b'urrainn duinn tuille dìoghaltais a dheanamh oirre. Thuig i 'n so gur sinne a bha tighinn a mharbhadh nan cearc ; agus dh'òrduich i gach brocair a bha 's an rìoghachd a chruinneachadh gu cur as duinn. Chasadh sinn an sin 'n ar triùir ri ailbhinn mhòir chreige, a bha ciad aitheamh os ar ceann, 's ciad aitheamh fodhainn, an fhairge fodhainn ann an aodann na creige ; 's bha sinn an sin a' dol bàs le cion a' bhìdh. Chuir sinn an so amach croinn, los gu'n aithnicheamaid am fear againn air an tigeadh an crann. Thàinig an crann orm fhìn ; 's mi 'bu shine na càch—agus thug mi leum, agus rug mi air sgòrnan air mo bhràthair agus mharbh mi e. Dh'ith sinn e 'n ar dithis. Bha sinn an sin co dona 's a bha sinn roimhe, gun bhiadh. Chuir sinn croinn amach a rìs, agus 's ann ormsa 'thàinig e 'n darna uair ; agus rug mi air mo bhràthair, agus mharbh mi e, mar a rinn mi air an fhear eile. Bha mi sin a' m' ònrachd, gun bhiadh gun ni. Bha so là a chunnaic mi soitheach dol seachad air an àite 'n robh mi ; agus smaointich mi nach robh ach am bàs romham 's am dhéigh, agus leum mi do 'n fhairge as déigh an t-soithich. Bhuail mi air glaodhaich leis an t-seòrsa glaoidh a bh' agam. Chuala sgioba[2] an t-soithich mi, agus dh'innis iad do 'n sgiobair gu'n robh iad a' cluinntinn glaoidh éigin. ' Theirigibh leis a' gheòla far a bheil e, dh' fhaicinn 'dé 'n duine 'tha 'n a éiginn.' Ràinig iad far an robh mi ; agus dar a chunnaic iad an creutair grannda 'bh' annam, dh'fhàg iad an sid mi, 's thill iad thun an t-soithich. Dh'innis iad do 'n sgiobair an creutair a chunnaic iad. ' O ! falbhaibh 's thugaibh air bòrd e", ars esan, " 'dé 'sam bith a th' ann. 'N uair a chaidh mi air bòrd, bhithinn 'g am shuathadh fhéin ris an sgiobair, agus a' mithlean ris, agus ghabh e tlachd mòr dhìom. Cha dealaicheadh e rium ;

---

[1] Madacha-allaidh.   [2] Crew.

bhithinn còmhla ris anns a' *chabin*,[1] gus an d'ràinig sinn dachaidh. Bha sinn an sin aig an tigh. Dh'fhàs an sin bean an sgiobair trom; agus 'n uair a thàinig àm a h-aiseid, fhuair iad mnathan-glùine dhi. Rug i leanabh mic. 'N uair a ghabh iad mu 'n bhean 's mu 'n leanabh, chaidil na mnathan-glùine. Bha mis' a 'm' laidhe fo 'n leabaidh: thàinig cròg mhòr a stigh air druim an tighe, 's thug i leatha an leanabh. 'N uair a dhùisg iadsan, cha robh an leanabh air faighinn. 'S e rinn iad fuil agus gaor a shuathadh riumsa, agus 'fhàgail orm gur mi a dh'ith an leanabh. Dh'innseadh so do'n sgiobair, gu 'n d'ith mise an leanabh. 'O! an creutair dona,' ars esan, 'tha e mòr leam cur as da, 's gur ro-thoigh leam fhìn e, 's leigidh mi sid leis.' Fad goirid 's a bha i gun fhàs leth-tromach, dh'fhàs i ann a rìs; 's cho luath 's a thàinig àm a h-aiseid, fhuair iad mnathan-glùine dhi. Rug i leanabh mic. 'N uair a ghabh iad mu 'n bhean 's mu 'n leanabh, chaidil na mnathan-glùine. Bha mis' a' m' laidhe fo'n leabaidh: thàinig cròg a stigh air druim an tighe, 's thug i leatha an leanabh. 'N uair a dhùisg iadsan, cha robh an leanabh air faighinn. 'S e rinn iad fuil agus gaor a shuathadh riumsa, agus 'fhàgail orm gur mi a dh'ith an leanabh. Dh'innseadh so do 'n sgiobair, gu 'n d'ith mise an leanabh. 'O! an creutair dona, tha e mòr leam cur as da, 's gur ro-thoigh leam fhìn e, 's leigidh mi sid leis fhathasd. An treas uair,' ars' an sgiobair, 'cuiridh sinn as da, ma dh'éireas a leithid amach.' Dh'fhàs is' an treas uair leth-tromach; agus 'n uair a thàinig an t-àm 's am biodh i air a h-aiseid fhuair iad mnathan-glùine dhi. Rug i leanabh mic. 'N uair a ghabh iad mu 'n bhean 's mu 'n leanabh, chaidil na mnathan-glùine. Bha mis' a' m' laidhe fo 'n leabaidh: thàinig cròg mhòr a stigh air druim an tighe; 's dar a chunnaic mise a' chròg a' tighinn, leum mi, 's rug mi air a' chròig; 's thug a' chròg mise suas gu druim an tighe; 's thug mise a' chròg o'n ghualainn deth, agus thug mi stigh fo 'n leabaidh i; agus chuir esan a stigh a' chròg eile, agus thug e leis an leanabh. Ghabh mise mach as a dhéigh, agus lean mi e dh'ionnsuidh a' chladaich. Bha'n sneachd air an làr, 's lean mi air 'fhuil e. Chunnaic mi eilean thall mu 'm choinnimh, 's shnàmh mi do 'n eilean. Chaidh mi stigh do'n uaimh a bh'aige; 's bha esan 'n a chadal ann am bràigh na h-uamha, agus an leanabh fo 'achlais, 's an dà phàisd eile 'thug e leis a' cleasachd air ùrlar na h-uamha. Thug mi leum suas 'n a sgòrnan, 's thug mi an sgòrnan as. Bha geòla bheag aige-san anns an eilen; 's fhuair mi 'n dà phàisd agus an leanabh

[1] Seòmar-luinge.

a chur anns a' gheòla, agus ghreas mi dhachaidh; agus bha mo mhaighstir an déigh éirigh an sin. Ghabh mi stigh, agus thug mi a' chròg air a bhialaobh. 'Tha so ag innseadh, a laochainn nach tusa 'bha ris a' chron; ach an fheadhainn a bha ris a' chron, théid iadsan a losgadh.' Rinn mi 'n so *sign* ris, agus lean e mi dh'ionnsuidh a' chladaich. Fhuair e a thriùir leanaban anns a' gheòla; 's ma bha gaol aige ormsa roimhe, bha 'sheachd uiread aige orm an sin. Thug e leis a' chlann dhachaidh, 's chruinnich e daoine 's cual chonnaidh, 's loisg e na mnathan-glùine 'bha mu thimchioll na mnà aige. Chaidh e an so là gu dìnneir gu tigh m'athar fhéin, 's chaidh mise leis—cha dealaichinn ris: agus bha leanabh òg a stigh a bha aig m'athair 's aig mo mhuime, agus bha 'n slacan draoidheachd a chuir mi fhìn fo na geasaibh 'n a làimh; 's bha mi smaointeachadh nam biodh an slacan air a bhualadh orm, gu 'm falbhadh na geasan dìom, 's gu 'm bithinn mar a bha mi roimhe. Agus bhithinn a' dol seachad air an leanabh dh'fheuchainn am buaileadh e orm e. Mu dheireadh, thug mi criomag as, agus bhuail e an slacan orm, agus dh'fhalbh na geasan dhìom, agus dh'fhàs mis' a'm' dhuine mar a bha mi riamh. An so, dar a bha mo mhaighstir a' falbh dhachaidh, cha robh fios c' àit' an robh mise. Bha iad 'g am iarraidh anns gach àit'. Rinn mise mi fhìn an so aithnichte do 'm mhaighstir; agus dh'innis mi dha mar a bha a' chùis, 's mar a thachair. Sin agadsa, a mhic rìgh Eirinn, mar a chaidh an Tuairisgeul Mòr a chur gu bàs; agus," ars' an seann duine liath, "cha 'n 'eil tuille saoghail agamsa: tilg anns a' choire ud mi." Dh'fholbh mac rìgh Eirinn an so, agus chrath e 'n t-srian, 's fhuair e 'n steud, 's ràinig e tigh 'athar mu 'n do stad e.

Choinnich a' ghruagach a dh'fhàg e aig an tigh e. "Thàinig thu," ars' ise. "Thàinig," ars' esan. "An d'fhuair thu a mach ciamar a chaidh an Tuairisgeul Mòr a chur gu bas?" "Fhuair," ars' esan.

"Falbh a nis agus ruig an tulaich air an d'fhàg thu 'n t-òlach dubh, agus innis dha gach car mar a dh'éirich dhuit." "O!" ars' esan, "dé a ni sin dòmhsa, 's nach 'eil cnàimh a chòir a chéile dheth 'n diu?" "Ruig thusa agus innis do 'n àit' a dh'fhàg thu mar a chaidh e gu bàs."

Dh'éirich esan beò slàn as an tulaich; 's phòs mac rìgh Eirinn agus a' ghruagach.

HOW THE GREAT TUAIRISGEUL* WAS PUT TO DEATH.

A WEST HIGHLAND TALE.

It was a son of the King of Ireland, and he was going to the hill to hunt (*lit.*, to the hunting hill); and young nobles used to meet him there. He was coming home one night, towards dusk, and saw a shower coming upon him from the west; and a big fellow came out of the shower, having a beautiful steed, and the most beautiful woman he ever saw behind him on the steed. "Is this you, son of the King of Ireland?" he said. "It is," said the son of the King of Ireland. "Will you play with me?" "I will," said the son of the King of Ireland; "I would not be worthy of my people if I would not play a game with you." They began to play, and the game was won by the son of the King of Ireland. "Take with you the reward of your play," said the fellow. "The reward of my play is, that I should have this beautiful woman going home with me." He went away, and took her with him, and reached home.

Early as the morrow came he made ready to go to the hill to hunt; and the woman said to him, "You are going to-day, and that fellow will meet you to-night again. He will play a game with you, and you will win, and take nothing but the steed he has under him." He went away, and betook himself to the hill to hunt; and when he was coming home late, he saw a shower coming upon him from the west, as he did before; and that fellow alighted, for he had the steed with him. "Is this you, son of the King of Ireland?" "It is I," said the son of the King of Ireland. "Will you play a game with me to-night, son of the King of Ireland?" "I will," said the son of the King of Ireland; "I would not be worthy of my people if I would not play with you." The game was won by the son of the King of Ireland. "Take the reward of your play." "That is," said the son of the King of Ireland, "that I should have this steed." He went away home, and reached the house.

Next day, he made ready to go to the hunting hill to meet other young nobles. The woman said to him, "You are going to-day again; but that man will meet you, and you will lose the game to-day; and he will lay as charms upon you that

* Description, report, calumny.

you do not stop, nor be at peace or rest, and that water leave not your shoe till you find out how the Great Tuairisgeul was put to death; and lay you as charms upon him that he leave not yonder hillock till you return. He will then say, 'Up and down with your charms;' and you will say, 'Neither up nor down, but as has been said.' He will then say, 'Let me go free, and I will let you go free.' You will then say, 'You will not set me free, and I will not set you free.'"

He went away to the hill; and when he was coming home, the big fellow met him, without horse, or steed, or anything. "Is this you, son of the King of Ireland?" "It is I," said the son of the King of Ireland. "Will you play with me?" said he. "I would not be worthy of my people if I would not play with you." They began to play, and the son of the King of Ireland lost the game. "I lay as crosses and charms upon you that water leave not your shoe till you find out how the Great Tuairisgeul was put to death." "I lay the same charms upon you," said the son of the King of Ireland, "that you leave not this hillock till I return." "Up and down with your charms," said he. "They will be neither up nor down, but as they are," said the son of the King of Ireland. "Set me free and I will set you free." "I will not set you free," said the son of the King of Ireland, "and you will not set me free."

They parted, and the son of the King of Ireland went home; and the woman said to him, "Well, you have come." "I have," he said. "You are going now to find out how the Great Tuairisgeul was put to death." "Yes," he said. "Many a king and squire's son have gone on that errand who never came back; but that will not be the end of your life-time to you, for all that." He prepared to start in the morning. "And you will take the steed under you," said she. "I have three brothers, and the Black Squire is the name of one, and the White Squire is the name of another, and the Brown Squire of another; and one of them surrounds the third part of the world, and another surrounds half the world, and the other surrounds the whole extent of the world. If you do not ascertain it from them, you may return home; and there is the distance of a day and a year between the house of each one of them; and if the steed has not gone back since my brother had it, it will be in the house of the first of them before the sun goes down: and when you arrive, you will ask of the groom for a stable for your horse; and the groom will say, 'What stable would you have but the stable our own horses have?' You will then give him a kick, and you will go in, and you will take the steed with you to the room in which you will be yourself; and you will have one bite for yourself, and the other bite the steed will have. My brother will then come to you, and will say to you, 'Where, my good sir, did you get this steed?' You will say to him, 'I got this steed in a herd of horses that my own father had; but wherever I got it, I wish all that I got with it were here to-night.' He will then say, 'I believe you.' Go now on horseback, and I will see if your journey will be successful."

He went on horseback. As he was about to go, the steed shook itself, and threw him down on its haunches; and it gave itself another shake, and threw him down on its mane; and on the third shake, he remained in his own place. "Oh!" said she, "your journey will be successful: have good courage."

He took his journey, and was ever going on; and he was in the Black Squire's house before the sun went down. He went to the groom: "Give me a stable where I shall put this steed." "What stable would you have but the stable our own horses have?" He gave him a kick and went in, and took the steed with him where he went himself. He had one bite himself, and the steed had the other. The Black Squire came where he was. "Where, my good sir, did you get this steed?" "I got this steed in a herd of horses my own father had; but wherever I got it, I wish I had all I got with it here to-night." "I believe you," he said; "and I know well the object of your going and journeying. You are going to find out how the Great Tuairisgeul was put to death; and many a king and squire's son have gone on that journey, and have not returned; but that will not be the end of your life-time to you. I surround the third part of the world, and I know nothing about it; but my other brother, who surrounds half the world, is a day and a year's distance from here, the White Squire; and if the steed has not gone any ways back since my brother had it, you will be there before the sun sets."

He went away in the morning, and made haste, and he was there before the sun went down. He went to the groom: "Give me a stable where I shall put this horse." "What stable," said he, "would you be wanting but the stable our own horses have?" He gave him a kick and went in, and took with him the steed where he went himself. He had the one bite himself, and the steed had the other. The White Squire came to him. "Where, my good sir, did you get this steed?" "I got this steed in a herd of horses my own father had; but wherever I got it, I wish I had all I got with it here to-night. "I believe you," said he; "and well do I know the object of your going and your journeying. You are going to find out how the Great Tuairisgeul was put to death; and many a king and squire's son went on that journey who never returned; but that will not be the end of your life to you. I surround half the world, and I have no knowledge of it; but my other brother, who surrounds the whole world, is the distance of a day and a year from here, the Brown Squire; and if the steed has not in any way gone back since my brother had it, you will be there before the sun goes down.

He went away in the morning, and made haste, and was there before the sun went down. He went to the groom: "Give me a stable in which to put this horse." "What stable would you ask but the stable our own horses have?" He gave him a kick and went in, and took the steed with him where he went himself. He had the one bite himself, and the steed had the other. The Brown Squire came where he was. "Where, my good sir, did you get this steed?" "I got this steed in a herd of horses my own father had; but wherever I got it, I wish I had all I got with it here to-night." "I believe you," he said, "and well I know the object of your going and journeying. You are going to find out how the Great Tuairisgeul was put to death; and many a king and squire's son went on that journey who never returned; but that will not be the end of your life-time to you. I surround the whole world, and I know nothing about it; but perhaps I can show you the way in which you can find out how he was put to death. When you go away to-morrow, you will take with you seven bottles of wine; and there is a loch before you, and when half-way you will rub three bottles to the steed against the hair and with the hair: and when you reach the side of the lake you will rub the other four bottles to it; and if the steed has not gone back since I had it, it will cut the loch; and when you have gone over the loch a young man will meet you, and will ask what you will take for the steed, and you will say that you will not take anything for it; and he will offer its weight in silver for it, and you will not take that. He will offer its weight in gold for it, and you will not take that. He will offer you half his kingdom for it, and you will not take that; but you will say that you will take the old grey man he has in the house for it: and when you give it to him, take the bridle off its head and keep it; and when you want the steed, shake the bridle, and you will have it." He now gave him the old grey-haired man. "Now, whatever the old grey man asks you to do, do you the contrary to that."

He went away having the old grey man astride on his neck (*lit.*, about the bone of his neck). The old grey man now said to him, "Do you see two roads there?" "I see them," said the son of the King of Ireland. "Is there a road going west and a road going east?" "Yes," said the son of the King of Ireland. "Take, then, the road that goes west." The son of the King of Ireland took the road that went east. "O! I don't think myself it is the right road you have taken; but that gives longer life to you, and shorter life to me. Do you see a house there?" said the old grey man. "I see it," said the son of the King of Ireland. "Two doors to it?" said the old grey-haired man; "go you in at the west door, and avoid the east door." He went in at the east door. "It was not at the right door you went in; but that gives longer life to you, and shorter life to me." They went in. "Are there two chairs there?" said the old grey-haired man. "Yes," said the son of the King of Ireland. He sat in the one chair, and the old grey-haired man in the other. "Do you see a cauldron there?" "I see it," said the son of the King of Ireland. "Put it on. Well do I know the object of your going and journeying. It is to find out how the Great Tuairisgeul was put to death you have toiled till now; and many a king and squire's son have suffered death in finding it out, if you can find it out. I am myself the son of a king; and my mother died, and left three sons, myself and two others; and my father married another queen, and 'Trouble-the-house' came to my father's house. She said to my stepmother that little good would her children get from anything that my father had, but that all the good would go to the other children. And she took a bribe from my stepmother to place us under enchantments; and she struck us with the divining rod (*lit.*, the beetle or mallet of Druidism), and made three wolves of us. We went away, and took to the hills as three wolves; and we used to come the way of the town, and kill her hens. We could not take more revenge upon her. She then understood it was we who came and killed her hens; and she ordered every vermin-killer that was in the kingdom to assemble to destroy us. We three were then hard pressed against a big precipitous rock, that was a hundred fathoms above us, and a hundred fathoms below us, in the face of the rock; and we were there dying from want of food. We then cast lots, that we might know which of us the lot might fall on. The lot fell on me. I was older than the rest; and I sprang and caught my brother by the throat and killed him. The two of us ate him. We were then as ill off as we were before, without food. We cast lots again, and it was upon me it fell a second time; and I caught my brother and killed him, as I had done to the other. I was now alone, without food or anything. One day I saw a boat going past the place where I was; and I thought there was nothing but death before and after me, and I jumped into the sea after the boat. I began to call out (*lit.*, I struck at calling out) with the kind of cry I had. The crew of the ship heard me, and they told the captain that they were hearing a cry of distress. 'Go with the skiff where it is, to see what man is in distress.' They reached where I was; and when they saw what an ugly creature I was, they left me there, and returned to the ship. They told the captain the creature they had seen. 'O! go away and take it on board, whatever it be,' said he. When I went on board, I used to rub myself against the captain and fawn upon him, and he took a great liking to me. He would not part with me; I used to be with him in the cabin, till we arrived at home. We were after this at home. The captain's wife then became pregnant; and when the time of her delivery came, they got midwives for her. She had a male child. When they had sorted the woman and child, the midwives slept. I was lying below the bed: a big fist came in through the roof of the house, and took away the child. When they awoke, the child was not to be found. What they did was to smear blood and filth over me, and accuse me of having eaten the child. 'O, the bad creature! I am loath to kill it, as I am myself very fond of it, and I will forgive it that.' Long or short as she might be in proving pregnant, she became so again; and when the time of her delivery came, they got midwives for her. She had a male child. When they had dressed the woman and child, the midwives slept. I was asleep below the bed: a hand came in through the roof, and took away the child. When they awoke, the child was not to be found. What they did was to smear blood and gore over me, and accuse me of having eaten the child. It was told to the captain that I had eaten the child. 'O, the bad creature! I am loath to kill it, for I like it very much myself, and I will

Reasonable by my friend the Minister but so far as it goes it is good and genuine. See my manuscripts and the 2d Volume of Popular Tales. for Xerxi Xerxius of the incidents. Compare Gelert — The Indian Versions of that myth. — J F Campbell. Nete November 11. 1883.

forgive it this time yet. The third time,' said the captain, 'we will destroy it, if the like happens.' She became a third time pregnant; and when the time came when she was to be delivered, they got midwives. She had a male child. When they had arranged about the woman and child, the midwives slept. I was lying below the bed; a big hand came in at the roof of the house; and when I saw the hand coming, I sprang and caught the hand; and the hand took me up to the roof of the house; and I took the hand from the shoulder off him, and I took it in below the bed; and he put in the other hand, and took the child away. I ran out after him, and followed him to the shore. There was snow on the ground, and I followed him by his blood. I saw an island over opposite to me, and I swam to the island. I went into the cave that he had; and he was asleep in the upper part of the cave, and the child under his arm, and the other two children he had taken with him playing on the floor of the cave. I sprang at his throat, and tore his throat for him (*lit.*, took the throat out of him). He had a little skiff in the island; and I got the two children and the babe put into the skiff and hurried home; and my master had then got up. I went in and took the hand before him. 'This shows, my good fellow, it was not you that was doing the mischief; but those that did the mischief—they will be burned.' I now made a sign to him, which made him follow me to the shore. He found his three children in the skiff; and if he loved me before, he loved me seven times more then. He brought the children home with him, and got men and bundles of fire-wood, and burned the midwives that were about his wife. He went one day to dinner to my own father's house, and I went with him—I would not part with him: and there was a young child there that my father and stepmother had, and the divining rod that had put myself under spells was in its hands; and I thought if I were struck with the rod, the spells would leave me, and I would be as I was before. And I was always going past the child, to see if it would strike me with the rod. At last, I took a bite out of the child, and it struck me with the rod, and the spells left me, and I became a man as I was before. Then, when my master was going away home, no one knew where I was. They were seeking me everywhere. I then made myself known to my master; and I told him how the matter stood, and how it happened. That is for you, son of the King of Ireland, the way the Great Tuairisgeul was put to death, and," said the old grey-haired man, "I am not to live any longer;

throw me into yonder cauldron." The son of the King of Ireland,
upon this, shook the bridle and got the steed, and reached his
father's house before he stopped.

The woman he had left at home met him. "You have come,"
she said. "I have," he said. "Have you found out how the
Great Tuairisgeul was put to death?" "I have," he said.

"Go now to the hillock on which you left the black fellow, and
tell him every turn that befel you." "O!" said he, "what is the
good of that when one bone of him does not stick to another to-
day?" "Go you and tell to the place you left how he was put
to death."

He rose alive and well from the hillock; and the son of the
King of Ireland and the woman were married.

DO MHORAIR GHLINNE-GARADH:
Le Iain Lom.

[The following poem by John M'Donald, the Keppoch bard, is
from a MS. collection of Gaelic poems, transcribed from an
older MS. by the late Mr. Ewen M'Lachlan of Aberdeen.]

1. Bidh an t-uidheamsa triall,
   Gu Ceann-uidhe nan cliar,
   Far 'm bu chubhaidh 's 'm bu mhiann le 'r scòd;

2. Gu tùr mheadhrach nach crìon,
   Am bi Ciun-fheadhna 's glan liomh,
   A chùirt ghreadhnach an rìoghail glòir.

3. Mi fada mu thuath,
   Gu'n lìon fadachd mi 's gruaim,
   Cha chadal dhomh uair air chòir.

4. Théid mi shealltainn a nunn
   Air nighinn Sheumais nan tùr,
   Gu 'm meall thu 'n *staoidhle* sin phùsd' ri d' bheò.

5. Gu mnaoi àillidh 'n fhuilt réidh;
   Cìr do 'n airgiod '...,
   Agus coinnlean d...chéir 'g a còir.

6. Gur tu 'n iuchair...bàth,
   'Chuir do fhradharc thar chàch—
   'S tu 'thaghainn do'n àls' 'tha beò.

7. Mach o Mhòrair nan steud,
   Nan organ, 's nan teud,
   'S tu 'b' *fhormaile* beus trà-neòin.

8. Théid eich sheanga 'n an leum,
   Dol 'n an deannaibh 's an réis,
   Fhir a theannaicheadh sréin mu 'm beòil!

9. B'fhearail t' fhaicinn air sràid,
   Le d' chiabh-fhalt cleachdach gu làr,
   Urla mhaisich, 's neo-thàireil oirnn.

10. B' ait leam torman do phìob',
    Creach 'g a togail le strìth,
    Le Mac aignidh bho 'n rìoghail stoirm.

11. Leat dh'éireadh na laoich,
    Clann Dòmhnaill an fhraoich,
    Sud na connsbuinn nach faoin 's an tòir.

12. Bu leat Bànich o thuath,
    Clann-'Ill-Andrais nan tuagh,
    Agus Ròdhaich le 'm buailtibh bhò.

13. Thig Mac-'Ic-Ailein o 'n chuan,
    Le 'loingeas daraich dubh luath,
    Buidheann bharrail le 'm buailteadh stròichd—

14. Buidheann alloil mo rùin,
    Cha laidh smal air an cliù,
    Leis an Alastair ùiseil òg.

NOTES ON GAELIC GRAMMAR AND ORTHOGRAPHY.

1. "De 'm bheil mòran air am baisteadh."
   (Of *whom whom* many have been baptised).

   In "de 'm bheil" the relative is repeated, for *bheil* = *bh-feil* is the verb *feil* = *velti or *velit (cf. Windisch in Beitr. z. Gesch. der Deutsch. Spr. und Lit., p. 228), from root *vel*, Skr. *var* (to choose, to will), Lat. *velle*, with *bh*, by which *f* of *feil* is eclipsed, representing *n* of the relative, and, therefore, forming really no part of the verb. But '*m*, after the preposition, is also the relative, and thus in "de 'm bheil," or, written in full, "de am bh-feil," the relative, occurs twice after the same preposition.

2. "Gu bheil," or, more correctly, "gu bh'eil."
   The above remarks shew that "gu bheil" ("gu bh'eil") in "gu bheil againn aitreabh o Dhia" (2 Cor. v. 1) is strictly correct, for the relative is concealed in the eclipsing *bh*. "Gu 'm bheil," sometimes used in both spoken and written Gaelic,

is a modern corruption, which ought to be discontinued.
3. "Gu 'n," "gu 'm," (that, lit., to that, *ad quod*).

Bh of *bheil* (for *bh-feil*) proves conclusively that *'n* of *gu'n* in "gu 'n dean," "gu 'n ith," "gu 'n ol," is the relative used as a conjunction (cf. Gr ὅτι, Lat. *quod*, Eng. *that*), and not, as Stewart supposed (cf. Gramm. 2nd ed. p. 176), a mere euphonic letter. It should, therefore, be written with an apostrophe—not a hyphen—before it, to mark the elision of the vowel of the relative.

4. In "gu 'n," "gu 'm," *gu* is a prep., the modern form of the old prep. *co* (to, *ad*) = **cot*, cognate with Gr. κατά. This prep. governs the accusative. In *gu'n, gu'm*, therefore, the relative is really the accusative, although it is now usually construed as the dative, the modern accusative, sing. and plur., being *a*.

5. It may be noticed here that the mod. prep. *gu* represents two distinct prepositions in ancient Gaelic, the prep. *co* (to, *ad*), referred to in the last note, and the prep. *co, con* (with), cognate with Lat. *con, cum*. These prepositions differ in their government and phonetic influence as well as in their meaning and etymology. *Co* (to) governs the accusative, but *co* (with) the dative. The former, having terminated originally in *t* (dropped by rule), does not eclipse; but the latter, having terminated originally in *n*, eclipses regularly. In "gu bheil," it is not the preposition but *bh = n* of the relative, as noticed above, that eclipses the initial consonant of the verb. These prepositions, having originally a consonantal termination, do not aspirate the word following. Hence "gu tìr" (to land), "gu fois" (to rest); "gu mall" (slowly), "gu tosdach" (silently).

6. The eclipses have long disappeared in Scotland from written Gaelic, except in some fossilised forms, such as *bheil*, above referred to, and *ma* in the phrases, "gu ma beannaichte," "gu ma h-amhlaidh 'bhios," "gu ma slàn a chi mi." In some of the remote Western Islands, they are still partially retained in the spoken language. A native of the Island of Lewis pronounces "mullach nam beann" (the top of the mountains) as "mullach na meann," "ar Dia" (our God) as "ar nia," "àireamh nan daoine" (the number of the men) as "àireamh na naoine."

(*To be continued.*)

COIR'-A'-CHEATHAICH—CORRIE OF THE MIST.

Mode of the 2nd of Scale.
Slowly, with marked accent.

FROM "THE THISTLE."
By the Editor's Permission.

LEABHAR COMUNN NAM FIOR GHÄEL—*Continued.*

"A BOOK WHICH SHOULD GREATLY INTEREST HIGHLANDERS.—This is the Book of the Club of True Highlanders, on which Mr. Macintyre North has been assiduously engaged for a considerable time, and which is on a good way towards completion. It consists of descriptions of rare objects of interest connected with the Highlands, illustrated with carefully executed etchings. It will rank in interest with Priolo's Illustrations from Ossian, and exceed that beautiful work in value, in that it does the next thing to placing in one's hand a large number of relics and other things which appeal to our patriotism, and cultivate our acquaintance with our country and our race."—*The Highlander.*

A FEW COPIES (ON INDIAN PAPER) OF LOGAN'S PORTRAIT WITH AUTOGRAPH, 7s. 6D. EACH.

Specimens of the PLATES may be seen at, and SUBSCRIBERS NAMES received by the following :—

LONDON :
The Author, 15 Boro' High Street, S.E.
Mr. W. Drewitt, bookseller, 48 Boro' High Street, S.E.
Messrs. Richardson & Co., 18 Pall Mall.
EDINBURGH :
Mr. Paterson, bookseller, Princes Street.
R. & H. B. Kirkwood, 68 Thistle Street.
GLASGOW :
D. Bryce & Son, booksellers, 128 Buchanan Street.
CRIEFF :
P. Comrie, bookseller.
PERTH :
Messrs. Wood & Son, booksellers, High Street.
BLAIRGOWRIE :
Mr. Macdoanld, Queen's Hotel.

BRECHIN :
Messrs Black & Johnston, booksellers, 40 High Street.
ABERDEEN :
Messrs. A. Brown & Co., booksellers, Union Street.
ELGIN :
J. T. Ferrier, bookseller, 62 High Street.
INVERNESS :
Messrs. A. & W. Mackenzie, *Celtic Magazine* Office, 2 Ness Bank.
Mr. J. Murdoch, *The Highlander* Office, 87 Church Street.
WICK :
Mr. P. Reid, *John O'Groat Journal* Office, Union Street.

TRÜBNER & CO.'S LIST.

THE GAELIC ETYMOLOGY OF THE LANGUAGES
OF
WESTERN EUROPE,

And more particularly of the English and Lowland Scotch, and their Slang, Cant, and Colloquial Dialects.

By CHARLES MACKAY, LL.D., F.S.A. of Denmark.

ROYAL 8vo., pp. xxxii.-604, CLOTH, 42s.

The Influence of the English and Welsh Languages upon each other, exhibited in the Vocabularies of the two Tongues. Intended to suggest the importance to Philologers, Antiquaries, Ethnographers, and others, of giving due attention to the Celtic Branch of the Indo-Germanic Family of Languages. Square, pp. 30, sewed, 1s.

LECTURES ON WELSH PHILOLOGY. By JOHN RHYS, M.A., Professor of Celtic at Oxford. Second edition, revised and enlarged. Crown 8vo, pp. viii. and 466, cloth 15s.

GOIDELICA—Old and Early-Middle Irish Glosses: Prose and Verse. Edited by WHITLEY STOKES. Second edition. Med. 8vo, pp. 192, cloth 18s.

BEUNANS MERIASEK. The Life of Saint Meriasek, Bishop and Confessor. A Cornish Drama. Edited with a Translation and Notes, by WHITLEY STOKES. Med. 8vo, pp. xvi. and 280, and Facsimile, cloth, 15s.

LONDON: TRÜBNER & CO., LUDGATE HILL.

MESSRS. MACMILLAN & CO.'S PUBLICATIONS.

SCOTCH SERMONS, 1880. By Principal Caird—Rev. J. CUNNINGHAM, D.D., Rev. D. J. FERGUSON, B.D., Professor WM. KNIGHT, LL.D., Rev. W. MACKINTOSH, D.D., Rev. W. L. M'FARLAN, Rev. ALLAN MENZIES, B.D., Rev. T. NICOLL, Rev. T. RAIN, M.A., Rev. A. SEMPLE, B.D., Rev. J. STEVENSON, Rev. PATRICK STEVENSON, Rev. R. H. STORY, D.D. 8vo. 10s. 6d.

The *Pall Mall Gazette* says: "The publication of a volume of Scotch Sermons contributed by members of the Established Church seems likely to cause as much commotion in that body as 'Essays and Reviews' did in the Church of England."

THE CHURCH OF THE FUTURE: Its Catholicity; Its Conflict with the Atheist; Its Conflict with the Deist; Its Conflict with the Rationalist; Its Dogmatic Teaching; Practical Counsels for its Work; Its Cathedrals. By ARCHIBALD CAMPBELL, Archbishop of Canterbury. Crown 8vo. 3s. 6d.

ENGLISH POETS: Selections, with Critical Introductions by various Writers, and a General Introduction by MATTHEW ARNOLD. Edited by T. H. WARD, M.A. 4 vols. Crown 8vo. Each 7s. 6d.

Vol. I. CHAUCER TO DONNE. | Vol. III. ADDISON TO BLAKE.
Vol. II. BEN JONSON TO DRYDEN. | Vol. IV. WORDSWORTH TO SYDNEY DOBELL.

"A work of the very highest excellence, which promises to be a most valuable addition to the standard criticism of English Literature."—*Academy.*

A DICTIONARY OF MUSIC AND MUSICIANS (A.D. 1450—1878). By eminent Writers, English and Foreign. With Illustrations and Woodcuts. Edited by GEORGE GROVE, D.C.L. In 3 vols. 8vo. Parts I. to XII., 3s. 6d. each. Vols. I. and II., 8vo, cloth, 21s. each.

Vol. I. A TO IMPROMPTU. Vol. II. IMPROPERIA TO PLAIN SONG.

"Dr. Grove's Dictionary will be a boon to every intelligent lover of music."—*Quarterly Review.*

ETIENNE DOLET: The Martyr of the Renaissance. A Biography, with a Biographical Appendix containing a descriptive Catalogue of the Books written, edited, or printed by DOLET. By RICHARD COPLEY CHRISTIE, M.A., Lincoln College, Oxford, Chancellor of the Diocese of Manchester. With Illustrations. 8vo. 18s.

"So conscientious and so successful have been the labours of Mr. Christie, his work stands in most important respects outside criticism, and his book may be cited as, in many respects, a model biography."—*Athenæum.*

ESSAYS ON ART AND ARCHÆOLOGY. By C. T. NEWTON, C.B., D.C.L., &c., Professor of Archæology in University College, London, Keeper of Greek and Roman Antiquities in the British Museum. 8vo. 12s. 6d.

THE YEAR'S ART. A Concise Epitome of all matters relating to the Arts of PAINTING, SCULPTURE, and ARCHITECTURE, which have occurred during the Year 1880, together with information respecting the events of the Year 1881. Compiled by MARCUS B. HUISH, LL.B. Crown 8vo. 2s. 6d.

"It is sold for half-a-crown, we would willingly have given a guinea for it."—*Portfolio.*

GOLDEN TREASURY SERIES (New Volume.)

ESSAYS OF JOSEPH ADDISON. Chosen and Edited by JOHN RICHARD GREEN, M.A., LL.D. 18mo. 4s. 6d.

"This is a most welcome edition to a most excellent series."—*Examiner.*

ENGLISH MEN OF LETTERS. Edited by JOHN MORLEY. New Volumes. Crown 8vo. 2s. 6d. each.

DRYDEN. By G. SAINTSBURY. [*Immediately.*

WORDSWORTH. By F. W. H. MYERS.

"Mr. Myers gives us a picture of the man and an estimate of his work, which is certainly not inferior to anything that has preceded it. . . . Probably the best chapter in the book—every chapter of which is excellent—is that on Natural Religion."—*Academy.*

THE STEAM ENGINE AND ITS INVENTORS. A Historical Sketch. By ROBERT L. GALLOWAY, Mining Engineer. With numerous Illustrations. Crown 8vo. 10s. 6d.

MACMILLAN & CO., LONDON.

THE

SCOTTISH CELTIC

REVIEW.

CONTENTS.   No. 2.   NOVEMBER, 1881.

                                                                                              PAGE

I.—The Laws of Auslaut in Irish,   - - - - - 81—106

II.—Gaelic and English; or the Etymology of the Celtic and Teutonic Languages, - - - - - - 106—115

III.—The Muileartach, a West Highland Tale, with Translation by Rev. John G. Campbell, Tiree, - - - - 115—137

IV.—Note on Tuairisgeul Mòr, by Mr. Alfred Nutt, - - - 137—141

V.—Miann a' Bhàird Aosda (the Aged Bard's Wish), with Translation by Rev. Hugh M'Millan, LL.D., D.D., - - 141—149

VI.—Notes on Gaelic Grammar and Orthography, - - - 149—157

VII.—Cumha Mhic-Criomthain (Macrimmon's Lament), &c., - - 157—159

VIII.—Music of Macrimmon's Lament, - - - - - 160

GLASGOW:
PRINTED BY ROBERT MACLEHOSE, 153 WEST NILE ST
MACLACHLAN & STEWART, EDINBURGH.
TRÜBNER & CO., LONDON.

1881.

Price to Subscribers 10s. for four Numbers.

Gaelic Literature.

MACLACHLAN & STEWART

HAVE always on hand a large collection of Works in the GAELIC LANGUAGE and on CELTIC LITERATURE, including those of Baxter, Bunyan, Dr. Norman Macleod, Grant, Macdonald, etc.; Confession of Faith; also M'Alpine's, and Macleod & Dewar's Gaelic Dictionaries, Stewart's and Macpherson's Gaelic Grammars, Catechisms, Song and Hymn Books. Catalogue on application. The "GAEL" for 1876 and 1877. Price, in cloth, 7s. 6d.

64 SOUTH BRIDGE (opposite the University), EDINBURGH.

CONTENTS OF No. I.

I.—Introductory Remarks: Place of Celtic in the Indo-European Family of Languages—Tests of Etymological Affinity—Grimm's Law—Illustrations of the Application of Grimm's Law.

II.—Indo-European Roots, with Derivatives and Analysis of some Gaelic Compound Words.

III.—The Laws of Auslaut in Irish. First Part.

IV.—Grammatical and Etymological Analysis of Gen. i. 1-8.

V.—Specimen of Old Gaelic: St. Patrick's Hymn, with Translation and Analysis of part of Hymn.

VI.—West Highland Tale: How the Tuairisgeul Mor was put to Death, with Translation.

VII.—Gaelic Song by John Macdonald (Ian Lom), the Keppoch Bard.

VIII.—Notes on Gaelic Grammar and Orthography.

IX.—Gaelic Air: "Coire-a'-Cheathaich," or "The Corrie of the Mist."

SCOTTISH CELTIC REVIEW.

No. 2.—NOVEMBER, 1881.

THE LAWS OF AUSLAUT IN IRISH.

Continued from Page 40.

(*Translated from an important paper by Profr. Windisch, of Leipzig, in the Beitr. zur Geschichte der Deutschen Sprache und Literatur*, Vol. iv., 1877, and revised by the Author.)

B. LOSS OF ORIGINAL FINAL SYLLABLES.

EVERY final syllable formed differently [from those of which we treated in the first part of this article] is lost as an independent syllable—not only every final syllable which consisted originally of a short or a long vowel, or of a diphthong, but also every final syllable which consisted of a short vowel with *s* or *t*, or of a short or long vowel with a nasal. But there still remain both regressive and progressive effects of the once existing syllable: regressive, when its vowel, in the form which it last assumed, has thrown its reflex into the preceding syllable, which has taken place invariably when the vowel was *i*; progressive, when an original vocalic auslaut, in certain combinations capable of being formulated, aspirates the anlaut of the following word, and when an original nasal auslaut is preserved at the beginning of the following word, if that word begins with a vowel or a medial.

a. TERMINATIONS WITH S- AUSLAUT.

I. *as* stood originally in auslaut. Before this syllable disappeared, its vowel, in some cases, was preserved as *a* (with perhaps a leaning towards *o*); but, in other cases, it was weakened to *e* or *i*. The agreement with Greek and Latin in this weakening of the vowel, is very striking.

F

Original *as*, represented in monosyllabic words by Old Irish *i*: *ni* (we) = Cymr. *ni* = Skr. *nas* (cf. Lat. *nōs*); *si*, *si-si*, *sissi* (ye, you) = Cymr. *chwi*, *chwi-chwi*, for original *svas*, related to Skr. *vas*, Lat. *vôs* (Z. 325). A pronominal *s* also appears in the fuller form *sni*, *sni-sni* (we).

Of polysyllabic forms there come here under consideration:—

1. The nom. sing. of the masc. stems in *a*. E.g., Old Ir. *ech*, for prehistoric *eq-as* = Lat. *equos*, Skr. *açvas*; *fer*, for prehistoric *vir-as* = Lat. *vir*, Goth. *vair*, Skr. *vîras* (the *e* of *fer* has originated from *i* through assimilation to the *a* of the once existing final syllable); *Corb-macc*, *Cormacc* = *Corpimaqas* in an Oghamic Inscription, which is older than our literary sources; *tarb*, for prehistoric *tarv-as* = Old Gaul *tarvos* (bullock)—Z. 222; Stokes in Beitr. i. 449, ii. 102; Becker in Beitr. iii. 168. In Old Irish, *e* represented two modifications of the *e* sound—one approaching to *i*, and the other to Germ. *ä*. In New Irish, the former is written *ei* and the latter *ea*; whence New Irish *fear* (without the softened pronunciation of *r*), *each*, etc.

2. The nom. and acc. sing. of the neutral stems in *as* (Z. 270), which were first recognised by Ebel in his able article in the Beitr. zur Vgl. Spr. vi. 222, etc. E.g., Old Ir. *tech* (house), for prehistoric *teg-as*, New Ir. *teach* = Gr. στέγος; Old Ir. *leth* (side), for prehistoric *let-as*, New Ir. *leath* = Lat. *latus*; *mach*, *mag* (a plain), for prehistoric *mag-as* (cf. Skr. *mahi*, earth); *nem* (heaven), for prehistoric *nem-as*, New Ir. *neamh*, perhaps identical with Skr. *namas*, cf. Old Ir. *nemed* = Old Gaul. *nemeton* (sanctuary), Skr. *namati* (to bow one's self), *namasyati* (to reverence, to worship). The usual comparison (defended by Ebel) of Ir. *nem* with Skr. *nabhas* conflicts with the phonetic laws of Celtic.

3. The gen. sing. of all consonantal stems.

E.g., *bethad* (nom. *beothu*, life), for prehistoric *bivatat-as* = Gr. βιότητος; *bráget*, *brágat* (nom. *bráge*, neck), for prehistoric *bargent-as*, Lat. *gurgitis*; *coimded* (nom. *coimdiu*, lord), for prehistoric *-medet-as* (cf. Gr. μέδοντος); *athar* (father), for prehistoric *ater-as* = Gr. πατέρος; *menman* (nom. *menme*, sense, mind) = Skr. *manmanas*; *er-miten* (nom. *er-mitiu*, reverence), for prehistoric *mentin-as* (cf. Lat. *mentiônis*).

The *e* in these forms is of different origin. In *bráget*, it is the *a* of the stem-forming suffix *ant*, weakened in prehistoric time to *e*; cf. Lat. *fer-ent*. In *coimded* (stem *con-mediat*), it is the representative of an original *ia*, the *a* of which changed the *i* into *e*, and then disappeared. In like manner, the *e* of *er-miten* has sprung from an original *i*, which, according to the phonetic laws of Irish, has been changed into *e*, as in *fer*, by the *a* of the once existing final syllable. For, the *-an* of the compound suffix *ti-an* is variable in Irish, like the Skr. primary suffix *an*: it has its vowel lengthened in the strong cases, and dropped in the weak cases (cf. Skr. acc. *rág-án-am*, gen. *ráj-ñ-as*), whilst in Latin the lengthened form has established itself for all cases. Therefore, the difference between Ir. *miten* and Lat. *mentionis*, consists in this, that the former presupposes a *man-tin-as*, but the latter a *man-tián-as*.

That, however, the *e* in *bráget*, *coimded*, *ermiten*, and in all similar genitives, was a broad *e*, is not proved so much by the form *brágat*, in which one might also assume the progressive influence of a long *a* in the root syllable, as by the spelling *ea* in later MSS., e.g., *lénead*, nom. *léine* (shirt); *tenead*, nom. *tene* (fire).

4. The 2nd per. sing. of the reduplicated perfect. Cf. Ztschr. für Vgl. Spr. xxiii. 229. E.g., *con-darc* = Gr. δέδορκ-ας.

5. The 1st per. plur. act. of the conjunct flexion.

Original *mas* represented by the Old Ir. *m*. E.g., *doberam* = Dor. φέρο-μες or Skr. *bhará-mas*. It cannot be determined whether Ir. *beram* is for *bhar-a-mas* or *bhar-á-mas*. The Irish has shortened the long *á* of an unaccented suffix-syllable in the stems in *tát*, e.g., *bethad* = Gr. βιότητος. In the following cases, the weakening of *-as* into *-es*, *-is*, was effected in prehistoric time.

6. In the nom. plur. of the mas. and fem. consonantal stems. The slender vowel has always entered into the preceding syllable, and has there become the characteristic mark of this case (internal flexion), e.g., *athir*, for prehistoric *ater-is* = πατέρες (cf. Osc. *censtur*, Umbr. *frater*, Lat. *quattuor*; see Bücheler's Lat. Decl., p. 16); *téit* (nom. *tee*, fervidus), for prehistoric *te(p)ent-is* = Skr. *tapantas*; *filid* (nom. *file*, poet), for prehistoric *velet-is*; *carait*, (nom. *cara*, friend), for prehistoric *carant-is* (cf. Gr. φέροντες); *coin* (nom *cú*, hound), for prehistoric *con-is* = Gr. κύνες; *teoir* (three, fem.), for prehistoric *tesor-is* = Skr. *tisras*; *cetheoir* (four; fem.), for prehistoric *cetesor-is* = Skr. *catasras* (cf. Ebel in Beitr. zur Vgl. Spr. i. 431). The forms *teora*, *cetheora* (Z. 302, 303) are formed after the analogy of the nom. plur. of the fem. stems in *á*.

7. In the 2nd pers. sing. pres. ind. of the conjunct flexion. The slender vowel has penetrated in the first conjugation (=3rd Lat.

conjugation) into the root-syllable. Cf. Beitr. zur Vgl. Spr., viii. 450.

E.g., *as-bir* (dicis), for prehistoric *ber-is* (cf. Gr. ἔφερες, Ved. *abharas*, *bharas*). Stokes infers also (Beitr. zur Vgl. Spr. vi. 465) *beris* as the original form.

In like manner are formed in the *t*-preterite, *as-ru-birt* (dixisti) Z. 454; in the *s*-preterite, *ro charais* (amasti; first pers. *ro charus*) Z. 462; in the *s*-future, *-téis* (cf. Beitr. zur Vgl. Spr. vii. 44), for prehistoric *(s)téx-is;* cf. Gr. στείξεις, which, however, has the primary ending.

8. Perhaps, in the adverbs in *th*, *d* (Z. 608), which I might regard as formations with the ablative-suffix *tas*, familiar to us in Sanskrit and Latin.

E.g., *ind óindid*, *ind óendaid* (semel, singulatim), adverb from *óinde* (singularis; stem *ainatia*); *óindid* for prehistoric *ointe-t-is* (gramm. groundform *ainatia-tas*); *samlid* (ita) Z. 610, for prehistoric *samali-t-is* (Lat. *simili-ter*, with another suffix), *cosmil* = Lat. *consimilis* (Z. 768). Cf. Lat. *primi-tus* (first), Skr. *sarvatas* (from all sides, everywhere). Only I cannot explain the form *in* of the art. *ind*. (*in tropdaid*, τροπικῶς).

II. *is* stood originally in auslaut. The *i* has penetrated into the preceding syllable. Here come under consideration:—

1. The nom. sing. of the masc. and fem. stems in *i*.

Examples—Old Ir. *fáith*, for prehistoric *vát-is* = Lat. *vátes*; *cosmail* (adj.), for prehistoric *con-samal-is* = Lat. *con-similis*; *cruim* (worm; fem.), for prehistoric *crom-is* = Skr. *krmis* (masc.); *buith* (to be; fem. infin.), *de-buith* (dissensio), for prehistoric *but-is* = Gr. φύσις; *súil* (eye; fem.), for prehistoric *súl-is;* cf. Corn. *heuul* (sun), Lat. *sol*, Goth. *sauil;* *com-bairt*, *compert*, for prehistoric *-bret-is* = Goth. *ga-baúrths*.

Aspiration appears at a later period after the nom. sing. of the fem. *i*-stems, according to the analogy of the fem. stems in *á*: *súil chairech* (the eye of a sheep), *gair choille loinche* (the voice of the wood [full] of blackbirds). See Beitr. zur Vgl. Spr. i. 335. In this case, aspiration has become the grammatical sign of the fem. gender.

2. The dat. plur. of all stems.

The more ancient form *-bis*, represented by Old Ir., *-b*, with a slender vowel in the preceding syllable; e.g., *feraib*, *tuathaib*, (*tuath*, fem. people), *súlib* (*súil*, fem. eye). The stems with consonantal auslaut follow the analogy of the stems with vocalic auslaut:

filedaib (*file*, poet), like *feraib; bráigtib* (*bráge*, neck), like *fáthib; athraib* (*athir*, father), alongside of *bráithrib* (*bráthir*, brother). In the Beitr. zur Vergl. Spr. i. 173, Ebel assumed *-bis*, as we have done, as the original termination of this case; but in his edition of the Gramm. Celt. (p. 222), influenced probably by Old Gaul. forms, like ματρεβo ναμαυσικαβo (Beitr. iii. 162), he has assumed *-bos* as the older form. That assumption, however, is not correct, according to the phonetic laws of Irish. The Irish prehistoric *-bis* may have, possibly, originated from an Indo-Germ. *-bhias* (like *-bim* in the dual form *-bhiam;* cf. B. VI. 2), so that, after all, it may be identical with the Gaulish *-bo* (=Lat. *-bus*); but, just as well, the Irish *-bis* may be a continuation of the Indo-Germ. *-bhis*. The latter assumption is supported by the fact that the Irish dative is used by itself (without a preposition) only in an instrumental sense, or to express time. Stokes has adduced from the older language a case of aspiration after the dative plural (Beitr. ii. 104, note); but in the face of the numerous Old Irish examples without aspiration quoted by Zeuss (p. 216), this single instance of it is of no weight against the original consonantal auslaut of this termination. May the *nab* (Z. 216), sometimes found in the article, contain the Gaulish termination *-bo?*

III. *us* stood originally in the last syllable. Of monosyllabic words, there comes here under consideration the particle *du-*, *do-*, which corresponds to the Skr. *dus-*, Gr. δυς- (Z. 863). No doubt, it has aspiration after it, as, e.g., *do-chruth* (turpis; *cruth*, forma) proves. I presume, however, that here the analogy of the particle *su-*, *so-* (=Skr. *su-*) may have had some influence. In polysyllabic words, the *u* has sometimes penetrated into the preceding syllable. Most frequently, the *u* of the secondary suffix *tu* has penetrated into unaccented suffix-syllables, which are short either by nature or by position.

1. The nom. sing. of the masc. stems in *-u*. E.g., *mug* (servus) = Goth. *magus; follus, sollus* (apertus), for *svalnast-us* (suff. *tu*), cf. Old Baktrian *qarenaç-ca* (brightness), gen. *qarenañhô; accus, occus* (vicinus), for *ancas-tus* (cf. Goth. *nehv*, nigh, near; Zeitschr. für Vergl. Spr. xx. 415); *cosmilius* (similitudo), for *-samaliast-us; imb-rádud* (cogitatio), for *-rádiat-us* (Goth. *redan*), cf. Lat. *vestitus*, Goth. *auhjodus* (noise); *fid* (tree), New Ir. *fiodh*, for prehistoric *vid-us* = O.H.G. *witu; bith* (world), New Ir. *bioth*, for prehistoric *bit-us* (cf. Gaul. *Bitu-riges*), belongs to Old Baktrian *jiti*, life; *molad* (praise; cf. Ch.-Slav. *-moliti*, to beg, to pray), for prehistoric

molat-us, a formation like Lat. *tractatus*, which in Irish has become *tractad*. Whether *molad* is to be traced back to *molâ-t-us* or to *molaja-tu-s* I leave here undecided. Cf. Stokes in Beitr. zur Vergl. Spr. i. 355.

b. TERMINATIONS WITH *M*- AUSLAUT.

The *m*, in prehistoric time, became *n*, and has been preserved in this form up to the present day in certain phonetic combinations at the beginning of the following word, before a vowel or a medial. Original *am* is preserved in the monosyllabic *co n-* = Lat. *cum* (Z. 640); as, e.g., *co n-eoch* (with a horse), but *co claidiub* (with a sword).

IV. *am* stood originally in auslaut. Before this syllable disappeared, it remained, in certain cases, unchanged (with perhaps a leaning towards *on*), but, in other cases, it became *en*, *in*. Here come under consideration :—

1. The acc. sing. of the masc. stems in *a*. *E.g.*, *fer n-aile* for *vir-an* = *virum alium*, but *in fer* (virum). The *e* of *fer* is to be accounted for as in the nom. sing. *fer* (B. I. 1). An unmutilated Old Celtic form we have, perhaps, in μάρκαν = ἵππον (Paus. x. 19; cf. Ebel in Beitr. zur Vergl. Spr. ii. 67).

2. The nom. and acc. sing. of the neut. stems in *a*, with the termination *on* in Old Gaulish.

E.g., Old Ir. *dliged n-aill* (lex alia), for *dliget-an* (cf. Goth *dulgs*, guilt, Ch.-Slav. *dlŭgŭ*, with suffix-formation as in Skr. *rajatam*, silver, Goth. *liuhath*, light); *biath*, usually *biad* (sustenance, food), for *bivat-an*, to be compared, without taking the difference of gender into account, with Gr. βίοτος (cf. Skr. *jîvitam*; *nemed* (sacellum) = Old Gaul. *nemeton* (Z. 801; Beitr. zur Vergl. Spr. iv. 130)—from the same root, Skr. *nam*, also *nem* (heaven), which has nothing to do with Skr. *nabhas*; *at-trab* (possessio; *atreba*, possidet, habitat, Z. 868), for -*treb-an*, perhaps = Goth. *thaurp*.

Following the analogy of the neut. *a*-stems, other neut. stems also have got *n* in Old Irish in the nom. and acc. sing. as a grammatical mark, although it did not originally belong to them. E.g., *tech n-oiged* (domus hospitum) Z. 270, although *tech* = Gr. στέγος; *leth n-gotho* (dimidium vocis), placed erroneously by Zeuss (p. 223) under the stems in *a*, although *leth* = Lat. *latus* (Z. 271); *muir n-Icht* (mare Ictium), although *muir* = Lat. *mare*. The *n* after *ainm* (name, stem *anmen* = Skr. *nâman*), is, perhaps, to be accounted for in the same way; as, e.g., in *ainm n-abstil* (nomen apostoli), Z. 269.

Probably the *n* in the nom. and acc. dual of neuters after *dá* (e.g., *dá n-grúad*, duae genae, Z. 228), of which Ebel (Beitr. zur Vergl. Spr. ii. 70) did not know what to make, is also to be explained in a similar manner. The cause of such an analogical construction, may partly be found in the nom. and acc. dual having frequently come to be of the same form as the nom. and acc. singular.

-am in prehistoric time became *-en, -in*:

3. In the acc. sing. of the consonantal stems of the masc. and fem. genders.

E.g., *brágit* (nom. *bráge*, neck), for prehistoric *brágent-in* (cf. Lat. *gurgitem*); *air-mitin* (nom. *air-mitiu*, reverentia), for prehistoric *-mentin-in* (cf. Lat. *mentionem*); *athir* (nom. *athir*, father), for prehistoric *(p)ater-in* = Lat. *patrem*, Gr. πατέρα.

V. *ám* stood originally in the last syllable. Before the syllable disappeared, the vowel was shortened, so that original *ám* could be treated as *am*. Here come under consideration :—

1. The gen. plur. of all nouns. The formation of this case is everywhere the same, as in Gothic (e. g., *fiske, balge, sunive, hanane, brothre*; *gibo, tuggono*).

E.g., *na n-ech n-aile* (aliorum equorum; nom. *ech*), New Ir. *na n-each*, for prehistoric *eq-an* = Gr. ἵππων ; *inna tuath* (nom. *tuath*, people; fem.), for prehistoric *tôt-an* = Goth. *thiudo*; *na m-ban* (nom. *ben*, a woman), for prehistoric *ben-an* (cf. Goth. *qene*); *filed* (nom. *file*, poet), later *fileadh*, for prehistoric *velet-an* (cf. Lat. *milit-um*); *con* (nom. *cú*, dog, hound), for prehistoric *cun-an* = Gr. κυνῶν; *anman* (nom. *ainm*, name), for prehistoric *anman-an* = Skr. *námnám*, Goth. *namno*; *bráthar* (nom. *bráthir*, brother), for prehistoric *bráter-an* = Lat. *fratrum*, Goth. *brothre*.

In the names of relationship, however, *bráthre* is found alongside of *bráthar* (Z. 263). It is remarkable that also the gen. plur. fem. of the numerals *trí* (three), *cethir* (four), has a vowel in the auslaut (Z. 302, 303): *teora n-ungae* (trium unciarum; *teoir, tos*; see B. I. 6), also *cetheora* (nom. *cetheoir*; see B. I. 6.) Perhaps the article may help to an explanation.

The article in the gen. plur. has the forms *inna* and *na*, with *n* following (Z. 215). As the dissyllabic *inna* is evidently the older form, and *na* only a shortened form, so likewise in *inna* we seem to have an instance of the violation of the laws of auslaut.

However, the phonetic relations are perfectly regular, if we start from the pronominal termination *sâm*. The fixed vowel *a* of *inna, na*, which never interchanges with another vowel, does not stand for *âm*, but for *-âsâm*.

Perhaps, then, the gen. plur. fem. of those two numerals, *teora* and *cetheora*, is formed after the analogy of the article. The same would then also be the case with the by-forms *teora* and *cetheora* in the nom. plur. fem., to which *inna* and *na* in the nom. plur. fem. of the article correspond. In the gen. plur., *inna* is the form of the article for the three genders. If my view of *teora* and *cetheora* be correct, one may assume that, in prehistoric time, *inna* was only the fem. form of the gen. plural, and that, therefore, the termination *sâm* occurred originally in Irish, as in Greek τάων, μουσάων, only in the feminine. The fem. *inna*, however, has forced its way into the two other genders in the gen. plur., as well as in the acc. plur. of which we have already spoken (A. II. 2).

Could the genitive forms *teora, cetheora*, have also influenced the genitive-formation of the names of relationship? The stems *teor-, cethcor-*, stood in a certain connection with these as *r*-stems by the genius of the language (sprachgefühl). The difference, however, between *teora* and *bráthre* in the modification of the final vowel, may have been caused by the *r* of *teora* being preceded by a broad vowel, whilst in *bráthre* an *e* has certainly been suppressed between *th* and *r*. [I do not believe this now; *ir-bráthre* is like the Gen. Pl. of the stems in -*i* and -*u* ; *fáthe* from *fáith* ; *moge* from *mug*. Also, in Gothic *brothar* follows in the Nom. Pl. *brotherjus*, and other cases the declension of *sunus*. E. W.]

Ebel supposed (Beitr. zur Vergl. Spr. i. 170, 172) that *athre* stands for a prehistoric *atrân*, and that it has preserved the vowel on account of the preceding double consonant. Of the correctness of this conjecture and of a supposed parallel case, I shall treat in the last Excursus.

The stems in *ia, i*, and *u*, have also the auslaut *e* in the gen. plural (see Excursus i. ii.); but it cannot be supposed that these stems influence the nouns of relationship in Irish.

2. The acc. sing. of the fem. stems in *â*. The vowel of the syllable -*âm*, before it was dropped, appears not only shortened, but also attenuated. In this prehistoric -*in*, the above mentioned feminines coincide with the consonantal stems (B. IV. 3) and the *i*-stems (B. VI. 1). [May it be taken from them?]

E.g., *tuaith-n-aili* (another people), for prehistoric *tót-in* = Goth. *thiuda; láim* (nom. *lám*, hand), for prehistoric *(p)lám-in* = Lat. *palmam*, O. H. G. *folma*, Gr. παλάμην.

VI. *im* stood originally in the last syllable. The *i* invariably penetrated into the preceding syllable. The following forms come here under consideration:—

1. The acc. sing. of the masc. and fem. stems in *i*. E.g., *in súil n-aili* (the other eye; nom. *súil*), for prehistoric *súl-in*. *VCVETIN* (Beitr. iii. 163), which is found alongside of *VCVETE* evidently as an inflected form, appears to be an Old Gaulish acc. of this kind. The form *ratin*, mentioned by Stokes (Beitr. ii. 104), is unfortunately only a conjectural reading of the Inscriptional *RATN* (Beitr. iii. 166).

2. The dat. dual of the numeral *deib, díb* (Z. 301), with a nasal following; e.g., *in dib n-uarib deac* (duodecim horis) Z. 246.

This *deib, dib*, stands for prehistoric *dveb-in*, the termination *bin* of which Ebel (Beitr. zur Vergl. Spr. ii. 70) has connected with Skr. *bhyám* in *dvábhyám*. Formally the Gr. φιν agrees more exactly with this Celtic *bin, bim*. From original *bhiám* we should expect, according to rule, to find *be* in Old Irish (cf. Excursus i).

The foregoing example, *in dib n-uarib deac*, proves, at the same time, that the nouns in the dative dual had already in Old Irish assumed the corresponding plural form. Had they preserved the proper dual form, it would have been *in dib n-uarib n-deac*. In the course of time, even the *n* after *dib* was dropped; for, as early as the Lebar Brecc (14-15 centuries), we find, e.g., *cona díb apstolu* (with his twelve apostles). The noun stands here even in the form of the acc. plural; from which it clearly follows that, according to Irish usage, the *apstalaib* of the dual was not different from the *apstalaib* of the plural.

The lengthening of the *i* in *díb* appeared, probably, only at a later period, perhaps after the analogy of the nom. plur. fem. *dí*.

VII. *um* stood originally in the last syllable. The *u* does not always penetrate into the preceding syllable. Cf. what has been remarked on -*us* (B. III).

1. Acc. sing. of the masc. stems in *u*; e.g., *in m-bith m-bras* (the great world), in which *bith* stands for *bit-un*.

c. TERMINATIONS WITH N- AUSLAUT.

VIII. *an* stood originally in the last syllable. The following cases come here under consideration:—

1. *Secht* (seven), for *secht-an; secht n-aisle* (septem articuli) Z. 303, 304; cf. Lith. *septyni*, Goth. *sibun*. That the vowel of the last syllable, before it was dropped, was a broad one, is proved by the modern spelling *seacht*. In the same way, *ocht* may be referred to *ocht-an; ocht n-aisle* (octo articuli). Cf. Lith. *asztůni*.

In the following cases, *an* was weakened in prehistoric time to *en, in*:—

2. *Nói* (nine), for *nov-in; nói m-bai* (nine cows); cf. Goth. *niun*, Lat. *novem;* *deich* (ten), for *dec-in; deich m-bai* (ten cows); cf. Goth. *taihun*, Lat. *decem*. Ir. *cóic* (five) for *cóc-i*, i.e., *quenque* = Old Gaul. *pempe-*, Cymr. *pimp*, shows just as little as Lat. *quinque*, Gr. πέντε, πέμπε, an auslauting nasal, although it appears in the Skr. stem *pañcan*.

3. Nom. and acc. sing. of the neuter stems in *n* (Z. 268); e.g., *ainm n-abstil* (nomen apostoli) in the Würzburg Codex; *ainm n-Aeda* in the Codex of the Cloister of St. Paul: *ainm* for a prehistoric *anm-in, anm-en* (cf. K.-Slav. *imę*).

I do not hold this opinion as absolutely established; for here also the *n* following might have been introduced only after the analogy of the neut. *a*-stems, as we have found already in the case of the neut. stems in *-as* and *-i* (B. IV., p. 86). In the same poem, from which we have quoted *ainm n-Aeda*, is found *inmain n-ainm* . . . *Aeda* (beloved the name . . . of Aed—Goid.,[2] 178), with *n* after the neut. nom. sing. of an adjective *i*-stem; and like this *n*, the *n* after *ainm* might also be a transported one. For, the neut. stems in *n* form in Sanskrit the nom. and acc. sing. without *n* (e.g., *náma*, name). Here may also be quoted the Old British form κοῦρμι, κόρμα (Z. 115),[1] which at the same time manifestly represents the prehistoric form of Ir. *coirm, cuirm* (beer; = *corm-i*), and that without *n* in auslaut. This renders of more importance the one passage, in the Codex of St. Gall, in which *ainm díles* (nomen proprium) is written without *n* (Z. 269, 984).

4. Stokes quotes (Beitr. zur Vergl. Spr. i. 341) *a dúlim na n-dúl*

---

[1] In the oldest authority, Dioskorides (40-60 A.D.) περὶ ὕλης ἰατρικῆς ii. 110, the nominative is κοῦρμι; the genitive in the heading is περὶ κούρμιθος. *Curmen* is probably only a Latinised form.

(O Creator of the elements) as voc. sing. of *dúlem* (creator), gen *dúleman*. Perhaps this *dúlim* is to be referred to a prehistoric *dúlem-in* (cf. Skr. *rájan*, O king); but *dúlim* may also be a later spelling for nom. *dúlem*, [and this is what I now believe.]

d. TERMINATIONS WITH *T*-AUSLAUT.

IX. *at* stood originally in auslaut.

Of monosyllabic words, there is to be considered here the prep. *co*, *cu* (ad, usque ad; Z. 647), reduplicated in *cucu-m* (ad me), *cucu-t* (ad te). This preposition terminated originally in a consonant, as shown by its not being followed by aspiration, and by its combining with the article to form *cossin n-*. This consonant was *t*, as is proved by *cucthu* (ad cos), which occurs alongside of *cucu*. Therefore Ir. *co* = Gr. κάτ. The *a* of κατά must have been dropped in Irish very early, even before the laws of auslaut began to operate.

Of polysyllabic forms there come under consideration here:—

1. The 3rd sing. pres. ind. of the conjunct flexion of the 2nd conjugation; e.g., *no chara* (amat), for prehistoric *cara-at*, *caraj-at*: cf. Hom. ὁράᾳ (with primary personal termination). See Excursus ii. 9.

2. The 3rd sing. conj. *fel* (sit), e.g., in the impersonal *con-dum-fel* (ut essem) Z. 491. This form stands for prehistoric *vel-at*, in contrast to the ind. *fil*, *feil*, for prehistoric *velt-i* (or *vel-it*). The root is Europ. *vel*, Skr. *var* (to choose, to will). To see the correctness of this etymology, one must know that *fil*, conj. *fel*, governs the accusative, e.g., *ni fil mnái*[2] *nachit charad* (there is not a woman who did not love thee). The Germ. "nicht gibt es eine frau" (there is not a woman, lit. it gives not a woman) is a counterpart to this Irish idiom: "There chooses not," or "there wills not a woman." The form *fel*, however, for prehistoric *vel-at*, is a reliable example of conjunctive-formation with a short vowel in the stem, like Ved. *asat*, Hom. ἴομεν, εἴδομεν. As these stand alongside of the indicative *asti*, ἴμεν, ἴδμεν, so *fel* stands alongside of the indicative *fil*, i.e., *velti*, Lat. *volt*. Cf. Curtius' Verb. ii. 55; Delbrück's Altind. Verb. 57.

In the following cases the original *-at* was weakened to *-et*, *-it*, the slender vowel of which penetrated into the preceding syllable:—

---

[1] *Mnai* is the acc. sing. of *ben* (woman). See A. II. 3.

1. The 3rd sing. pres. ind. of the conjunct flexion of the 1st conjugation (= Lat. 3rd conjugation). This form has a secondary personal termination, as has been already pointed out in the Beitr. viii. 450.

Old Ir. *no beir* (fert), for prehistoric *ber-it*, cf. Skr. *abharat;* *not ail* (alit te), for prehistoric *al-it;* *ni ib* (he drinks not), for prehistoric *(p)ib-it*, = Lat. *bibit.* Cf. B. I. 7. The same primitive forms have been inferred also by Stokes (Beitr. zur Vergl. Spr. vi. 465).

In the same way is formed the 3rd sing. of the *t*-preterite; e.g., *birt* (she brought forth), for prehistoric *bert-it;* cf. Gr. ἔκοπτε (Beitr. zur Vergl. Spr. viii. 451). But most verbs have in this tense *a*, also *e*, in the root-syllable, without *i* penetrating into it (Z. 455). Either the *-at* had not been here so decidedly weakened to *-it*, or the double consonants (*rt, lt, cht*) prevented the penetrating of *i*.

The 3rd sing. of the conjunct-flexion of the *s*-future has suffered a specially remarkable mutilation. This tense is formed in Irish in a way similar to that in which it is formed in Greek, only that in Irish it is limited to the roots with a guttural, a dental, or *s* in auslaut. A guttural or a dental with *s* becomes in Irish *ss*, or *s*. The 2nd sing. fut. of the conjunct-flexion of *tiagaim* (στείχω) according to rule, is *téis*, for prehistoric *téss-is*, of which the corresponding form in Greek would be *στείξες. Likewise, in the 3rd sing. we should expect *téis* for prehistoric *téss-it;* but, generally, this has been mutilated to *téi, té* (Z. 467). Consequently, even the *ss, s*, has also been dropped, which has otherwise happened only in the case of a primitive final *ss*, e.g., *rí* = Lat. *rex*, *a* from *ass* = ἐξ, Lat. *ex*.

2. The nom. and acc. sing. *traig* (foot) Z. 255, for prehistoric *trag-it*. Ebel, in Beitr. i. 170, took this word as a neuter. *Traig* would, therefore, correspond in its formation to Skr. *bharat*, the neuter of the participle. Cf. Beitr. ii. 68. [A very doubtful case.]

e. TERMINATIONS WITH VOCALIC AUSLAUT.

The word-forms coming here under consideration, have the peculiarity that, in certain positions, they aspirate the anlaut of the following word.

X. *a* stood originally in the last syllable.

1. The 1st pers. sing. of the reduplicated perfect. See Ztschr. für Vergl. Spr. xxiii. 229. E.g., *con-darc* (conspexi), for pre-

historic *dedarc-a* = Gr. δέδορκα, Skr. *dadarça*; *seslach* for prehistoric *seslac-a* (cf. Goth. *sloh*). [I believe that this *a* was originally long.]

1a. *can* (unde) Z. 356, for prehistoric *can-a*? This word, according to its form, is to be compared with Goth *hvan*, but according to its signification, with O. H. G. *hwanana*. Its ablative character is based upon the pronominal-stem *na*.

Perhaps certain prepositions ought to be mentioned here; e.g., *ar* (before, for; Germ. *vor, für*) Z. 622, for prehistoric *(p)ar-a*, Gr. παρά. The Old Gaul. *are-* in *Are-moricae civitates* (Glück's Kelt. Namen, p. 31) seems to indicate a short vowel in auslaut. Since, however, Irish has dropped even long *â* in auslaut, and since, in Gothic, *faura* occurs alongside of *faur*, *ar* might have also originated from *(p)ar-â*.

In all the following cases, *a* was weakened to *e, i*:—

2. In the voc. sing. of the masc. stems in *a*. A similar weakening has taken place in the corresponding Greek and Latin forms, -ε, -e.

E.g., *a maicc, micc* (O son), for prehistoric *maq-i* nom.) *macc*, for prehistoric *maq-as*), cf. Gr. φίλ-ε, Lat. *amic-e*; *a dé* (O God), for prehistoric *dév-e* (nom. *día*, for prehistoric *dév-as*) = Skr. *dev-a*; *a fir* (O man) = Lat. *O vir* = Skr. *vira*.

3. In the nom. and acc. dual of all consonantal stems. Similarly, -ε occurs in the corresponding Greek forms.

E.g., *di siair* (duas sorores), for prehistoric *sesar-e* (nom. sing. *siur*, for prehistoric *sesur*) Z. 263, cf. Gr. θυγατέρ-ε; *di sligid* (duas vias), for prehistoric *sliget-e* (nom. sing. *slige*) Z. 259; *di tiprait* (duo fontes), -*ait* for prehistoric -*ant-e* (nom. sing. *tipra*) Z. 259, cf. Gr. γέροντ-ε.

We are justified in assuming here a special dual-formation distinct from the plural, because the accusative has in the plural a form distinct from the nominative: nom. sing. *slige*, nom. dual *sligid*, nom. plur. *sligid*; acc. sing. *sligid* with *n* following, acc. plur. *sligeda*, acc. dual *sligid*.

4. In the 2nd sing. imperative of the 1st conjugation. Similarly, the Lat. has -*e* in the 3rd conjugation, and the Greek -ε in the corresponding forms.

E.g., *beir*, for a prehistoric *ber-i*, Gr. φέρ-ε (Z. 443).

5. In the 2nd plur. imperative. Original -*ta* represented by Old Ir. -*d*, with slender vowel penetrating into the preceding syllable; similarly in Greek -τε, and in Lat. -*te*.

E.g., *berid*, for prehistoric *beret-i* = Gr. φέρετε, cf. Lat. *ferte;* *ibid* (drink ye), for prehistoric *pibet-i* = Lat. *bibite.*

6. In the 2nd plur. of the conjunct-flexion of nearly all tenses. Here, likewise, the Greek has -τε, whereas the Skr. has -*tha* and -*ta*.

E.g., pres. *do-berid* (Lat. *date*), for prehistoric *beret-i* = Gr. φέρετ-ε; fut. *for-tésid* (succurretis), for prehistoric *tésset-i* = Gr. στείξετε, etc.

7. In the 3rd sing. of the reduplicated perfect. The stem -*a* of Skr. forms like *dadarça* was here, before it was dropped, weakened to *e* or *i*, in beautiful accordance with the Gr. ε in λέλοιπε. Cf. Ztschr. xxii. 229.

E.g., *con-daire* (conspexit), for prehistoric *dedarc-i* = Gr. δέδορκε, Skr. *dadarça;* *cechuin* (cecinit), for prehistoric *cecani*. Curtius holds (Verb. der Griech. Spr. ii. 173), but incorrectly, that this form ended originally in *t*—(*ce-cani-t*). The aspiration proved (Z. 181) so often after *bo* (fuit; shortened for *bói*, for prehistoric *bebovi*, root *bhû*), in the ancient language, and still used in the modern language (O'Donovan's Ir. gramm. 386), shows that the 3rd sing. perf. in Irish, as in Sanskrit and Greek, was formed without *t*.

8. *Cóic* (five), for prehistoric *cóc-i*, that is, *cuenq·e* = Cymr. *pimp*, Lat. *quinque*, Gr. πέντε, πέμπε.

XI. *â* stood originally in the last syllable. It is preserved in the monosyllabic vocative-particle *a* (sometimes *á*) = Gr. ὦ, Lat. *ó*, with aspiration after it (e.g., *a chossa*, O foot!) Z. 246, which is still an established law in New Irish. The Indo-Germ. *â* was split up on Irish territory into *â* and *ô*. Before these vowels were dropped in the auslaut of polysyllabic words, they were shortened into *a* and *u*. The following forms come here under consideration :—

1. The nom. sing. of the fem. stems in *â*.

E.g., *tuath* (people), for prehistoric *tót-a* = Goth. *thiuda; froech* (heath, heather), for prehistoric *vroik-a* = Gr. ἐρείκη; *lám* (hand), for prehistoric *(p)lâma* = Gr. παλάμη, Lat. *palma; rún* (secret, mystery), for prehistoric *rún-a* = Goth. *runa; fedb* (widow), for prehistoric *vidv-a* = Lat. *vidu-a; ingen* (daughter), New Irish *inghean* with *n* not softened, because it was followed in prehistoric time by a broad vowel. See Ebel in Beitr. zur Vergl. Spr. i. 179

2. The nom. and acc. dual of the masc. and neut. stems in *a*,

The original long *á* of this form has been preserved in the monosyllabic *dá* = Ved. *dvá*, Gr. δύω, Lat. *duo*.

Old Ir. *dá ech* (two horses), for prehistoric *ech-a* = Ved. *açvá*, Gr. ἵππω. The original vocalic auslaut of *dá* is shown by the aspiration following it; e.g., *eter dá son* (inter duos sonos) Z. 228. In regard to the *n* in the neuter *dá n-grúad* (duae genae), see under B. IV. 2.

3. The nom. and acc. plur. of the neut. stems in *a*, and of the neut. consonantal stems.

The neut. stems in *a* certainly follow in these cases, even in Old Irish, the analogy of the fem. stems in *á* (A. ii. 2); but there have also been preserved alongside of these some genuine neut. forms: *grán*, for prehistoric *grán-a* = Lat. *grána*; *nert* (virtutes), for prehistoric *nert-a* (as in Patrick's Hymn in the Liber Hymnorum; but in a more recent MS., we have in the same passage the later form *neurta*) Z. 228; *trí chét* (Z. 307, 1087) = Ved. *trí çatá, trí thráth* (three times), and others.

Of consonantal stems: *anman, anmann* (nom. sing. *ainm*, name), for prehistoric *anman-a*, cf. Lat. *nomina*; *bémen, bémenn* (verbera; nom. sing. *béim*, connected with *benim*, ferio), for prehistoric *bémen-a; drommann* (terga; nom.*druimm*), for prehistoric *drommann-a* (assimilated from *drosmann-*, like ἔμμεναι from ἐσμεναι, cf. Lat. *dorsum* for *droso-*) Z. 269. Instead of these, we find in later MSS. forms ending in *a* following the analogy of the neuter stems in *a*: *anmana, béimeanna* (cf. O'Donovan's Ir. Gramm. p. 98). The doubling of the *n* in the auslaut of the suffixes *an* and *man* has not yet been explained.

4. The nom. sing. of the masc. stems formed by the suffix *man* (Z. 264a). This suffix serves in Irish for the secondary word-formation (Z. 775), but has had *má* in the nominative, like the primary *man* of Sanskrit and Latin: *brithem* (judex; from *breth*, judicium), for prehistoric *brithem-a* (cf. Skr. *brahmá*, gen. Ir. *bretheman*, Skr. *brahman-as*; *flaithem* (dominus; from *flaith*, dominion), for prehistoric *vlatim-a*; *Airem*, nom. propr., for prehistoric *Arem-a*, (*Ariam-á*), gen. *Aireman, Eremon* (cf. Skr. *Aryamá*, stem *Aryaman*). The lost broad vowel is clearly shown by the modern spelling *breitheamh, flaitheamh*. To this class belongs also *talam* (earth), for prehistoric *talm-a*, gen. *talman*, reminding us, as to its root syllable, of Lat. *tellus*, but, as to its stem-formation, of Skr. *stariman, starîman*, (couch; cf. Commentary on the Unâdis.), locative *starîmaṇi*, Ved. infinitive to the root *star*.

On the nom. sing. of the remaining stems in *n*, mentioned in Z. 264a, see Excursus iii. 2.

5. The instrumental sing. of the fem. stems in *â*, preserved in isolated forms. See thereon under 9.

6. The conjunct-form of the 1st pers. sing. pres. conjunctive.

E.g., *co n-aer-bar* (donec dicam), *coni eper* (ut non dicam) Z. 440; *-bar* for prehistoric *ber-a*, orig. *bharâ*. This person is rarely met with in the 1st conjugation, as the old conjunctive was already in Old Irish nearly extinct. The question now is whether the original termination of this form was *â* or *âm*. In the latter case, we should be reminded of Lat. *feram*. But, on the other hand, Vedic forms, like *nir ayâ* (I will go out), *stavâ* (I will praise),[1] and Gr. φέρω, belong to a very ancient type; and for this latter I decide, since a nasal has not been proved after any of the Irish examples, whilst aspiration has been proved after, at least, one of them: *ni ta chumme-se friu-som* (non fuerim ego par illorum; *tau, tao* indicative, *tâ* conjunctive) Z. 490. In Irish, therefore, in prehistoric time, the common ground-form for the 1st pers. sing. indicative and conjunctive assumed different forms, so that the latter became *berâ* and the first *berú* (B. XI. 8), whilst Greek has φέρω in both cases.

In some verbs, whose present-stem is formed with *ia*, we find also in the conjunctive indications of a tendency towards the obscuring of the vowel: *do-gnéo* (faciam) beside *do-gníu* (facio), *beo* (sim) beside *bíu* (sum), Z. 492. The modified form *eo* in the conjunctive beside *iu* in the indicative, shows that here also the *a* was preserved pure in the conjunctive longer than in the indicative. How it is that *gnéo, beo*, by the preservation of the last vowel, do not conflict with the laws of auslaut, will be explained in Excursus i., 2.

7. The conjunct-form of the 1st sing. of the reduplicated future, which, in nearly all instances, has a conjunctive-flexion. This form may be more correctly regarded as the conjunctive of a reduplicated perfect or aorist, the indicative of which is not always preserved in Irish.

Of these forms more numerous examples can be adduced, since they belong to a favourite formation which has been preserved down to the modern language: *as-bér* (dicam), originating out of *bebr-â*; *nad cél* (quod non celabo), originating out of *cecl-â* (Z.

---

[1] See Delbrück's Altind. Verb. 26.

452; Beitr. zur Vergl. Spr., vii. 16). The Vedic *prá ná vocá* (I will announce; R.V. vi. 59, 1; Delbrück's Altind. Verb. 26) is precisely the same formation; for *vocá* is contracted from *va-uc-á*, Indo-Germ. *va-vak-á*, from which also Gr. εἶπω (for ϜεϜεπω) has originated. On this *é* in Irish, originating through compensation-lengthening, see Ztschr. für Vergl. Spr. xxiii. 246.

Original *á* was modified to *ó*, and then shortened to *u*, before it was dropped.

8. In the 1st sing. pres. ind. act. of the conjunct-flexion, which may be best observed in the 1st conjugation. The *u* has almost always entered into the preceding syllable.

E.g., *as-biur* (dico), for prehistoric *ber-u* = Lat. *fero*, Gr. φέρω; *for-chun* (praecipio), for prehistoric *can-u* = Lat. *cano*; *con-riug* (ligo), for prehistoric *rig-u* (or *reg-u*) = Lith. *riszù*; *ar-riuth* (adorior), for prehistoric *rit-u* = Lith. *ritù*.

With these, moreover, agree the 1st pers. sing. of the *t*-preterite *as-ru-burt* (dixi; cf. Gr. κόπτω), 3rd pers. *birt*, *bert* (Z. 454; Beitr. zur Vergl. Spr. viii. 450); the 1st pers. of the conjunct-flexion of the *s*-preterite *ro-charus* (amavi) Z. 461; the 1st person of the conjunct-flexion of the *b*-future *for-chanub* (docebo; Beitr. zur Vergl. Spr., vii. 33; Z. 458), although this tense has a conjunctive character in the other forms. Also, the 1st pers. sing. of the conjunctive-flexion in the *s*-future, comes under this head. The reflex of the *u* is seen in *nocho n-crus* (I shall not rise; 2nd pers. *cris*), for prehistoric *eress-u* = ὀρέξω; *at-chous* (exponam), for prehistoric *cóss-u* (i.e., *cód-syá*) Beitr. zur Vergl. Spr., vii. 45. The *u* does not enter into syllables with long *í*, *ó*, *ía*, whence *ria tías* (before I shall go), for prehistoric *téss-u* = Gr. στείξω.

Of the reduplicated future, there come under this head only *as-ririu* (impendam) Z. 452, and the 3rd. pers. *as-riri* (appendat; Ml. 30 c) of the perf. *as-rir* (dedit), pres. *as-renat* (reddunt), which I have connected with Gr. πρίαμαι and πέρνημι (Beitr. zur Vergl. Spr. viii. 11; Ztschr. für Vergl. Spr. xxiii. 214). But, as in the perfect, the simple *rói-r* (i.e., the verbal particle *ro*, with the reflex of the lost reduplication-syllable *ri*, *r* being the last relic of the verbal form)[1] belongs to the compound *as-rir*, so the simple forms *ni ria* (ne emat), *ni riat* (ne dent, vendant),[2] which have likewise lost the reduplication syllable, belong in the future to

---
[1] See Ztschr. xxiii. 225.
[2] See Beitr. zur Vergl. Spr. vii. 7; Z. 447.

the compounds *as-ririu, as-riri*. These forms show the conjunctive-flexion; *riu* (i.e., prehistoric *ridt*) stands in the same relation to *riri* (i.e., prehistoric *riri-it*), in which in the present the conjunctive *móidea* (i.e., *módiát*) stands to *móidi* (gloriatur; i.e. *módi-it*). See A. II. 4, B. IX., and Excursus i. 1. The reduplicated future has everywhere else the conjunctive-flexion; and it is remarkable that this future *ririu, riri*, standing beside a perfect, shows an indicative-flexion. We may here refer to the relation of the Vedic forms of the ind. perf. *jaghána*, and of the conjunctive *jaghanat* (Delbrück's Altind. Verb. 57), and assume that in Irish a further trace has been preserved of the conjunctive with a short vowel in the stem (see B. IX. 2).[1] By means of Skr. forms, the original relation of the connected indicative and conjunctive forms, may be represented in the following manner—

IND. PERF.	CONJ.
jaghana.	(*jaghaná*) cf. *vocá.*
jaghantha.	(*jaghanas.*)
jaghána.	*jaghanat.*

All Indo-Germanic languages realise, in the course of time, a tendency to distinguish, as a general rule, the conjunctive by the length of the stem vowel. In this way, the more distinctly conjunctive *riu* has been formed alongside of *riri*.

According to Stokes, *ibiu* is another example of a future formed like *ririu: ní praindigiub-sa ocus ní ibiu* (I will not eat and I will not drink) Beitr. zur Vergl. Spr. vii. 16. The passive form *ebar*, which occurs in the Leb. Brecc. p. 9b (Facs.), proves that Ir. *ibimm* (I drink) is a pres. tense formation, like Skr. *pibámi*, Lat. *bibo*. Now, one might suppose from the gloss, *deugaigfit i. ibait*, on *potabunt* in the Lat. Text of the Milan Codex, fol. 30ᶜ (Goid.[2] p. 35) that the pres. ind. of *ibimm* had been used as a future; but, on the one hand, the glosses are not always accurate as to tense, and, on the other hand, *ibiu* would be a present-form, which we would have to put into the 3rd conjugation. The comparative philologist is here readily reminded of Gr. πίομαι, the πι-ο

---

[1] If we trace *riri* to *riri-it*, but, on the other hand, *fel* to *vel-at*, we must admit that certainly a want of agreement appears, in these prehistoric forms, in the treatment of the conjunctive vowel: *ririu, riri*, might be connected, according to the phonetic relations, with the pres. of the 3rd conjugation (*rádiu, rádi*), whilst *vel-at* could only have been connected with the pres. of the 1st conjugation (*beir* for *ber-it*); but, then, *vel-it* would have become *feil, fil*, as in the indicative.

of which beside the $\pi\iota$ contained in πi-$\theta\iota$, could very well be taken as an original conjunctive-formation. Ir. *ibiu*, originating, according to the Celtic phonetic laws, from *pibiu*, would have differed in the stem-formation from $\pi i o \mu a \iota$ only by the reduplication, which, by the bye, we find also in Greek in the instance of the root-form $\pi\iota$ in $\pi\iota\pi i\sigma\kappa\omega$.

The absolute form *tíasu* (with *u* in the auslaut), which has been compared by Stokes (Beitr. zur Vergl. Spr., vii., 45) with Gr. $\sigma\tau\epsilon i\xi\omega$, I shall endeavour to explain in Excursus iii.

9. In the instrumental sing. of the masc. and neut. stems in *a*.

In the so-called dative (characterized by *u*) of this stem, two different cases, in my opinion, have come to coincide in form, and those certainly not, as Ebel is inclined to assume, the dative and ablative, but the old dative and the old instrumental. Why it cannot be the ablative-form is stated under (A. II. 6). As regards the laws of sound, no objection can be urged against the opinion that, e.g., *fiur* (nom. *fer*., masc. man), *niurt* (*nert*, neut., strength), may have originated, on the one hand, from *vir-di*, *nart-di*, an Indo-Germ. dative-formation, but also, on the other hand, from *vir-â*, *nart-â*, an Indo-Germ. instrumental-formation. The latter hypothesis commends itself especially on this account, that it enables us to understand why the Irish dative without a preposition, is used only with an instrumental signification (e.g., *nach cruth ailiu* [in any other way] Z. 608), and requires, when used with a purely dative function, the preposition *do* before it.

Here I might especially point out as an old instrumental the *u*-case when it expresses the compared object after the comparative; e.g., *ba mó amru arailiu*, (greater than another miracle was; nom. sing. *amre*, *araile*, from stems in *ia*). For other examples see Z. 917.

In the same way, I explain the adverbs formed from adjectives, as *in biucc* (paulum; for prehistoric *bicc-u*), which are treated in Z. 608. In regard to its formation and vowel modification, this Irish instrumental is to be compared with the O. H. G. instrumental in *u*; e.g., *mit muatu* (cf. Erdmann's Syntax der Sprache Otfrids, ii. 248).

As an instrumental of a fem. stem in *â*, I regard *ind ór sa* (hac hora), quoted as an ablative in Z. 244. The instrumental agrees here in form with the nominative. Similarly, e.g., the Vedic *barhaṇâ* ("mit macht," with might) is not different in form from the nominative *barhaṇâ*. So, likewise, we may take the form *ancreitmech* in the sentence *creitmech sin as messa ancreitmech* (fidelis haec quae est deterior quam infidelis) Z. 917, for an instrumental; also, *ind adaig thússech* (in the first night) Fled Bricr. 83; *in tan* (when; *tan* fem., time), alongside of the dative in *iar tain*. In the course of time, this old instrumental was entirely supplanted by the dative-form: alongside of *lia turem* (Fled Bricr. 28), appears *mo turim* (greater than can be told) Hy. 5, 18.

On the other hand, we have the real ablative of *ór* in the conjunction *óre*, *úare* (because) Z. 708. In the declension-paradigm, this form must be given in the first place, as a genitive; but similarly in Sanskrit the genitive and ablative sing. of the feminines in *â* coincide. Also the accusative (or dative) *úair* is used as a conjunction in the sense of " because."

XII. *i* stood originally in the last syllable. It penetrated into the preceding syllable, and was dropped in the auslaut. To this class belong the following cases:—

1. The nom. and acc. sing. of the neut. stems in *i*. E.g., *muir*, for prehistoric *mori*, = Lat. *mare*; *guin* (wound), for prehistoric *gon-i*; *búaid* (victory), for prehistoric *bód-i*. Cf. Ebel in Beitr. zur Vergl. Spr., vi. 223.

After the analogy of the neut. stems in *a*, an *n* has crept in after these forms, as if to mark the neuter: *muir n-icht* (mare Ictium) Z. 235; see B. iv. 2.

2. The 2nd sing. of the absolute-flexion of the present, which may be best observed in the 1st conjugation (= Lat. 3rd). The single *s* of the termination must have fallen away, according to the Irish laws of sound. E.g., *beri* (thou bearest), for prehistoric *beres-i*, = Gr. φέρεις.

Similarly, the same person in the *s*-future: *tési* (thou wilt or shalt go), for prehistoric *tésses-i* = Gr. στείξεις (Beitr. zur Vergl. Spr. vii. 46).

3. The 3rd sing. of the absolute-flexion of the present. The *t* of the termination -*ti* is represented by *th*, generally *d*. E.g., *berid* (he bears), for prehistoric *beret-i*, = Gr. φέρει, Skr. *bharat-i*; *ibid*, for prehistoric (*p*)*ibet-i*, = Skr. *pibati*. Likewise, whenever -*id* appears in any 3rd pers. sing., e.g., in the *b*-future *predchibid*.

Under this head comes likewise *is*, for prehistoric *est-i*, = Gr. ἐστί, Skr. *asti*; also *jail, feil, fil* (there is, "es gibt"), for prehistoric *vel-ti*, Lat. *volt*. Whilst in *is* (*iss*) the *t* of the personal-termination -*ti* has been assimilated to the preceding *s*, in *fil* the *t*, having come into the auslaut, was dropped. If *feil, fil*, occurred only conjunctly (*ní fil, a fil, con fil*), it might be referred to *vel-it*; but then *fil* appears in the ancient language also absolutely. For the absolute *fil*, however, we must, according to the analogy of *berid*, assume a ground-form with a primary personal-termination, and are thus led back to a prehistoric *velti*, a form which is also demanded by the thereto belonging conjunctive *fel*, for prehistoric *vel-at*. See B. IX. 2.

4. The 3rd pers. plur. of the absolute-flexion of the present.

Original *anti* represented, according to the Irish phonetic laws, by *-it*. E.g. *berit* (they bear), for prehistoric *berant-i*, = Dor. φέροντι; *tíagait* (they go), for prehistoric *tégant-i*, = Gr. στείχουσι.

5. The dat. sing. of the consonantal stems. By this assumption we take, as Ebel does (Beitr. zur Vergl. Spr. i. 169), this case to be, according to its form, an original locative, like the dat. of the Greek 3rd declension. But since also *ai*, the termination of the Indo-Germ. dative, must have led to the Old Ir. forms before us, it is possible that here, cases, which differ both in function and in form, may have been blended into one case. E.g., Old Ir. *dond athir* (patri), for prehistoric (*p*)*ater-i*, = Gr. πατέρι; *do fili* (poetae), for prehistoric *velet-i*; *do menmain*, for prehistoric *menman-i*, = Skr. *manman-i*.

The neuter stems in *man* (*ainm*, name ; *cuirm*, beer, Z. 268) have, however, preserved in the dative an old instrumental-form, as was already seen by Siegfried (Beitr. zur Vergl. Spr. i. 452): *anmaimm* for prehistoric *anmamm-i*, originating out of *anman-mi*, with suffix *mi* like Lith. *akmen-i-mi*.

6. Some prepositions, viz. :—

Imb, imm, for prehistoric *amb-i*, = Gr. ἀμφί, Z. 654.

The original final vowel is occasionally preserved in composition, e.g., in *imme-churetar* (negotiantur) Z. 876. *Imm, im,* because originally ending in a vowel, aspirates the following word : *im charpat* (circa carpentum) Z. 654.

Aith, for prehistoric *at-i*, corresponding etymologically to Skr. *ati*, Gr. ἔτι, but used like Lat. *re-*, *iterum* (Z. 869). This particle is found only in composition. For *aith-* we find also *aid-*, *id*, and, before a syllable with a broad vowel, occasionally even *ad-*.

E.g., *aid-chrochad* (crucifixio iterata) ; *aith-rech* (paenitens), cf. Goth. *id-reiga* (repentance), *id-reit* (disgrace). Whether *aithirge*,

ithirge (repentance) stand for *aithi-rige* or *aith-rige*, cannot be decided.

The Gaulish forms of these two particles are *ambi-*, *ate-*, e.g., *Ambi-rénus*, *Ate-gnâta* (Glück's Kelt. Nam., pp. 18, 97). The weakening of the final *i* to *e* occurs also in Irish in *imme-churetar*, and also in *ci*, *ce*, related to Lat. *quis*, *quid*.

The Irish preposition *ind-* (Z. 877), related both etymologically and as to usage to Goth., *and*, *anda-* —e.g., in *ind-rid* (incursus ; *ar-riuth*, for *ret-u*, adorior) to be compared with Goth. *and-rinnan*, —might have originated out of *and-i*, but also out of *and-a*, since *a* before *nd*, *nn*, has been attenuated even without the influence of an *i* in the following syllable (Z. 5). The Gaulish form is *ande-* (Glück, p. 24, &c.), e.g., *Ande-ritum* ; *ritum* = Cymr. *rit* (vadum),[1] Old High German *furt*, Old Baktrian *peretu* (bridge).

7. *onn urid* (ab anno priore) Z. 611; *urid* for prehistoric (*p*)*arut-i* = Dor. πέρυτι, Ion. πέρυσι.

8. *Cethir* (τέσσαρα, neutr. Z. 303) aspirates the anlaut of the following word, and may, therefore, stand for prehistoric *cetar-i* = *catvâri*; *cethir chét* = Ved. *catvâri çatâ*.

XIII. *i* stood originally in the last syllable. It has been preserved in the monosyllabic forms *sí* (ea) Z. 326 = Goth. *si*, and *trí* (tria) Z. 302, 1087, since *trí chét* = Ved. *trí çatâ*. In polysyllabic forms *i* has been lost, having first been shortened and having penetrated into the preceding syllable. Here come under consideration :—

1. The nom. and acc. dual of the stems in *i*.

E.g., *di súil* (duo oculi), for prehistoric *sûl-i* (cf. Ved. *kavi*, K.-Slav. *nošti*, Lith. *nakti*. See Leskien's Die Decl. im Slaw.- —Lith. und Germ. p. 107 ; Ebel in Beitr. ii. 73).

2. The dat. sing. of the stems in *i*.

E.g., *fáith* (nom. *fáith*, poet), for prehistoric *vât-i; súil* (nom. *súil*, eye, fem.), for prehistoric *sûl-i; muir* (nom. *muir*, sea, neut.), for prehistoric *mor-i*.

Certainly, an *i* stood in the last syllable before it was lost; but for an explanation of this *i*, we have a choice of several possibilities. It might have been shortened from an original *î*, as in the nom. and acc. dual. In that case, this so-called dative would be, as to its form, an instrumental, like the Vedic instru-

---

[1] If this Gaulish *ritum*, therefore, be etymologically related to O.H.G. *furt*, we would have here a farther proof that the Indo-Germ. *p* was lost also in Gaulish (cf. Gaul. are-, p. 229).

mental of the *i-* stems in *î*; e.g., *matî* from *matis* (see Grassmann's Wörterbuch). This supposition is supported by the fact that, so far as I know, the Irish dative without a preposition occurs only with the function of an instrumental. It is, however, possible that this *i* may have originated from a primitive *i-i*; in which case, this Irish dative would be an original locative, like the Ionic πόλῑ. But the locative form πόλει for πολεjι also would have led in Irish to a similar contraction, since from *tegesi*, the locative of an *as-* stem, the Irish *tig* has been formed (see Excursus ii. 6). Of an original *i-ai*, or even *-aj-ai*, which would be a genuine dative-formation, more would probably have survived than the mere penetrating of *i* into the preceding syllable. Finally, we have to mention that the dat. sing. of the consonantal stems and of the fem. *a-*stems, is, likewise, characterised by internal *i*, and that the force of analogy may have contributed its part to give, as far as possible, one form to this case.

XIV. *u* stood originally in the last syllable. In the monosyllabic particle *su*, *so* = Skr. *su* (Z. 863), it is either preserved as *u* or weakened into *o*. In polysyllabic words, the *u* more frequently, but not always, penetrated into the preceding syllable. Cf. the remarks on *-us* and *-um* under B. III. and VII.

Here come under consideration :—

1. The nom. and acc. sing. of the neut. stems in *-u*.

E.g., *suth* (fetus), for prehistoric *sut-u* (related to Skr. *sútus*, fem. pregnancy), cf. Lat. *corn-u*; *dorus* (door), for original *dvarust-u*. Cf. Ebel in Beitr. zur Vergl. Spr. vi. 223.

2. The 3rd pers. sing. and plur. of the imperative.

E.g., *berad* for prehistoric *berat-u* = Skr. *bharatu*; *berat* (they shall bear), for prehistoric *berant-u* = Skr. *bharant-u*. In any case, this *u* would have been lost without a trace; but, especially, the 3rd pers. sing. is hardly to be explained otherwise, since its *d* or *th* (for original *t*) could not have been the original auslaut of this form, but must necessarily have had a vowel after it. That the dropped *u* does not always influence the *a* of the preceding syllable, is proved by the short word *cath* (fight, combat), for prehistoric *cat-us* (cf. Old Gaul. *Catu-rix* in Glück's Kelt. Namen, p. 47), O. H. G. *hadu-*, A. S. *headho-*.

XV. *û* stood originally in the last syllable. Before it disappeared it was shortened to *u*. Here come under consideration :—

1. The nom. and acc. dual of the stems in *u*.

Of this case very few examples are quoted by Zeuss (pp. 240 241); but *dá atarcud* (duo relationes; nom. sing. *atárcud*, relatio Z. 882, with -*ud* for prehistoric -*atu*) is certainly, as to its formation, to be compared with Skr. *úrú* (the two thighs). Cf. Ebel in Beitr. ii. 73, 74.

2. The dat. sing. of the stems in *u*. This case I mention here, but only with hesitation. From *isin biuth* (in mundo; nom. *bith*), it is evident that, in prehistoric time, this case terminated in *u* (*biuth* for prehistoric *bit-u*). In the other examples mentioned by Zeuss (239), it does not differ in form from the nominative. Also, the dat. sing. of the masc. and neut. *a*- stems is distinguished by *u*, e.g., *don fiur* (viro). See B. XI. 9, and B. XVII. There is, moreover, a coinciding of the *a*- and *u*-stems in the acc. plural, as, e.g., in *firu* = Goth. *vairans* and *mugu* = Goth. *maguns* (A. I. 1). But as the *u*- stems nowhere show any tendency to pass over into the inflection of the *a*-stems, I might, likewise, regard the agreement in the dat. sing. as accidental. If we, therefore, try to explain organically the *u* of *biuth*, I think we must leave out of view *u-i* or *av-i* (with slender vocalic termination); for this would be the only case known to me, in which an *i* in the termination has been lost, without a trace remaining. It appears, therefore, that the only other alternative is to try the instrumental *u-â*, *vâ-* (Ved. *madhvâ* from *madhu*). The phonetic combination *uâ* (*uó*?) is represented in the monosyllabic *cú* (hound) = Skr. *çvá* (see Excursus iii. 2) by long *ú*. Such a *ú* might, in the auslaut of a polysyllabic word, have easily disappeared, without leaving a trace except its reflex in the preceding syllable. Supported by the Old Bactrian, we may even assume a very ancient instrumental formation of the *u*- stems in *ú* (like the *i*- stems in *î* and the *a*- stems in *â*): Old Baktr. *khratú*, instrumental of *khratu* (wisdom); *danhu*, instrumental to *danhu-s* (district, province). See Justi's Handb. der Zendspr. p. 390.

If, finally, we would assume for *biuth* a ground form *bitvá*, we would then have another example in support of the loss of *vá* in the auslaut: Ir. *árd* (high) goes back in the fem. to a ground-form *ardhvá* = Lat. *ardua* (cf. Old Baktr. *eredhwa*, Skr. *ûrdhva*, Gr. ὀρθός).[1] By this hypothesis, the *u* preserved in *biuth* would

---

[1] In other words, however, *b* (*bh*) has originated from -*vas*, ·*vá*, after a single consonant: Ir. *tarb* = Gaul. *tarvos*, Ir. *fedb* = Lat. *vidua* (cf. Stokes in Beitr. ii. 101).

not be the reflex of the original *u* or *v*, but of the *á*, which was obscured in the instrumental. Cf. B. XI. 9; XIII. 2; XVII.

XVI. *ai* stood originally in the last syllable.

In the root syllables this diphthong is represented generally by *é*, from which the new diphthong *ia* originated, when the following syllable contained a broad vowel. This substitution of *é* for *ai*, is seen also in the monosyllabic *é* (he) = Old Lat. *cis*. The *ai* in the auslaut of inflected words, however, became early in Irish an *í*, and was then treated as an original *í*.[1] Here come under consideration:—

1. The nom. and acc. dual of the fem. stems in *á*. The more ancient *í* is preserved uncurtailed in the monosyllabic *dí*, which Ebel (Beitr. zur Vergl. Spr. ii. 70) already compared with Skr. *dve*. This diphthongal origin of the *í* is clearly and distinctly proved by the corresponding *dui*, *duy*, the *ui*, *uy* of which usually represent an original *ai*. In polysyllabic words only the internal *i* is now preserved; e.g., *dí choiss* (duo pedes; nom. sing. *cos*), for prehistoric *coss-i* (cf. Skr. *kukshe*). The aspiration after *dí* proves that the original termination was vocalic. Very interesting is the fact, that in Lithuanian the original *ai* in this case has been treated in quite the same way; for *mergì* stands for *mergë*, as *dvì* (= Ir. *dí*) stands for *dvë*. The more ancient form has been preserved only in the pronoun; e.g., *të-dvi*. Cf. Leskien's Die Declination, p. 106.

2. The nom. plur. of the masc. stems in *a*.

E.g., *eich* for prehistoric *equ-i* = Lat. *equí*, Gr. ἵπποι; *fir* for prehistoric *vir-i* = Lat. *virí*. That this case terminated originally in a vowel (not, as we might have supposed, in *s*) is evident from the fact that aspiration can be proved after it; as, for instance, after the nom. plur. of the article, which, of course, is formed in the same way: *in chnamai* (ossa) Z. 215, 236.

XVII. *ái* stood originally in the last syllable. Of this *ai* there remained, in prehistoric time, in the one case an *i*, in the other case a *u*. How *ái* became *i* may be explained by reference to Gr. *η* (pronounced, at a later period, like *í*); and how *ái* became *u*

---

[1] In the ancient language *é* is also used for the plural: at a later period *iat*=Cymr. *wynt* (Z. 372), formed, probably, after the analogy of the 3rd plur. in the verb (*doberat*), appears as the plural. The interrogative pronoun *cía* (who, what) reminds one of *día* (god), and may, possibly, contain the stem *cai-a*, as the latter contains the stem *daiv-a*. The Cymr. *puy* (= Ir. *cía*) does not furnish any argument against this hypothesis.

may be explained by reference to Gr. φ. Here come under consideration:—

1. The dat. sing. of the fem. stems in *â*. The original *âi* passing through the intermediate stages of *éi, é*, had become *i* in prehistoric time. It penetrated into the preceding syllable, and disappeared altogether in the last syllable.

E.g., *tuaith* (nom. *tuath*, people), for prehistoric *tôt-i* = Goth. *thiudai*; *láim* (nom. *lám*, hand), for prehistoric *(p)lám-i* = Gr. παλάμῃ; *fróich* (nom. *froech*, erica,), for prehistoric *vroic-i* = Gr. ἐρείκῃ. The original vocalic auslaut of this form is shown by the aspiration after it, e.g., *ina láim chlí* (in his left hand). As an Old Gaulish dative of this kind, Stokes regards (Beitr. ii. 103) Βηλησαμι (Belesama is the Gaulish Minerva). Cf., however, Becker in Beitr. iii. 353, 354. On *i* in an Old Gaulish dative of this kind, see H. d'Arbois de Jubainville in Rev. Celt., i. 326.

2. The dat. sing of the mas. and neut. *a*-stems. The original *âi*, passing through *ôi, ô*, had become *u* in prehistoric time. It penetrated before it was dropped into the preceding syllable, except when that syllable contained a long vowel or a diphthong. In Mod. Irish, it has wholly disappeared.

E.g., Old Ir. *fiur*, for prehistoric *vir-u* = Lat. *viro*; *coch*, for prehistoric *eq-o* = Lat. *equo*; *biuth* (dissyllabic), for prehistoric *bivat-u* = Gr. βιότῳ. The original vocalic auslaut of this case is shown by the aspiration after it; e.g., *on mud chetna* (eodem modo). As Old Gaulish forms of this kind are regarded *ALISANV*, *ANVALONNACV* (cf. Stokes in Beitr. zur Vergl. Spr. ii. 103; Becker, ibid. iii. 189).

That the Irish dative, not only as to meaning, but also as to form, may be a mixed case, I have remarked under B. XI. 9.

(The first and second "Excursus" added by Professor Windisch to the above article will appear in our next number.)

GAELIC AND ENGLISH; OR, THE AFFINITY OF THE CELTIC AND TEUTONIC LANGUAGES.

(*Continued from p.* 21).

WE intend to give in this article illustrations of the affinity of the Celtic and Teutonic languages, and more especially of Gaelic and English, as shown by the application of the general principles of etymology stated in the opening article of our first number.

We begin with the Celtic tenuis *c*, which, according to Grimm's Law, corresponds to *h* (sometimes *g*) in the Teutonic languages. To facilitate reference, the examples are arranged alphabetically, words with initial *c* being placed first, whilst words with *c* in the middle or at the end are put in a separate list. A few doubtful examples, which, however, are pointed out as such, are included; but most of the Gaelic words compared are genuine Celtic words.

It is necessary to keep in view that it is only the fact, and not the precise degree, of relationship of the Celtic and Teutonic languages we are dealing with in these articles. The position of Celtic in the Indo-European family of languages will be considered in separate articles.

I. Words beginning with *c*.

1. *Càch, gach,* and *who?*

Càch (the rest, others; = O. Gael. *càch*) and *gach* (each, every; = O. Gael. *cach*) are cognate with Skr. *ka-* in *ka-s* (who), Gr. κο- (= πο-) in κότε for πότε (when), πύ-τερος (which of two), Lat. *quo-* in *quod*, *-que* in *uter-que*, Lith. *kà-s* (who), Goth. *hva-s* (who), A.S. *hwa*, O. Eng. *hwa*, Eng. *who*.

Gael. *càch* and *cach* are reduplicated forms from the root *ca* = Indo-Europ. *ka*. *Càch* = W. *paup*, Mod. W. *pob*, Corn. *pop, pup, pep,* Mod. Corn. *py*, Arm. *peb*.

2. *Cacht* and *haft*.

Cacht (a maid-servant, a bond-woman), if not borrowed from, is cognate with Lat. *capta,* from *capio* (I take). The latter view has been maintained by Windisch, who refers (Beitr. viii. 17) *cacht* and Goth. *hafts* to a common base *kapta*. If this view be correct, the combination *cht* represents an original *pt*, as in *secht* (seven) and *necht* (grand-daughter). *Capio* is connected with Gr. κώπη (handle), Goth. *hafja* (I lift), *hafts* (joined together), Ice. *haft-r* (one who is taken, a prisoner), Germ. *heft* (that which is taken hold of, a handle), A.S. *haeft* (a handle), Mid. Eng. *heft, haft,* Mod. Eng. *haft*. The root is *kap* (to take, seize, bind).

Cacht = W. *caeth* (a slave, a captive), Corn. *caeth* (a captive), Arm. *kez, keaz* (miserable).

3. *Cai, ceardach,* and *home*.

Cai (a house) is given in the Highland Society's Dictionary, but it is not used in the spoken Gaelic of Scotland. It forms, however, the second syllable of *ceardach* (a smithy) = O. Gael. *cerdcha* and *cerdd-chae,* of which *cerd-* is connected with Lat. *cerdo* and Gr. κέρδος, while *cae* (house) is cognate with κεῖ- in κεῖμαι (I lie), κοί-τη (bed), κώ-μη (village), Lat. *qui-es* (rest), Skr. *çi* (jacere, dormire), *célé* (κεῖται), Lith. *ke-mas* (a village), Goth. *hai-va* (house), *hai-ms* (village), O.H.G. *hî-wo* (spouse), Ice. *heim-r* (an abode, village), *heima* (home), A.S. *ham* (home, dwelling), Scott. *hame*, Eng. *home*. The root is *ki* (to rest).

4. *Cailleach* and Goth. *huljan*, O. Eng. *hulen*, Eng. *hull*.

Cailleach (an old woman, a nun), a derivative from *caille* (a veil), is connected by Windisch (Beitr. viii. 18) with Goth. *hulister* (a veil), O.H.G. *hulla* (a veil), N.H.G. *hülle*, O. Eng. *hulen* (to hide), Eng. *hull*. *Cailleach* would thus belong to the root *kal*, from which are derived Gael. *ceil*, Lat. *celo*, &c. See p. 110. Stokes regards *caille* as a loan-word from Lat. *pallium* (a coverlet, a mantle).

5. *Cainb* and *hemp*.

Cainb (hemp, canvas) is cognate with, if not borrowed from, Lat. *cannabis* (hemp) = Gr. κάνναβις, with which are connected Skr. *çanam* (hemp), Ice. *hanp-r* (hemp), O.H.G. *hanf*, N.H.G. *hanf* (hemp), A.S. *haenep* (hemp), Eng. *hemp*. According to Fick, the Europ. base is *kanapi*, from root *kan* (to sting).

6. *Can* and *hen*.

Can (to sing) is cognate with Lat. *cano* (I sing), Gr. κανάζω (I sound) from root καν, καναχή (noise), Skr. *kan-kan-i* (bell), *kvan* (to sound), Goth. *hana* (a cock, lit., the crier), Ice. *hani* (a cock), *haena* (a hen), N.H.G. *hahn* (a cock), A.S. *hana* (a cock), *hen* (a hen), Eng. *hen*. The root is *kan* (to sound, to sing). *Can* = W. *canu* (to sing), Corn. *cane* (to sing), Arm. *kana* (to sing).

Derivatives from *can* are *foirceadul* (instruction, doctrine), in O. Gael. *forcital, foircheadlair* (instructor), *forchun* (I teach), &c. To *can* may also, probably, be referred *caint* (speech).

7. *Caoch* and Goth. *haihs*.

Caoch or *caech* (blind), in O. Gael. *coech*, W. *coeg* (foolish, vain), Corn. *cuic* (blind of one eye), are connected with Lat. *caecus* (blind), Goth. *haihs* (half-blind, with one eye), Cf. Corn. Gloss., p. 31.

8. *Caoin* and *whine*.

Caoin (weep, lament, wail), in O. Gael. *cáinim*, or *cóinim* = W. *cwyno* (complain, bewail), Corn. *cyny* (to lament), Arm. *keina* or *krini* (to lament), *keinvan* (lamentation), has lost a *p* as shown by W. *cwyno*, and may, therefore, be connected with Skr. *kvan*, *kvanati* (to sound, to lament), Ice. *hvina* (to give a whizzing sound), A.S. *hwinan* (to utter a hissing sound), O. Eng. *hwinen*, Eng. *whine*. The root is *kan* (to sound).

9. *Caor* and *hearth*.

Caor or *caoir* (a brand, a burning coal) seems cognate with Goth. *hauri* (burning coals), Ice. *hyr-r* (embers), A.S. *heor-dh* (hearth), O. H.G. *heerd* (fire-place), O. Eng. *her-th*, Eng. *hear-th*.

10. *Carr* and *horse*.

Carr (a waggon, a cart) = Lat. *carr-us* (a kind of two-wheeled cart for heavy burdens), probably a Gaulish word, but cognate with *curr-ere* (to run), *curr-us* (a chariot, a car), Skr. *car*, *carati* (to go), from root *car* (to move, to run). With this root Fick has connected Ice. *hross* (horse), O.H.G. *hros*, A.S. *hors*, O. Eng. *hors*, Eng. *horse*, N.H.G. *ross*, all from a Teutonic base *horsa*, root *hor* or *har* = Indo-Europ. root *kar*. Cf. Fick's Wört., i. 521. *Carr* is identical with Welsh and Armoric *carr*.

11. *Cas* and *haste*.

Cas (rapid, sudden, quick), *cais* (haste), and *caise* (a stream) are connected by Pictet (Beitr. i. 97) with O. Swed. *hasta* (to haste), O. Fries. *hast* (haste), N.H.G. *hast* (haste), Eng. *haste*. The root is *kas* (to go), with which Skr. *çaç* (to jump) is connected. Cf. Skeat's Dictionary. The *s* of *cas* may be for *st*.

12. *Cas* and *hate*.

Cas (gnash with the teeth, to be angry, to scorn) agrees with W. *casdi* (to hate, detest, abhor, to be disgusted at or with), Corn. *case* (to hate, detest), Arm. *casaat* (to hate, to have aversion to). *Casdi* is referred by *Rhys* (cf. Lect.[2] p. 12) to a base *cad-sa* cognate with Goth. *hat-is* (hate, wrath, anger), *hat-an* (to hate), A.S. *hat-ian*, Ger. *hass*, Eng. *hate*. The root is *cad*, and *cas* is for *cad-s*.

13. *Casd* and O. Eng. *host(e)*, Scott. *host* or *hoast*.

Casd or *casad* (a cough), W. *pás* (chin-cough), *pesuch* (cough), Corn. *pas* (a cough), Arm. *pás*, *páz* (cough) are connected with Ice. *hosti* (a cough), *hosta* (to cough), Suio-Goth. *hosta* (a cough), A.S. *hwosta* (a cough), O. Eng. *host(e)* (a cough), Scott. *host* or *hoast*. Other cognates are O.H.G. *huosten* (to cough). N.H.G. *husten* (to cough), Dan. *hoste*.

14. *Cath* and A.S. *headhu*, O.H.G. *hadu*.

Cath (battle) = Gaul. *catu-* in *Catusloji*, *Caturiges*, is cognate with O.H.G. *hadu* (battle, war), Ice. *höðh* (war, slaughter), N.H.G. *had-er* (contention, quarrel), A.S. *headhu* (war). The base of *cath* is *catu*, probably from the root *ka* (to sharpen). The W., Corn., and Arm. common form is *cad* (battle, war), with *d* for *t*.

Cearc (hen) = O. Gael. *cerc* is connected with Gr. κέρκος (hen; cf. Hesychius' Lexicon), κρέξ, gen. κρεκός (a bird with a sharp notched bill), κρέκ-ω (to strike or touch a stringed instrument, to sound), all of which words are referred by Fick (cf. Wört. i. 42) to an Indo-Europ. base *kark* (to sound, to laugh), from the root *kar* (to sound, to call out). With this root are connected Goth. *hlah-jan* (to laugh), Ice. *hlaeja* (to laugh), A.S. *hlih-an*, *hleh-an* (to laugh), O. Eng. *hluhh-en* (to laugh), Eng. *laugh*, with loss of initial *h*. The Teutonic words may be referred to a base *hlah* = Indo-Europ. *krak*. The derivatives of the root *kar* (to cry) are very numerous.

16. *Ceil*, *cleith*, and Eng. *hele*, *hill*.

Ceil (to conceal), *cleith* (concealment), W. *celu* (to hide), Corn. *celes* (to hide, conceal) are connected with Lat. *celo* (I conceal), Gr. καλ-ια (hut, store-room), Skr. *khalas*, *khalam* (threshing-floor, shed), Goth. *hul-jan* (to veil or cover), O.H.G. *hëlan*, N.H.G. *hehlen* (to conceal), A.S. *hel-an* (to conceal, cover), Eng. *hele*, *hill* (to conceal). The root is *kal* (to hide).

Other connected Gaelic words are *celt*, (vestis), *fo-ro-chlad* ("had been shut up"). Cf. Stokes in Beitr. viii. 311.

17. *Cél* and *hale*.

O. Gael. *Cel* (omen), W. *coel* (an omen), *coel-fain* (glad tidings) are connected with Ice. *heill* (an omen, auspice, foreboding), Goth. *hail-s* (sound, healthy) = *hal-jas*, Mid. Eng. *heil*, *heyl*, Eng. *hale* (healthy). The root is *kal*, whence Skr. *kal-jas* (healthy, pleasant) and Gr. καλός (beautiful). Cf. Fick's Wört. i. 530, and Curtius' Gr. Etym., p. 139.

18. *Cer-*, *ciar-*, and Scott. *harns*, O.E. *herne*.

Cér- or *ciar-* in *cér-chaill* (pillow) or *ciar-chaill* (head protection) is connected by Stokes (Cf. Corm.'s Gl. p. 38) with *cere-* in Lat. *cere-brum* (the brain), Goth. *hvair-nei* (skull), O.H.G. *hirni*, N.H.G. *hirn* (brains), Ice. *hjarni* (the brain), Scott. *harns*, O. Eng. *herne* (the brain). The common root is *kar* (head), whence Gr. κάρα (head), Skr. *çiras* for *karas* (head), Zend. *çara*, *çaranh* (head).

19. *Cét* and *Ice. hnjodhu*, Goth. *hnutho*.

Cét (a blow), in O'Clery's Glossary *ceud* (a blow) with loss of *n* before the tenuis, is cognate with Gr. κεντ-έω (to goad, sting), Ice. *hnjodhu* (to strike with a hammer, rivet, clench), Goth. *hnutho* (a thorn, prick, sting). Cf. Beitr. viii. 352 and Cleasby's Dictionary. *Cét* = *centa* = *kantu* (a bar), from root *kant* = *knat* (to strike, push, sting).

20. *Ceud* and *hund-red*.

Ceud (hundred), in O. Gael. *cét*, W. *cant* (hundred), Corn. *cans* (hundred), Arm. *cant*, are cognate with Lat. *centum* (hundred), Gr. ἑ-κατ-όν, Skr. *çat-am*, Zend *çat-em*, Lith. *szimt-as*, Goth. *hund* (hundred), A.S. *hund-red*, compounded of *hund* (hundred) and *réd* or *ráed* (speech, reckoning or rate), Eng. *hund-red*.

Eclipsis occurs after *cét*, because it originally terminated in a nasal. *Cét* = *cétan* = *kantam*, from a root *kant*.

21. *Cia* and *he*.

Cia (who, what) is cognate with Lat. *qui-* in *qui-s, qui-d*, Gr. τί-ς (who), τί (what), Skr. *na-ki-s* (nemo), *má-ki-s* (nequis), *ki-m* (quid), Zend *má-ci-s* (quid), Goth. acc. m. *hi-na*, neut. *hi-ta*, A.S *hi, hë*, Eng. *he*. The root is *ki*, a pronominal base preserved in *ki-m, ki-s*, &c.

In W. *pui, puy* (who), Corn. *py* (who, which), Arm. *pa* (when), original *k* has become *p*.

22. *Ciad-* and *heath*.

Ciad- in *ciad-cholum* (wood-pigeon), W. *coed* (wood) = O. W. *coit*, Corn. *coid* (wood), Arm. *coat* (wood) are from a base *céto* = *-cetu-m* in Lat. *bucetum* (pasture for cattle), and are cognate with Goth. *haithi* (heath), Ice. *heidh-r*, Germ. *heide*, A.S. *haedh*, Eng. *heath*. Cf. Beitr. viii. 39, and Zeitschr. zur. Vergl. Spr. xxi. 368. The common Europ. base is *kaita* (pasture).

23. *Ciar* and *hoar*.

Ciar (dusky, dark-brown, dark-grey) = *céra* seems connected with Ice. *har-r* (hoary), A.S. *hár* (hoar), Eng. *hoar*. With the Teutonic words, Fick compares Skr. *çára* (variegated, spotted).

24. *Claidheamh* and *hilt*.

Claidheamh (sword), in O. Gael. *claideb*, is cognate with Lat. *gladius* (sword), for *gladius* = *kaldios*, which Fick (Wört. ii. 58) connects with Ice. *hjalt* (mas., sword), *hjalt* (neut., the boss or knob at the end of a sword's hilt), O.H.G. *hëlza* (sword-hilt), A.S. and

Eng. *hilt*. The root is *kal* (to strike, smite). The British forms are W. *cleddyf*, *cledd* (sword), Corn. *cledhe*, plur. *cledhyow*, Arm. *clezef*, *clezé*.

25. *Claon* and *lean* (to incline or bend).

Claon (incline), in O. Gael. *clóen*, *clóin*, is cognate with O. Lat. *clino* (I incline), *in-clino* (I incline, bend), Gr. κλίνω (I lean or bow down), κλίνη (bed), O.H.G. *kliném* (lean), Goth. *hlain-s* (hill), A.S. *hlyn-ian* (to lean), Eng. *lean* with loss of initial *h*. The Indo-Europ. root is ḳri (to go, to lean against, to bend, to incline). Cf. Fick's Wört. i. 62.

26. *Clí* and *hlei-* in Goth. *hleiduma*.

Clí (the left), in O. Gael. *clé*, is cognate with *hlei-* in Goth. *hleiduma* (the left, on the left). The corresponding British forms are W. *cledd*, Corn. *cledh*, Arm. *cleiz*.

27. *Cliath* and *hurdle*.

Cliath (a hurdle) = *cléta (cf. Mid. Lat. *cleta*) is connected with Lat. *crates* (wicker-work, a hurdle), Gr. κάρτολος (a basket), Skr. *cart*, *crtati* (to connect together, to weave), Goth. *haurds* (a door made of wicker-work), M.H.G. *hurt*, N.H.G. *hürde* (a hurdle), Ice. *hurdh* (hurdle), A.S. *hyrd-el*, Mid. Eng. *hurd-el*, Eng. *hurd-le*. The root is *krat* = Europ. *kart* (to weave). The British forms are O. W. *cluit*, Mod. W. *clwyd*, O. Corn. *cluit*, Arm. *cloued*, *clud*.

28. *Cliù*, *cluas* and Eng. *loud*.

Cliù (fame, praise), in O. Gael. *clú*, is cognate with Lat. *clu-o*, *clu-eo* (I hear), *in-clu-tus* (celebrated), Gr. κλύω (I hear), κλυ-τός (renowned), κλέος (fame) = κλεϝος, Skr. *çru* (hear), *çru-tis* (reputation), *çrav-as* (fame), Ch.-Slav. *sluti* (distinguished), *slava* (fame), Lith. *szlové* (honour), *klausaú* (hear), Goth. *hliu-ma* (hearing), O.H.G. *hlû-t* (loud), N.H.G. *lau-t*, A.S. *hlú-d*, Eng. *loud* = (h)*lou-d*. The root is *ḳlu* = Indo-Europ. *ḳru* (to hear). To this root or extended forms of it, belong the Gaelic words *cluas* (ear) = *closta, *cloth* (renowned) = Gr. κλυτύς, *cloor* (I hear) for *closor, *cluinn* (hear), and *claistin* (hearing). Brit. forms are W. *clôd* (praise), *clust* (ear), *clyw* (the hearing), *clywed*, Corn. *clewas* and *clowas* (to hear), *clos* (glory, praise), *clowans* (hearing), Arm. *klévout* (to hear), *kléved* (hearing).

29. *Cloch* and Goth. *hallus*.

Cloch or *clach* (a stone) is connected by Stokes with Gr. κρόκη (a rounded or rolled stone, a pebble), κροκάλη (a pebble), which, along with Skr. *çarkará* (flint) and Zend *çraçe* (hail-stones), are referred by Fick (Wört. ii. 54, to a base *kurki* (gravel), from root, *kar* (cf. Curt. Gr. Etym. p. 144). With these words are connected Lat. *calx* (the heel), *calculus* (a pebble), and Goth. *hallus* (a rock, a stone). Pictet connects also Gael. *carraig* (a rock). The fundamental idea, according to Curtius, is hardness.

30. *Cluaidh* and O. Eng. *hlutter* (pure).

Cluaidh (the river Clyde), in O. Gael. *Cluad* (cf. *A il-cluade*, the rock of Clyde, now Dumbarton), has been connected by Stokes (Beitr. viii. 314), with Lat. *cluere* (to wash), Gr. κλύζω (I wash), Goth. *hlutrs* (pure), O.H.G. *hlûtar* (pure), N.H.G. *lauter* (pure), A.S. *hlutor* and *hluttor*, O. Eng. *hlutter* (pure). Literally, therefore, the *Clyde* signifies "the pure river"! The common root is *klu* (to wash).

31. *Clúi* and *ladder*.

O. Gael. *clúi* (plur., nails) = *clovi* is connected with Lat. *clavus* (a nail), *clavis* (a key, *claudo* (I shut). Gr. κλεί-ς, κλη-ῖ-ς (a key), for κλαϝ-ι-ς, κλεί-ω (I close), Ch.-Slav. *klju-čĭ* (a hook, a key). With κλείω are connected κλεῖθρον κλῆθρον (bar, bolt), Lat. *clathri* (plur., grate, set of bars); and with these we may connect O.H.G. *hleitra*, N.H.G. *leiter* (a ladder), A.S. *hlaeder* (a ladder), Mid. Eng. *laddre*, Eng. *ladder*. The Mod. Gael. *cleith* (a stake) and *cláithean* (a bar or bolt) seem connected. Curtius (Gr. Etym. p. 149) gives *sklu* as the root. Cf. W. *cloi* (to lock, close).

32. *Cnáimh* and *ham*.

Cnáimh (bone), in O. Gael. *cnáim* = *cnámi*, is connected with Gr. κνήμη (the shin, the shin bone), and is cognate with O.H.G. *hammua* for *hanma*, M.H.G. *hamme* (the hind part of the leg), A.S. *hamm* for *hanm* (back part of the knee), Mid. Eng. *hamm* and *hamme* (the inner or hind part of the knee, the thigh), Mod. Eng. *ham*. Cf. Ztschr. für Vergl. Spr. xxi. 368.

33. *Cneadh* and *nit, nettle*.

Cneadh (wound, hurt), in O. Gael. *cned*, seems connected with Ice. *hneit-a* (to cut, wound), *hnit-a* (to strike), A.S. *hnit-an* (to butt, gore), from stem *hnita*, to which Skeat refers Mid. Eng. *nite, nyte*, Eng. *nit*. Gr. κνίδη (nettle), κνίζ-ειν (to scrape, to cause to itch) for κνίδjειν, O.H.G. *nazza* (nettle), dim. *nezzila* (nettle), N.H.G. *nessel*, A.S. *netle, netele*, Mid. Eng. *netle, nettle*, Eng. *nettle*, belong to the same root *knid = knad* (to bite, sting, scrape).

34. *Cno* and *nut*.

Cnò (nut) is connected by Stokes (cf. Cormac's Glossary) with Lat. *nux* (nut) for *cnux, Ice. *hno-t*, A.S. *hnu-tu*, Eng. *nut* (with loss of initial h). The connection with Lat. *nux* is doubtful. The Teutonic base is *hnoti* from root *hnat* = Europ. root *knad* above noticed. The Brit. forms are *cnau* (nuts), sing. *cneuen* (a nut), Corn. *cynyfan*, Arm. *cnaouen, craouen*.

35. *Cochull* and O. Eng. *hakele*.

Cochull (cowl, hood, mantle) = Lat. *cucullus* (cowl, hood), cognate with Goth *hakul* (a cloak), Ice. *hökull* (a mantle), O.H.G. *hachul*, A.S. *hacele* O. Eng. *hakele* (vestis). Cf. W. *cochl* (a cloak).

36. *Coileach* and *hale, haul*.

Coileach (cock), in O. Gael. *cailech* = *calicos* (Stokes), is cognate with Gr. καλέω (I call), Lat. *calare* (to call, call out), *calendae* (the calends), O.H.G. *halón* (to call, summon, fetch), N.H.G. *hol-en* (to fetch), O. Sax. *hal-ón* (to bring, fetch), A.S. *hol-ian* (to acquire), Mid. Eng. *hal-ien, hal-en*, Eng. *hale, haul*. The root is *kal* (to call). The Brit. forms are W. *ceiliog*, Corn. *celioc, colyec*, Arm. *cilec, cilok*.

37. *Coille* and Eng. *holt*.

Coille (wood), O. Gael. *caill*, gen. *caille, calle*, dat. *caill, caillid*, dat. plur. *cailtib*, is referred by Stokes to a stem *caldit*, connected with Gr. κλάδος (young branch or shoot), and A.S. *holt* (grove), O.H.G. *holz*, N.H.G. *holz*, Eng. *holt* (a wood, a woody hill, a grove). The root is *kal* (to hide) = Indo-Europ. *kar* (to cover), the same to which belong Gael. *ceil, cleith*, Lat. *celare*, &c., noticed above. Cf. Skeat's Dictionary s. v. *holt*. Brit. forms are W. *celli* (a grove), Corn. *celli* or *cilli* (a grove).

38. *Coire* and A.S. *hver*, Eng. *ewer* (?)

Coire (a kettle) and W. *pair*, were connected by Siegfried with A.S. *hver* (a ewer, kettle), Ice. *hver-r* (a kettle, cauldron). Fick connects Eng. *ewer*, but Skeat assigns to this word a different origin. Cf. Cormac's Glossary, p. 41. Fick compares Skr. *caru* (kettle). The root is *kar* (to pour).

39. *Colainn, creabh* and A.S. *hreaw* (carcase).

Colainn (body), in O. Gael. *colinn*, gen. *colno*, dat. *colain*, is related to Lat. *caro* (flesh), gen. *carn-is, cruor* (blood), Gr. κρέας (flesh), Skr. *krav-jam, kravis* (raw flesh), *crū-ra-s* (sore, bleeding), Ch.-Slav. *krŭvĭ* (blood), Lith. *kraújas* (blood), Goth. *hraiw* (carcase), O.H.G. *hrév*, A.S. *hréaw* (carcase). *Créubh* (body) is cognate with Goth. *hraiw*, A.S. *hréaw*. The Indo-Europ. stem is *krav* (blood), from root *kru* (to bruise, to make sore, to make or become hard). Cf. Fick's Wört. i. 52, and Curt. Gr. Etym. pp. 154, 155. Cf. W. *crau* (blood), Corn. *crow* (blood).

(To be continued.)

THE MUILEARTACH.*

THIS tale has been selected as a fair specimen of tales at one time common in the Western Islands and Highlands of Scotland, and still to be occasionally fallen in with. It relates, as almost all the popular tales of the Scottish Celts do, to Ireland. Copies in print of the tale, or parts of it, are to be found in Campbell's *West Highland Tales*, iii., 122; several versions in *Leabhar na Féinne*, by the same excellent collector; and one in Gillies' Collection. Of the version here given, Part I. has never appeared in print. It was written many years ago from the dictation of Duncan M'Fadyen, Caolas, Tiree, and has been compared with other oral versions; and Part II. from Duncan Cameron, constable, Tiree, in 1871.

In the translation, "Fin-Mac-Coul" is adopted as a better rendering of *Fionn Mac Cumhail* than the more familiar and euphonious Fingal, a name which had its origin with Macpherson. Similarly, "Fians" is adopted for *Féinne*, a collective noun, and *Fiantan*, a plural noun, instead of Fingalians or Fenians, names which have other ideas now associated with them. "Fin-Mac-Coul" has more of the ludicrous idea attached to it than belongs to the Gaelic name. It is as old as Barbour, who uses it in the poem of "The Bruce" (circ. 1380).

Historically, this tale is worthless, as it cannot be accepted as a *memento* of, or in any way relating to, a sea fight between Norsemen and Celts. It is, however, of considerable interest to the student of history, as showing personification at work, and the manner in which the creations of fancy harden into acceptance as historical facts. The tale is a myth, in the true sense of

---

* The name of the principal character in this tale is pronounced indifferently, and by the same reciters, *Muireartach* and *Muileartach*, and is construed by them sometimes as a masculine, but most commonly as a feminine noun. There is no difficulty in deriving it from *Muir Iartach*, the Western Sea.

that word. Of the reciters, some believed it to record a real, some a possible event—thus agreeing with Mr. Campbell, who says (*West Highland Tales*, iii., 144), "I suspect the poem was composed in remembrance of some real invasion of Ireland by the sea-rovers of Lochlann, in which they got the worst of the fight, and that it has been preserved traditionally in the Hebrides ever since." The *Muileartach* (Western Sea), here personified, is appropriately represented in the tale as the nurse or foster-mother of Manus, King of Lochlin, who falls to be identified with Magnus Barefoot, King of Norway. That potentate is said in history to have made, towards the end of the eleventh century, extensive conquests along the north and west coasts of Scotland, and also in Ireland. He was killed near Dublin, in 1103. The epithets applied to the *Muileartach* leave no doubt as to the personification. The sea-rover is her foster-child. She is ill-streaming (*mì-shruth*), abounding in seas (*muir-each*), bald-red (*maol-ruadh*), white-maned (*muing-fhionn*). She has long streaming hair, and is finally subdued by being let down into the ground to the waist, the mode in which water is best subdued. She is also represented as terrific (*uamhannach*), as having a roaring wide-open mouth (*bha gàir 'n a craos*), &c. Any one, who has seen the sea in a storm, will understand the appropriateness of the description. It is also to be observed that, uniformly in popular lore, she is slain by Fin-Mac-Coul himself, and not by the band of men of whom he was leader. Fin was not the strongest of the *Féinne* or Fian-band, but the solver of questions (*fear-fuasgladh ceisd*) and adviser. The blades of the Fians passed as harmlessly through the body of the *Muileartach* as a knife through flame. Fin, who represents brain, intellect, subdued her by letting her down into the ground. Manus, who was acquainted with northern seas, imagines, as the only way in which she could be killed, (1) her being swallowed by a hole in the ground, or (2) her being frozen over.

It is said that this was the first day on which the Fian fair-play (*cothrom na Féinne*) was broken. Previously, it was a law of the band to oppose only one to one; but this day, Fin told them to attack the *Muileartach* before and behind (*air a cùlthaobh 's air a beulthaobh*).

Another tale of popular lore relating to the Fian-Band, in which personification is unquestionably at work, is that of *Ciuthach mac an Doill*, whose name is but a slight alteration from *Ceathach*, and means, "Mist, son of the Blind Man." He came in from the sea to the cave in which Diarmid and Graine had taken refuge, in a night so stormy that Diarmid, the third best hero of the Fians, would not on any account venture out of the cave.

In the whole of the Fian lore, there is much that seems purely imaginative. And it is upon this supposition of personification that the localisation in so many places of the Fian traditions, and their strange extravagances, are best explained. The classical reader will remember how Hercules, also a personification of bodily strength, was found by the Romans in every place they visited.

Upon this view—the supposition that the incident is entirely the work of imagination—the ballad is interesting and poetical. The Western Sea, in one of the gloomier aspects which it frequently presents among the Islands of Scotland, a bank of mist, a darkening shower, a high tide, or a fierce gale is converted by the poet's fancy into an old woman who is the foster-mother of the Pirate King who infests the coast. A solitary star twinkling through the darkening clouds, becomes an eye glimmering in her gloomy forehead; the agitation of the sea, waves swept into spindrift or breaking wildly on the rocks, the roaring of the waves, and the Skerries covered with tangle, are readily converted into her rocking motion, streaming hair, gloomy looks, projecting red teeth, and loud laughter. Following up the idea, the superiority of the Norsemen at sea is represented by the old woman taking away the Cup of Victory. Betrayed into over-confidence the Norse king engages in battle on land and is defeated. This is represented by the poet as an inroad of the Personified Sea.

The explanation of the Muileartach is further strengthened by the representation of an enclosure having been made for the great fight, denoting the confining of water within manageable limits, by the Muileartach being called *sgleò* a spectre, a film, a vapour, or an indistinct appearance, and by her combating the heroes like a flame.

At the same time, while there is much in the stories of the Fians that can be explained as personifications and poetical fancies; there is much, such as the death of Oscar, that appears as like real history and tradition as anything to be found in authentic records.

For archæological or other scientific purpose, it is essential that ballads of this kind, and indeed everything got from oral sources, should be presented to the reader "uncooked," that is, without suppression or addition, or alteration, which is not pointed out.

A' MHUILEARTACH.

A' Cheud Earann.

Bha na Fiantan airson an rìoghachd a chumail bho na Lochlainnich.[1] Bha Fionn 'na righ orra. Bha blàr eatorra fhéin agus Mànus aig Dùn-Chinn-a'-choire ann an Éirinn. Dar a chaidh Mànus dhachaidh, thuirt a mhuime, "A' Mhuileartach," gu'n rachadh i thoirt blàir do Fhionn agus gu'n tugadh i uaithe an Corn-Buadhach,[2] soitheach creadha, air an robh e air 'fhàgail, gur ann le deoch òl as a bha an Fhéinn' daonnan a' faotainn buaidh. Thuirt Mànus gu'n cuireadh e daoine leatha, ach dhiult i. Cha tugadh i leatha ach an duine aice, Gobhainn-nan-Cuan, agus lùbiarruinn, ris an abradh iad, an Trosdan beag, druimneach. Ghabh iad gu astar gu Dùn-Chinn-a'-choire. Chunnaic an Fhéinn' rud mòr duaitheil a' tighinn, agus thuirt Fionn, "Ma shiubhail e'n domhan, agus ma chuairtich e'n saoghal, is i muime Mhànuis a th'ann, is tha rud sònruichte a dhìth oirre." Chaidh an Fhéinn' a stigh do'n tigh; agus chuir naoi naoinear an druim ris an dorus, agus chuir iad naoi slàbhraidhean iarruinn an glacaibh a chéile.

Spìon i craobh agus sgrios i dhi na meanglain, agus bha i aice 'na bata. Dh'fhuirich Gobhainn-nan-Cuan aig a' bhàta. Chuir iad naoi druill air an dorus, is naoi troidhean an cloich 's an aol, is chaidh naoi caogad[3] le an dromannaibh ris an dorus.

Bha Fionn a' seallltuinn a mach, agus thàinig ise, agus thuirt i an guth ìosal—

Ise.
Is mise cailleach thruagh, thruagh,
'Thàinig air a dian-ruaig;
Shiubhail mi còig-chòigeamh[4] na h-Éirinn,
'S cha d' fhuair mi tigh a leigeadh a stigh mi.

Fionn.
Ma shiubhail thusa sin gu h-uilidh[5]
'S comharra sin air droch dhuine;
'S ged uainicheadh do spuir fodhad,
Uam-sa cha'n fhaigheadh tu fosgladh.

Ise.
'S olc an cleachdadh sin do mhac rìgh,
Do'm bu dual gaisg' agus mòr-ghnìomh;
Mac rìgh 'ga ràdhainn riut,
'S nach tugadh tu cuid oidhche do chaillich.

Fionn.

Ma 'se modh, no biatachd, no fialachd,
'Tha dhìth ort, a chailleach!
Cuiridh mise thugad biadh cheud fear,
'S tog dhìom do sheanchas, a chailleach!

Ise.

Cha'n'eil mise 'm feum do bhìdh bhochd,
'S cha mhò a's àill leam do mhòr sprochd;
B'fheàrr leam a bhith am blath's do theine mhòir,
'S a bhith an comith ri do chonaibh.

Fionn.

Nach fhadaidh thusa teine dhuit féin,
Far an séid thu e le t' anail?
'S cuir cual chonnaidh ri d' gharbh-chneas,
[*Variation*—Pronn geugan beaga ri do chruit]
'S dean gu crìonna ris do gharadh.

Ise.

An t-seisear laoch a's fheàrr 'san Fhéinn',
Faic thusa air an raon a mach iad;
'S 'nuair 'ruigeas an sneachd an crios doibh,
Cha'n urrainn iad teine fhadadh.

[*Var.*—An naoi naoinear 'ga bheil a stigh
Eadar an tugha 's an fhraigh;
Ruigeadh an sneachd dhoibh an crios,
'S cha rachadh leo teine fhadadh.]

Thug a' chailleach, 'bu chruaidh còmhrag,
Breab a dh'ionnsaidh na còmhla;
'S mu'n d'thill i bun-dubh[6] a coise,
Bhrist i na naoi slàbhraidhean iarruinn á glacaibh a
 chéile, [agus thilg i na laoich air an druim-dìreach
 air an ùrlar].

Sheachainn Fionn an rathad oirre; is ghabh ise gu ciste nan seud,
agus thug i leatha an Corn-Buadhach.

Dh'éirich na daoine,
Dh'éirich Caoilt'[7] is dh'éirich càch;
'S dh'éirich fear-iomairt nan ràmh,[8]
A dh'fhalbh an déigh na caillich.

Cha b' urrainn doibh breth oirre. Chaidh Oscar, am fear 'bu làidire do'n Fhéinn' as a déigh. Rug e oirre air chois aig uchd Beinn-Eadainn*. Bha 'falt liath a' slaodadh rithe, agus rug Oscar air. Thug e dùi'-leum, agus chuir e tri duail do fhalt cas, liath na caillich m'a dhorn. Mu'n tug e sreamadh aisde, chaidh iad fodha gu 'm meadhon an sneachda. "Ud! ud! a laochain!" ars' ise, "ghortaich thu mi. Ma's e biadh no deoch a tha dhìth ort, gheibh thu e 'nuair a ruigeas mise an iùbhrach." [Ruig Gobhainn-nan-Cuan 's gheibh thu e.] " Cha'n e sin a tha dhìth orm, ach t'fhalt liath a thoirt a dh'ionnsaidh mo sheanair." "Ho! ho! an ann diubh sin thu ?"

Tharruing i nall a falt cas, liath, o 'gàirdean toisgeil, agus leag i a làmh gu h-eutrom air, agus chual e fhéin fuaim a h-uile cnàimh.

"Ma tha spionnadh agad a dhol dachaidh, innis do Fhionn gu bheil an Corn-Buadhach agam-sa."

Thill e, agus chaidh ise do Lochlainn. Chuir Mànus roimhe blàr a thoirt do Fhionn. Chruinnich e a dhaoine, agus chaidh e gu Dùn-Chinn-a'-choire a thoirt blàir do Fhionn.

Choinnich iad, agus thoisich iad air a chéile. Bha na Lochlainnich uile air am marbhadh, agus bha an Corn-Buadhach air 'fhaotainn air 'ais. Chaidh Mànus a cheangal, agus chaidh mionnan a chur air. 'S ann an sin a thuirt Conan[10]—

"A leigeil gu Mànus nan lann
'S gu'n sgaradh e 'cheann o 'chorp."

Thuirt Mànus an sin[11]—

"Buille bheag a' t'aghaidh, Fhinn,
'S aithreach leam na riun mi ort."

Chaidh e dhachaidh lom, falamh. Dh'fhoighneachd a mhuime airson a dhaoine, agus thuirt e gu'n robh iad air an call.

"A righ!" ars' ise "gu'n tug mi riamh sùgh mo thaoibh dhuit, is nach rachadh agad fhéin air Fionn a mharbhadh, 's gun ann ach leth-dhuine.[12] Bithidh mise nis' a' falbh, agus uirread 'sa chaill thusa bheir mise as an Fhéinn' an ceithir uairibh fichead."

"Togaidh mise," arsa Mànus, " mo chuid loingeis, agus théid mi leat." Cha chluinneadh i so, ach an Gobhainn a dhol leatha. Bha esan math gu naigheachdan innseadh, agus dh'innseadh e do Mhànus a h-uile ni dar a thigeadh iad air an ais. Cha robh an

* Beinn-Eadair (The Hill of Howth, near Dublin).

Gobhainn toileach falbh, ged nach d'rinn e ach cluinntinn mu
Fhionn ; ach rug ise air, agus thilg i e anns a' bhàta. Ghabh iad
an turus-cuain. Thàinig soirbheas beag ciùin as an déigh o ìsle
nam beann, is o àirde nan craobh, a bheireadh duilleach á beinn
is soileach á craoibh, agus luachair bheag, òg, as a bun agus as a
freumhach. Thòisich iad air tilgeadh na fàirge fiolcanaich, falcan-
aich, fualcanaich, air dubha a sean-chloich, 's air piceadh a sonna
chloich, a' bhéisd 'bu mhò 'g itheadh na béisd 'bu lugha, 's a bhéisd
'bu lugha a' deanamh mar a dh'fhaodadh i. Càllaga beaga a'
chuain a' gabhail fàil agus fasgaidh ann an sop a' chroinn-mhòir
aice. Ghearradh i 'n coinnlein caol, cruaidh, coirce, roimh a dubh-
thoiseach, aig ro fheabhas a stiùramaiche.[13] " Seall suas," ars'
ise, ri Gobhainn-nan-Cuan, " is feuch am faic thu am fearann."
'Nuair a sheall esan thuige is uaithe, chunnaic e fearann is thuirt
e, "Ma's fearann e, is beag e, agus ma's feannag e, agus mòr e." " Is
fìor sin, a laochain," ars' ise, " cha'n'eil an iùbhrach aig astar
ceart leinn."

Chuir iad a mach na ràimh bheaga, bhaisgeanta, dhruimneach ;
's cha robh sìneadh a bheireadh iad air an druim, nach tugadh iad
uisge stigh air beul-mòr a' bhàta. H-uile uile no urbhaidhe 'gan
d'fhuair iad, ràinig iad tìr ; is tharruing iad an iùbhrach am bràighe
a' chladaich, far nach deanadh macan a' bhaile-mhòir bùird no
magadh oirre.

Dh'òrduich ise do Ghobhainn-nan-Cuan dol air cnocan, air cùl
gaoithe 's air aodann gréine, far am faiceadh e a h-uile duine,
's nach faiceadh duine idir e.[14] Rinn e sin, is chaidh ise air a
h-aghaidh. Gu mi-fhortanach, bha na Fiantan 'nan codal air an
cuid àrm, agus bha ceithir-ar-fhichead dhiubh air an uchd.
Thòisich i air am marbhadh leis an lùb iarruinn. Mharbh i—

> " Ceithir-ar-fhichead de'n Fhéinn',
> 'S Ailbhinn féin air thùs,
> Thuit air làimh na h-Iorghuil mhòir,
> Mu'n deachaidh na seòid 'nan dlùth's."

An sin thòisich na Fiantan is a' chaillcach, 's bha iad a' sliocart-
aich, 's a' slacartaich, 's a' gabhail d'a chéile. Bha i 'gan ceapadh
mar lasair shìos is shuas. Bha i àrd. An sin dh'iarr Oscar e
bhith air a chur 'na h-aghaidh, e féin ; 's bha i 'ga throm-liàbadh,
's 'ga iomain an comhair a chùil ; agus ghabh Fionn lag-mhisneach.
Dh'iarr e orra spaidean a ghabhail is iad a ghearradh foidhpe 's a
cur air a h-ais, gus am faigheadh iad cothrom iomain no bualaidh

oirre. Rinn iad toll, agus dh'iomain iad air a h-ais i gus an deachaidh i ann. Bha i fhathast 'gan ccapadh mar lasair, ach na h-uile
h-uile no h-urbhaidhe 'gan d'fhuair iad, mharbh iad a' chailleach
mu'n do stad iad. Thog iad an sin gaoir-chatha le toilinntinn;
agus an sin ceithir-ar-fhichead do na Fiantan a bha an Coire-
Ghlinne, 'nuair a chual iad e, bha fhios aca gu'n robh fargradh
air teachd air an Fhéinn'. Ruith iad a null, is thuirt fear dhiubh
ri 'chompanach:—"A rìgh fhéin! nach innseadh tu dhomh ciamar
a bha i 'nuair a bha i air a casan?" "Cha'n'eil mise an urrainn
sin innseadh ach do neach a bha 'ga faicinn."

['S e so an t-àite ceart air son Duan na Muilcartaich aithris.]

    Latha dhuinn air tulaich shoir,[15]
      'Scalltainn Éirinn mu'n cuairt;
    Thàinig oirnn bharr muir sleamhain trom,
      Atharnach[16] trom, neò-ghlas.
    Dà fhiacail seachad siar air a craos,
      'S ceithir aimhlean 'na màs:
    Ceithir-ar fhichead de'n Fhéinn',
      'S Ailbhinn féin air thùs,
    'Thuit air làimh na h-Iorghuil mhòir,
      Mu'n deachaidh na slòigh an dlùth's.[17]
    Sin 'nuair a labhair Goll,
      An sonn nach robh riamh 'sa chùil:
    "Leigibh mi 'ga h-ionnsuidh greis,
      'S gu feuchainn ri cleas lùgh's."

Bha a' chailleach 'ga riabadh, 's 'ga iomain an coinneamh a chùil.
Agus ghabh Fionn lag-mhisneach an uair sin. Sin an uair a
dh'òrduich e an talamh a ghearradh o 'bonn, 's a leigeadh gu ionad a
crios 'san làr. Bha i 'gar ccapadh shìos is shuas mar lasair; 's na
h-uile h-uile no h-urbhaidhe 'gan d'fhuair sinn, sin dar a mharbh
sinn a' chailleach, 's thug sinn an gaoir-chatha asainn.

Dar a chual Gobhainn-nan-Cuan, a bha air cùl gaoithe 's ri
aodunn gréine gu'n do mharbhadh a' Mhuileartach, ghabh e mach
gu cuan. [Rann mu thurus-cuain.] Ràinig e Lochlainn leis fhéin:
choinnich Mànus e, agus dh'fhoighneachd e dheth, c'àit' an
d'fhàg e a' chailleach. "Mharbhadh i," thuirt Gobhainn-nan-
Cuan.

"O bhéisd! cha do mharbhadh; ach dar a chunnaic thusa
eaghnadh a bha i deanamh, theich thu."

"O! mharbhadh i."

"Cha do shluig an talamh-toll'i, 's cha do bhàthadh i air muir sleamhuin lom, 's cha robh do shluagh air an domhan na mharbhadh mo Mhuileartach."

"Cha do mharbh i ach an Fhéinn',
An dream air nach do thàrladh buaidh ;
'S aon riamh cha deach' as
Air an dream fhalt-bhuidhe chas."

Mar sin chrìochnaich a' chailleach a turus.

AN DARA EARRANN.

Latha do'n Fhéinn air tulaich shoir[18]
Ag amharc Éirinn m'a timchioll,
Chunncas a' teachd bhàrr thonn,
Arrachd éitidh, creadhall, trom.
'S gu'm b'e b'ainm do'n fhuath nach robh tiom,[19]
A' Mhuileartach mhaol, ruadh, mhuing-fhionn.
Bha 'h-aodann dubh-ghlas air dhreach guail,
Bha deud a carbaid claon-ruadh,
Bha aon shùil ghlogach 'na ceann,
'S gu'm bu luaith' i na rionnach madhair ;
Bha greann glas-dhubh air a ceann,
Mar choille chrìonaich roimh chrith-reotha ;
Ri faicinn na Féinne bu mhòr goil,
Shanntaich a' bhéist a bhith 'nan innis.
An toiseach mire agus àir,
Rinneadh leatha gion gun chomain ;
Mharbh i le 'h-àbhachd ceud laoch,
'S a gàire 'na garbh chraos.

. . . .

Caillidh tu dosan do chinn chrionaich
Air son deagh mhac Oisein iarraidh.

. . . .

Thairg iad dhi cumha, 's i thilleadh an taobh a thàinig i. Cha ghabhadh i sid na bha sheudaibh buadhach an Éirinn gus am faigheadh i—

Ceann Oscair, Oisein, is Fhinn,
Ghoill, agus Choirill.

. . . .

Rinn iad crò airson a' chatha mhòir
Mu'n atharraichte air faiche na sgleò,

A' cheathrar laoch a b'fheàrr 'san Fhéinn,
Gu'n còmhraigeadh i iad gu léir;
'S fhrithealadh i iad mu seach,
Mar ghath rionna na lasrach.
Thachair Mac-Cumhail an àigh
Is a' bheist làimh ri làimh;
Bha taobh-'cholluinn ri guin bualaidh,
'S bha braon d'a fhuil air na fraochaibh.
Thuit a' Mhuileartach le Fionn;
Ma thuit cha b'ann gun strìth;
Deuchainn cha d'fhuair e mar sin,
O latha ceardaich Lon-'ic-Lìobhainn.
Thog iad a' chailleach air bharraibh an sleagh,
'S thug iad 'na mìreanaibh as a chéil' i.

Ruith an naigheachd ud mu thuath,
Gu crìoch Lochlainn nam mòr-shluagh;
'S chaidh an Gobhainn leis a' bhrìgh,
Gu teach aobhair an Àrd-Rìgh.
"Rinneadh beud," deir Gobhainn-nan-Cuan,
"Mharbhadh a' Mhuileartach ruadh."
"Mur do shluig an talamh-toll i,
No mur do bhàth muir leathan lom i,
C'àit' an robh do dhaoin' air domhan,
Na mharbhadh a' Mhuileartach mhuing-fhionn?"
"Thuit a' Mhuileartach leis an Fhiann,
A' bhuidheann leis nach gabh-te fiamh.
Cha tig fuath no atharrach as,
Air an t-sluagh àluinn, fhalt-bhuidhe, chas."
"Bheiream-sa briathra a rìs,
Ma mharbhadh a' Mhuileartach mhìn,
Nach fàg mi'n Éirinn àigh
Tom, innis, no cilean,
Nach tog mi ann an crannagaibh mo long,
Éirinn coranta, co-throm;
Mar deanadh i breabanaich air muir,
'Ga togail as a tonna-bhalla,
Cròcain chroma ri tìr,
'Ga tarruing as a tàdhaibh."
"Is mòr an luchd loingeis, a Mhànuis,
'Thogadh còigeamh a dh'Éirinn,

'S cha'n'eil do loingeis air sàile,
Na thogadh còigeamh a dh'Eirinn."
  Ochd agus ochd fichead long
  Thogadar a dh'fheachd 's bu trom,
  Thoirt a mach éirig a' Mhuileartaich.[20]

. . . .

  Chaidh iad air tìr an cala Beinn-Eadainn.* Chaidh Fearghus mùirneach mac Mòirne air theachdaireachd 'gan ionnsuidh; thairg e dhoibh cumha gun fheall, 's iad a thilleadh an taobh a thàinig iad.

  Thairg e dhoibh ochd ciad bratach,[21]
  Caoin-daithte, agus lùireach;
  Ochd ciad conair mheangain;[22]
  Ochd ciad mean do ionndrainn;
  Ochd ciad gearr-fhaltach, gruaidh-dhearg;
  Ochd ciad làn clogaid de'n òr dhearg;
Ged gheibheadh iad sin, cha tilleadh iad gus am faigheadh iad—
  Ceann Oscair, Oisein, 's Fhinn,
  Ghoill, agus Choirill.

. . . .

  "Gearraidh sibh 'ur teann-leum thar muir,
  Ar neò fanaidh sibh ri'r n-aimhleas;
  An long a 's mò a thug sibh thar muir,
  Le goinealadh,
  Ma tha a dh'fhuil 'n'ur collainnibh,
  Snàmhaidh i air 'ur dromannaibh."
Sin 'nuair a thug iad an latha mòr agus ro-mhòr—
  Latha catha Beinn-Eadainn,
  Far am bu lìonar ceann 'ga chromadh,
  Agus muineal 'ga mhaoladh.
  Cha deachaidh aon riamh as,
  Ach leth-chiad fear,
  'Chaidh mar thriall srutha gu sùil',
  'S gaoir-chatha 'gan iomain.

  [Sin dar a thug a' Chailleach bu mhòr fearg
  Breab o dh'ionnsuidh na còmhla,
  'S bhrist i na naoi ceanglaichean a sìos
  Mu'n deachaidh stad air a teann-ruith;

  * Beinn-Eadair.

'S chaidh i stigh do mhùr Fhinn,
'S rug i air cuach Fhinn 'na croma-chròig.
Leum i air eas ruadh nan ràmh,
'S cuach Fhinn na deas làimh.
Leum Fionn gu cas, cas,
An déigh chas na Caillich
'S rug e air a' chuaich
O'n 's ann leis 'bha 'buaidh 's a brìgh.
Rug Caoilte Mac Ròin
Air a chlaidheamh mòr 's a dhà shleagh ;
'S rug an t-Oscar meamnach òg
Air an léine shròil a bha mu cneas.
Thug iad an t-ubhal o'n bhéist ;
'S ma thug cha b' ann gun streup ;
'S mar deachaidh an ceann air colluinn eile,
Cha d'fhuair a h-anam riamh tròcair.
B' àrd a h-ionad, 's b' ard a fàs,
B' àrd a cuid siùil ri h-aois,
Geamhlag iaruinn fo 'màs,
'S da fhiacail siar o 'craos ;
Leithid na ciaraig chaillich,
Cha'n fhacas o linn Chuchullin].*

TALE OF THE MUILEARTACH (WESTERN SEA).
[TRANSLATED.]
PART I.

THE Fians were for keeping the kingdom from the Lochlinners. Fin was their king. There was a battle between them and Manus at Dun Kincorry in Ireland. When Manus went home, his foster-mother (nurse), the *Muileartach*, said that she would go to fight Fin, and to take from him the " Cup of Victory "—a vessel of clay, of which it was said that it was by drinking from it, the Fians were always victorious. Manus said he would send men with her, but she refused. She would take with her only her husband, the Ocean Smith, and a loop of iron, called the Little Ridged Crutch. She went at full speed to Dun Kincorry. The Fians saw something big and monstrous coming; and Fin said, " If he has traversed the universe, and gone round the world, it is Manus's foster-mother,

* See p. 119, 6th stanza, and p. 137, last Note.

and she wants something particular." The Fians went into the house and nine times nine of them put their backs to the door, and put behind it nine chains interlacing each other. (She pulled a tree, and swept off the branches, and had it for a stick. The Ocean Smith stayed at the boat. They put nine wooden bars behind the door, and nine feet in stone and lime, and nine times nine put their backs to the door.)

Fin was looking out, and she came and spoke in a low voice:—

She.
I am a poor, poor old woman,
That have come hotly pursued;
I have travelled the five-fifths of Ireland,
And found not a house to let me in.

Fin.
If you have travelled all that,
It is the mark of a bad man;
And though your claw grow green beneath you,
You will not get an opening from me.

She.
That is an evil custom for a king's son,
Who ought to show heroism and great deeds;
That you should be called a king's son,
And not give a night's lodgings to an old woman.

Fin.
If it be manners, or meat, or hospitality
You want, old woman!
I will send the meat of a hundred men,
And take away from me your talk, old woman!

She.
I am not in need of your wretched meat,
Neither do I care for your great sadness;
I would prefer the warmth of your great fire,
And partake with your dogs.

Fin.
Will you not kindle a fire for yourself,
Where you can blow it with your breath;
And put a load of fuel to your stout body,
[*Var.*—Break down small branches against your hump]
And wisely warm yourself at it?

She.

The six best heroes among the Fians,
Put you them out on the sward;
And when the snow reaches their waist,
They cannot kindle a fire.

[*Var.*—The nine nines who are within,
Between thatch and wattled-wall—
The snow would reach their waist-bands,
And they could not kindle a fire.]

The old woman of hardest conflict,
Gave a kick towards the door;
And before she turned back the sole of her foot,
She broke the nine chains of iron from their interlacings.
[And she threw the heroes on the breadth of their backs
on the floor.]

Fin avoided her way; and she went to the chest of jewels, and took with her the "Cup of Victory."

The men arose—
Thinman[7] rose, and the rest rose,
And rose the plier of the oars,[8]

to go after the old woman.

They could not overtake her. Oscar, the strongest of the Fians, went after her. He caught her by the foot at the brow of the hill of Howth. Her grey hair was hanging behind her, and Oscar caught it. He sprang, and put three plies of the grey wreathed hair of the old woman about his fist. Before he in any way checked her (lit., put a wrinkle in her), they sank to their waists in snow. "Ho, ho," she said, "young man, you have hurt me! If it be food or drink you want, you will get it when I reach the boat." [Al., reach the Ocean Smith and you will get it.] "It is not that I want, but to take your grey hair to my grandfather." "Ho, ho, are you one of that sort?" She drew over her wreathed grey hair below her left arm, and she laid her hand gently upon him; and he himself heard the noise of every bone. "If you have strength to go home, tell Fin that I have got the 'Cup of Victory.'"

He returned, and she went to Lochlin. Manus resolved to fight Fin. He gathered his men, and went to Dun Kincorry to fight Fin.

They met, and commenced at each other. All the Lochlinners were killed, and the "Cup of Victory" was recovered. Manus was bound, and put under oaths. It was then that Conan[10] said—

"Let me to Manus of the swords,
That I may separate his head from his body."

Manus then said—"

"A little blow against thee, Fin,
I repent me of what I have done to you."

He went home bare and empty handed. His foster-mother asked for his men; and he said they were lost. "King!" she said, "that ever I gave the juice of my side to you when you could not kill Fin, seeing he is only a halfman" (*i.e.* one of twins).[12] "I shall go now; and as many men as you have lost I shall take from the Fians in twenty-four hours." "I shall raise," said Manus, "my ships and go with you." She would not hear of this, but that the Smith should go with her. He was good at telling stories, and would tell everything to Manus, when they came home. The Smith was not willing to go, though he had only heard of Fin; but she caught him, and threw him into the boat. They took their sea journey. A little gentle breeze came after them from the lower part of the hills and from the heights of the trees, that would take foliage from a hill, and willows from a tree, and little young rushes from their base and roots. They began to throw the sea aside, flashing, flapping, foaming, against the blackness of the old stone, and the pitch-blackness of the boulder stones, the biggest beast eating the smallest beast, and the smallest beast doing as best it could; the little sea-birds betaking themselves to rest and shelter in the wisp of the main-mast. She (the boat) would cut the hard slender stalks of oats with her very stem, for the great excellency of her steersman.[13] "Look up," she said to the Ocean Smith, "and try and see land." When he looked all round about him, he saw land and said, "If it be land it is small, and if it be a crow it is large." "That is true, my good fellow," she said, "we have not the boat at its proper speed." They put out the small broad-bladed, ridged oars, and every time they stretched their backs, they took in water over the gunwale of the boat. For all the evils and tossings they got, they reached land and drew up the boat above the beach (lit. "in the top of the shore"), where the boys of the town could not make sport or

laughing-stock of it. She bade the Ocean Smith go behind a
hillock at the back of the wind and in front of the sun, where he
could see everybody and nobody could see him.¹⁴ He did this,
and she went on. Unfortunately, the Fians were sleeping on their
arms, and twenty-four of them were on their breasts. She began
to kill them with the iron loop.

> "She killed twenty-four of the Fians,
> Alvinn himself foremost
> Fell by the hand of the great Conflict,
> Before the warriors came to close quarters."

Then commenced the Fians and the Carlin wife, and were thrash-
ing and slashing and working away at one another. She was intercepting them like a flame down and up. She was tall. Oscar
asked to be sent himself against her, and she was heavily
buffetting him, and driving him backwards; and Fin's courage fell.
He told them to take spades and cut below her, and drive her
backwards to get a chance of engaging and striking her. They
made a hole and drove her back, until she fell in. She was still
intercepting them like a flame; but for all the evils and tossings they
got, they killed the old woman before they stopped. It was then
they raised a battle-shout for joy; and then twenty-four of the
Fians, who were in Corry Glen, when they heard it, knew that
some trouble had come on the Fians. They rushed over, and one
of them said to a companion, "King! wilt thou not thyself tell me
how she was when she was on her legs?"

"I am not able to tell that to any but to one who saw her."

[This is the proper place for the lay of the Muileartach.]
> A day we were on Eastern hillock,
> Looking on Erin all around,
> There came upon us over a slimy heavy sea,
> A spectre[16] heavy and not grey;
> Two teeth protruding westward from her gaping mouth,
> And four fathoms from around her lower part.
> Twenty-four of the Fians,
> And Alvin himself foremost,
> Fell by the hand of the great Brawler
> Before the people closed.[17]
> Then spoke Goll,
> The hero who was never behind—

"Let me towards her for a while,
That I may shew her a feat of strength."

The old woman was tearing at him and driving him backwards; and Fin lost courage at that time. It was then that he ordered them to cut the earth below her sole, and to let her to the place of her girdle into the ground. She was intercepting us down and up, like a flame; but for all the evils and tossings we got, it was then we killed the old woman and raised the battle-shout.

When the Ocean Smith, who was behind the wind and in front of the sun, heard that the *Muileartach* had been slain, he put out to sea [here repeat the rhymes descriptive of sea journeys] and reached Lochlin alone. Manus met him, and asked where he had left the old woman. "She has been killed," said the Ocean Smith.

"Wretch, she has not been killed; but when you saw the doughty deeds she was doing, you fled."

"Oh, she has been killed!"

"Hole of earth has not swallowed her, nor has she been drowned on brown slippery sea, and there were not people in the univefse who could kill my *Muileartach*."

"No one slew her but the Fians, the people who were never overcome; and never one has escaped from the people of the yellow wreathed hair."

Thus the Old Woman finished her journey.

Part II.

A day the Fians were on an Eastern knoll [18]
Gazing at Erin all around,
There was seen coming over the waves
A hideous apparition—a heavily rocking object.[19]
The name of the dauntless spectre
Was the bald-red white-maned *Muileartach*.
Her face was dark grey, of the hue of coals,
The teeth of her jaw were slanting red,
There was one flabby eye in her head,
That quicker moved than lure-pursuing mackerel.
Her head bristled dark and grey,
Like scrubwood before hoar frost.
When she saw the Fians of highest prowess,
The wretch coveted being in their midst.

At the outset of fury and slaughter,
She performed an over-keen thankless deed;
She slew in her frolic a hundred heroes,
While loud laughter was in her rough mouth.

. . . .

You will lose the forelock of your scrubby head,
In lieu of having asked for Oisian's goodly son.

. . . .

They offered her compensation, if she would turn back the way she came. She would not take all the valuable jewels in Ireland till she would get—

The heads of Oscar, Oisian, and Fin,
Goll, and Corral.

. . . .

They made an enclosure for the great fight,
Lest the apparition on the field should change.
The four best heroes among the Fians,
She would combat them all together,
And attend them each by turns,
Like the shimmering beam of a flame.
Mac-Coul of good fortune met
The wretch, hand to hand.
Her flank was exposed to the violence of the blows,
And there were drops of his blood on the heath tops.
The *Muileartach* fell by Fin,
If she did, it was not without strife;
A trial like this he did not get
Since the day of Lon MacLioven's smithy,
They lifted the Old Woman on the point of their spears,
And tore her asunder in pieces.

The tale ran northwards
To the borders of Lochlin of many people;
And the Smith went with its purport
To the palace of the High King.
"A mischief has been done," said the Ocean Smith,
"The red *Muileartach*[20] has been killed."
"If the porous earth has not swallowed her,
Or the broad bare sea drowned her,
Where were the people in the universe
Who could slay the white-maned *Muileartach?*"

"The *Muileartach* fell by the Fians,
The company that never was touched with fear;
Nor hatred nor change comes
On the comely people of yellow wreathed hair."
" I will give words again,
If the smooth *Muileartach* has been killed,
That I will not leave in Fair Erin
Hillock, place of shelter, or island,
That I will not lift in the cross-trees of my ships,
Erin fairly-balanced, full weight;
If it does not take to kicking at sea
When it is being lifted from its sea-walls,
I shall put crooked hooks into the land,
To draw it from its fastenings."
" Numerous are the shipmen, O Manus!
That could lift the fifth-part of Erin;
And there are not as many ships on salt water
As would lift a fifth-part of Erin."
Eight and eight-score ships,
Were raised of forces, and they were numerous,
To raise the ransom of the *Muileartach*.

. . . .

They went ashore at the harbour of the Hill of Howth. The well-beloved Fergus, the son of Morna, went on a message to them; he offered them satisfactory indemnity [21] if they would return the way they came.

He offered them eight hundred banners
Beautifully coloured, and war-dresses;
Eight hundred dogs on leashes (?); [22]
Eight hundred close searchers (?);
Eight hundred short-haired, red-cheeked men;
Eight hundred helmets-full of red gold,
Although they got that, they would not return till they
    got
The head of Oscar, Oisian, and Fin,
Goll, and Corral.

. . . .

" You will betake yourselves smartly across the sea,
Or remain to your hurt.
The biggest ship you have taken across the sea,

With winds hard blowing,
If there be as much blood in your bodies,
It will swim on your backs."

Then fought they the great day, and very great day—the day of the battle of the Hill of Howth,

Where many a head was lowered,
And neck was rendered bare.
Not a single man escaped
But half a hundred men,
That went like the current of a stream seaward,
With the battle-shout driving them.

[Then when the old woman of great fury
Gave a kick to the door,
She broke the nine fastenings
Before her full speed was checked;
And she entered the dwelling of Fin
And caught Fin's Cup in her crooked claw.
She leapt upon the red rushing water of the oars,
With Fin's Cup in her right hand.
Fin leapt quick, quick,
After the feet of the old woman,
And caught the Cup,
Since to him belonged its Virtue and Power.
Thinman,[23] son of Roin, caught
His big sword and his two spears;
And the active, youthful Oscar caught
The embroidered skirt that was round her body.
They took the apple from the wretch;
And if they did, it was not without a struggle:
And if her head was not put on another body,
Her soul never obtained mercy.
High was her place, and high her growth,
High were her sails for age,[24] (?)
An iron crowbar under her,
And two teeth westward from her open mouth;
Such a darksome old woman
Was not seen since the days of Cu-chullain."] *

* See p. 128, 3rd stanza, and p. 137, last note.

NOTES.

1. Reciters are not agreed as to this being the purpose for which the Fians were. Some (and this is the most rational of the realistic explanations) say they were a body of hunters that followed the chase both in Ireland and Scotland. As to their having a separate kingdom, tradition makes no mention.

2. More correctly "Cup of Virtues," or precious cup.

3. *Caogad* is explained in dictionaries as meaning fifty. It was explained by the person from whom this portion within brackets was heard, that the number who put their backs to the door was nine times nine; and there are other confirmations of an explanation heard from an old man, chat *taogad* was used to signify nine days or times.

4. In the twelfth century, Ireland was divided into five kingdoms—Ulster (*Còige-ulainn*), Leinster (*Còige-Laighinn*), Meath (*Mith*), Connaught (*Conach*) and Munster (*Còige-Mumha*). The rulers of these divisions were styled kings; and over all was the one called the "High King of Ireland," *Ard righ Eirinn*. Cairbre, who slew Oscar, was one of these; and Fin's own genealogy is traced up to the same royal line.

5. The common form is *uile*, but the various reciters said *uilidh*. This may have been merely the attraction of the emphasis. At all events not much weight is to be placed upon the peculiarity.

6. The usual phrase is *bonn-dubh*, "the black sole," which is explained to be the heel.

7. *Caoilte* (Thinman) was called *Daorghlas* (Thorough-grey) till the day when the swords of the Fian chiefs were made in the magic smithy of Lon MacLiovnn, of which there is an account in a separate ballad.

8. This expression is noticeable, as a reference to its being a sea fight. There does not seem to have been any one in particular of the Fian band to whom this post was assigned.

9. This sentence, and the others within brackets, are from other oral versions.

10. *Conan* was the crossest of the Fians, and is said, in popular lore, not to have been worth anything till he got over the first disgrace. Any one, even a woman, could overcome him at first; but after that he was as good as another man; and there was a man's death on his hands if he struck. ("*Bha bàs duine air a dhòrn nam buaileadh e.*") He never saw a door open but he thought he should enter; and he never saw a man frown but he thought he ought to strike him. When he went to hell, he gave "blow for blow and scratch for scratch." (*Buille air son buille agus sgrìobadh air son sgrìobadh.*) The evil spirits could not tolerate him.

11. There is a much longer poem about this incident.

12. Fin's mother was the daughter of the Ulster smith (*An gobhainn Ultach*), and the ugliest woman in all Ireland. His twin sister was Diarmid's mother.

13. *Stiùramaiche*, in the Hebrides, denotes the steersman of a particular boat, *stiùradair* a steersman generally.

14. Rhymes or "runs" (*ruitheannan*), such as this and those preceding, in the description of the sea-journey, are common in Gaelic Tales, and are made use of by the reciter on every suitable occasion. They are more or less full, according to the skill of the reciter.

15. The version which the reciter himself gave, is evidently very much fallen to pieces. It is bald in Gaelic, and much more so in English. Translations, at the best, have not the "taste" (*blas*) of the original.

16. This word and *Arracht*, which is used by other reciters, is most probably from *athar* (the air), and merely denotes an aerial phenomenon.

17. This is a piece taken unconsciously by the reciter from another Fian ballad, called Ailvinn or Iorghuin.

18. In various printed versions of the tale, this hillock is called *tulaich oirill*, which may be correct.

19. The meaning of this line is not very clear; and it is a mere matter of inference from the sound and collocation of the letters, that they denote some monstrous, lumbering, heavy-moving object, rocking from side to side.

20. This word, like some others, is conventionally used both in a masculine and feminine form.

21. Other versions, such as that given by Mr. Campbell in his West Highland Tales, vol. iii., 135, make the indemnity ten hundred instead of eight hundred of each article. They all agree in making fine-coloured flags, and dogs, and gold, part of the ransom.

22. *Conair mheangain*, is most probably *coin air mheangain* (dogs on branches), *i.e.*, on withes, or leashes, a most valuable ransom in the days of the Irish wolf-hounds and stag-hounds. In the Long Island, among the Roman Catholic population, a rosary is called *Conair Mhoire*, the beads of S. Mary. *Meangain* is the designation of a certain kind of heather (*fraoch meangain*), and universally in the Highlands, *meangan* means a branch, so that the expression may denote some kind of bead. In early times, before the days of coinage, and to the present day among savage tribes, beads are valuable as a circulating medium, and as personal ornaments.

In regard to "close" searchers, the existence of *fiondruine* as a name of a metal renders it highly probable that a tribute of it was here meant. The reciter did not know the meaning of the words, though, as in other instances of popular recitation, the sound of the correct words is retained.

In the Island of Tiree, pins or small skewers—of some composite metal resembling bronze—about three inches in length, are occasionally found. They are called by the natives, *Prine fionndrainn*.

The "close" searchers may be the smaller dogs.

The short haired men are doubtlessly slaves or bondsmen, long hair being much affected by Chiefs.

23. Thinman (Caoilte) is more commonly called Mac Rònain. He was the weakest, but the fastest of the Fian band.

By reference to Leabhar na Féinne and Popular Tales, and my manuscripts it will be seen that this orally collected version is a jumble of a whole series of heroic ballads written down long ago

[handwritten margin note top: in scraps, and recited in fragments in the West. The stuff is the foundation of many MacPhersons]

[handwritten margin note right: Fingal — My friend the Minister did his best, and did well.]

24. The meaning of the word age (aois) is not evident.

25. In tradition Cuchulin is not mentioned in connection with the Fians. The lays about himself or his chariot are different from anything to be found in Macpherson.

With our explanation, in our introductory remarks, of this tale as a myth, descriptive of a contest between the Sea violently invading the Land, and Human Might, will fall to be compared an anecdote frequently met with, also further illustrative of the popular view of the Fians as the representatives of bodily strength. One of the Fians (aon de'n Fhéinn), looking at the sea breaking in foam, was told that it was laughing at him. He was for rushing out to chastise it.

The idea of personification is, however, entirely lost sight of by reciters, and it belongs to the poet's skill that, while his words are singularly descriptive of the angry Sea, such should be the case. The last lines, enclosed within brackets, written down in 1870, from the dictation of James Cameron, a native of Morven resident in Coll, is illustrative of this, and of the manner in which modern ideas become involved with old tradition.

JOHN G. CAMPBELL.

The Manse, Tiree.

NOTES ON THE TUAIRISGEUL MÒR.

No. 1, p. 61.

THIS curious and valuable tale consists of two distinct stories—the one dealing with the adventures of the hero in search of the Tuairisgeul Mòr, the other being the recital of the old man. The first belongs to what may be called the "task" group of Märchen, in which the fulfilment by the hero of a given task is the main incident; the second to the "calumniated wife" group. The connection between the two is very well managed, and the whole tale is of the greatest interest. The opening incident is especially Celtic in character; the hill upon which the hero goes to hunt may be compared to that upon which Pwyll, Prince of Dyfed, walks, and to which it is peculiar "that whoever sits upon it cannot go thence without either receiving wounds or blows, or else seeing a wonder" (*Mabinogion*, p. 344). The same magic hill appears in *Campbell*, 38; *Murachaidh MacBrian;* and in *Connala of the Golden Hair; Joyce, Celtic Romances*, No. 4. In each case the hill is haunted by a supernatural maiden of great beauty; in the Mabinogi, as in our story, she is on horseback; in Joyce and Campbell on foot apparently, but unaccompanied in all three versions. The coming of the magician out of a shower from the west may be compared to the opening of *Campbell*, 52, *The*

Knight of the Red Shield, where the king, *seated upon a hillock*, sees the "shadow of shower coming from the western airt, and the rider of a black filly coming cheerily after it." The gambling between the magician and the hero takes the same course as in *Campbell, No. 1, The Young King of Esaidh Ruadh*. There, as here, the prince wins twice and loses the third time, takes the woman as his first stake, and, by her advice, the horse as his second. In Campbell, however, the hero is helped by a "scanagal," and the woman does not instruct him beforehand how he may guard against the magician's winning the third time. In the Y. King of E. R. the magician lays it as crosses and as spells upon him that he get the Glaive of light. Our story is here more like *Campbell, No. 46, MacIain Direach* (the best and fullest task märchen in Campbell's collection); the terms of the spell, "I am setting it as crosses and as spells, and as the decay of the year on thee; that thou be not without a pool in thy shoe," etc. are almost the same, and in both stories the hero foils his adversary by forcing him to remain on the same spot until the task be accomplished. The referring of the hero to three brothers is perhaps the commonest incident in the "task" series: it appears, though in different form, in the oldest task story known, that of Perseus, where the hero must seek aid and counsel from the Graiai and the Hesperides. In the Norse tale of *East o' the Sun and West o' the Moon*, the three brothers are the winds. In French folk-tale the brothers, or brother, are almost invariably hermits, as, for instance, in *Luzel, Veillées Bretonnes, No. 1, La Princesse Blondine*. The hero then starts off upon the steed he had won from the magician. In many task stories it is noticeable that the hero acts entirely under the advice and aid of his horse, as, for instance, in the Norse Dapplegrim, in *Luzel, Veillées Bretonnes, No. 4, Petit Louis*. This is not the case in our story, where the horse plays a comparatively small part. The adventure at the houses of the three squires is, I believe, not found in any variant. The curious method by which the hero is to strengthen his steed before passing the loch is found likewise in *Campbell, 51, The Fair Gruagach*, in which the hero, transformed into a brown ambler, carries Fionn to the house of the Tree Lion, and requires three wheaten loaves, three stoups of wine, and to be combed against and with the hair before scaling the fortress of the Tree Lion. Common likewise in folk-tales is the advice given to the hero not to take gold or silver, but some seemingly worthless person or object in exchange for the steed. Thus, in *Campbell, No.* 1, the young king is to take no fair woman, but the "cropped, rough-skinned maid." The bargain, too, is no fair one, as the hero keeps the bridle, which, being shaken, brings back the steed. This may be compared to *Campbell, No.* 46, where the "Gille Martean" takes the shape of the persons or objects promised by the hero to those who had spared his life, but speedily returns to his master. In *Grimm's No.* 68, *Der Gaudeif*, the hero turns himself into a hound, is sold for a large sum of money by his father, to whom he comes back upon the first occasion. Compare, likewise, *Der Hasenhirt, Wolf, Deutsche Hausmärchen*, p. 134, where the hero sells the hare, but immediately recalls him with his magic whistle. Of frequent occurrence, too, is the injunction laid on the hero to do the contrary of what he is told. Thus, in Pwyll, Prince of Dyfed, Arawn directs Pwyll not to strike Havgan a second time, however much the latter may entreat him to do so. Cf. also *Ralston, Russian Folk-Tales*, pp. 238, 239. The calumniated wife story told by the old man presents the closest analogies with the third incident in the Mabinogi of Pwyll —a fact of great interest, considering the other points of contact already dwelt upon between the two tales. The opening incident may be compared to *Joyce, No.* 1, *The Fate of the Children of Lir*, in which the wicked step-mother changes her step-children into swans. Wolves are animals of equal importance with the latter in folk-literature, and the traditions of their transformation into men, or *vice versa*, which in the Middle Ages assumed a peculiarly ghastly shape, are very widespread. Cf. *Baring Gould, Curious Myths*, and *Liebrecht Fur Volkskunde*, p. 17. The subject is an obscure and complicated one, upon which little light is thrown by our story. The Persian, Roman, and Teutonic forms of the Aryan Expulsion and Return-Formula may be examined with advantage in this connection, and in particular that portion of the Teutonic Heldensage which deals with the transformation into wolves of Siegmund and Sinfiötli. Another point, which may be of great importance, should be noticed : the transformed sons, unable to take any other revenge, come and kill the hens of their step-mother. Now it is a common incident in folk-tales that a bespelled animal comes by night and ravages the field or the orchard of the hero's or heroine's family (cf., among the countless variants, *Campbell, No.* 41, *Grimm, No.* 66, and *Asbjörnsen and Moe, No.* 31), being eventually released from the spells by the

> *This is a very good note. I don't know the writer but he knows my work & books referred to me in it. J.F.R.*
>
> *Nov 11. 1893 —*

hero's action. The bespelling is not *motivé* in the same way as in our story in any variant that I know. The incident of the three brothers casting lots which should eat the other may be compared with the well-known ballad of the "sea-faring man" (which exists in French as "Le petit navire"). Cf. Folk-Lore Record, vol. iii., part ii., pp. 253 etss. The very unusual form of the calumniated wife story which follows is of the utmost interest owing to close similarity in many details to the Mabinogi of Pwyll, Prince of Dyfed. There, as here, a gigantic hand comes through the roof and carries off, twice running, the new-born foal in the one, the new-born child in the other story. The third time Teirnyon cuts off the monster's arm, taking it off at the elbow, just as the wolf "took the hand off at the shoulder." In the Mabinogi nothing further is told respecting the monster, nor does it actually appear as carrying off Pwyll's child; the latter disappears, however, at the same time as Teirnyon's foal, and certainly by the same agency. The carrying off of St. George, in the English ballad, may perhaps be mentioned in the same connection. The Welsh Gellert story may possibly be related to ours, or at all events have been influenced by a similar version of the calumniated wife. The close agreement between Pwyll and the Highland tale makes it not improbable that a genuine folk-tale, constructed on precisely the same lines as the latter, existed formerly in Wales. As regards the remaining incidents of the story, the magician and the great Tuarisgeul would seem to be identical (perhaps the old man, too, is the same?), the familiar cauldron of renovation appears, and the horse which the hero wins from the magician, and upon which he accomplishes his task, is quite forgotten. As a rule he turns out to be the bespelled brother of the heroine—*e.g.*, in the already quoted *Petit Louis, filleul du roi de France*, in the Irish *Conn-Eda* (Folk-Lore Record, vol. ii. pp. 180 etss), and in the Danish *Mons Tro* (Folk-Lore Record, vol. iii., part ii., pp. 214 etss). The same thing happens to the fox, who, in *Grimm's* 57, *Der Goldene Vogel*, is the helping animal. For variants, see Grimm, vol. iii., p. 98.

ALFRED NUTT.

270 STRAND, LONDON.

[NOTE.—In the introductory remarks to the tale of the *Tuairisgeul Mòr*, in the first number of the *Review*, there is a misprint of Lamhanaich for *Samhanaich*, the giants who dwelt in caves by the sea. It is a common expression to say of any strong offensive smell, *mharbhadh e na Samhanaich*, it would kill the giants who dwell in caves by the sea. *Samh* is a strong oppressive smell, and in the Western islands *Samh a' chuain t-shiar*, the strong smell of the western sea, is a common expression.

It is an addition to the tale that the one who imposed upon the Son of the King of Ireland the task of finding out how the great Tuarisgeul was put to death, and over whose place of decay and disappearance the King's son—by his wife's instructions—recounted, after his long search, the manner of the Giant's death, was himself a son of the Great Tuairisgeul, and that as the story was being told he gradually rose out of the ground. Also, by the wife's instructions, his head was cut off before he got entirely clear of the ground, for then no one could withstand the young Giant's prowess.—J. G. C.]

MIANN A' BHAIRD AOSDA.

(THE AGED BARD'S WISH.)

[Transcribed from Gillies' Collection of Gaelic Poetry, published at Perth in 1786, and compared with the version contained in R. M'Donald's Collection, published at Edinburgh in 1776.]

O ! càiribh mi ri taobh nan allt,
A shiùbhlas mall le ceumaibh ciùin ;
Fo sgàil' a' bharraich leag mo cheann,
'S bi thus', a Ghrian, ro-chàirdeil rium !

Gu socair sìn 'san fheur mo thaobh,
Air bruaich nan dìthean 's nan gaoth tlàth ;
Mo chos 'ga slìobadh 'sa' bhraon mhaoth,
'S e lùbadh thairis caoin tro'n bhlàr.

Biodh sòbhrach bhàn a's àillidh snuadh
Mu'n cuairt do m' thulaich 's uain' fo dhrùchd,
'S an neòinean beag, 's mo làmh fo chluain,
'S an ealbhuidh ri mo chluais gu cùbhr'.

Mu'n cuairt do bhruachaibh àrd' mo ghlinn,
Biodh lùbadh gheug is orra blàth ;
'S clann bheag nam preas a' tabhairt seinn
Air chrengaibh aosd', le h-òrain ghràidh.

Briscadh tre chreig nan eidheann dlùth,
Am fuaran ùr le torrghan trom ;
Is freagradh Mac-talla gach ciùil,
Ri srann-fhuaim sruthadh dlùth nan tonn.

Freagradh gach cnoc agus gach sliabh,
Le binn-fhuaim ghéir nan aighean mear ;
'N sin cluinnidh mise mìle geum,
A' ruith mu'n cuairt dhomh 'n iar 's an ear.

Sruthadh air sgéith na h-osaig mhìn
Glaodhain mhaoth nan crò gu m' chluais,
'N sin freagraidh 'mheanbh-spréidh 'nuair 'chluinn
An giucil, 's iad a' ruith a nuas.

Mu 'n cuairt domh biodh lùth-chleas nan laogh
Ri taobh nan sruth, no air an leirg ;
'S am minnean beag, de'n chòmhrag sgìth,
A' m' achlais a' codal gun cheilg.

O ! ceum an t-sealgair ri mo chluais,
Le srannaibh ghath is chon feadh sléibh ;
'N sin deàrrsaidh 'n òige air mo ghruaidh,
'Nuair 'dh'éireas fuaim air sealg an fhéidh.

Dùisgidh 'n smior a'm' chnàimh 'nuair 'chluinn
Mi tailmrich dhos, is chon, is shreaug ;
'Nuair 'ghlaodhar, "Thuit an damh," tha m' bhuinn
A' leum gu beò ri àird' nam beann.

An sin chi mi, ar leam, an gadhar
A leanadh mi anmoch is moch,
'S na sléibh 'ba mhiann leam bhi tadhall,
'S na creagan a fhreagradh do'n dos.

Chi mi 'n uaimh a ghabh gu fial
'S gu tric ar ceuma o'n oidhche,
'Dhùisgeadh ar sunnd le blàth's a crann,
'S 'na sòlas chuach bha mòr aoibhneas.

Bhiodh ceò air lleadh a bhàrr an fhéidh,
Ar deoch a Tréig, 's an tonn ar ceol ;
Ged sheinneadh tà'isg, 's ged rànadh sléibh,
Sìnte 'san uaimh bu shèimh ar neòil.

Chi mi Beinn-àrd a's àillidh sniamh,
Ceann-feadhna nam mìle beann ;

Bha aisling nan damh 'na ciabh,
'S i leabaidh nan nial a ceann.
Chi mi Sgur-Eilt air bruaich a' ghlinn'
'San gair a' chuach gu binn an tòs,
Is Gorm-mheall àilt nam mìle giùs,
Nan luibh, nan earba, is nan lon.

[1] Biodh tuinn òg' a' snàmh le sunnd
Thar linne 's mìne giùs [2] gu luath ;
Srath ghiubhais [2] uaine air a ceann,
Is lùbadh chaoran dearg air bruaich.

Bidh nighean àlainn an uchd bhàin,
A' snàmh le spreigh air bhàrr nan tonn ;
'Nuair thogas i a sgiath an àird'
A measg nan nial, cha 'n fhàs i trom.

'Stric i ag astar thar a' chuan
Gu aisridh fhuair nan ioma ronn,
Anns nach togar bréid ri crann,
'S nach do reub sròn dharaich [3] tonn.

Bidh tusa ri dosan nan tom,
Le cumha [trom] do ghaoil a'd' bheul,
Eala, 'thriall o thìr nan tonn,
'S tu seinn domh ciùil an àird' nan speur.

Cò an tìr o'n d' ghluais a' ghaoth,
'Tha giùlan glaoidh do bhròin o'n chraig,
Oigfhir, a chaidh uainn a thriall,
'S a dh' fhàg mo chiabha glas' gun taic ?

Bh-'eil deòir do roisg mu thùs na rìoghain,
A's mìne mais', 's a's gile làmh ?
Sòlas gun chrìch do'n ghruaidh mhaoith,
A chaoidh nach pill o'n leabaidh chaoil.

---

[1] After the 15th stanza the following lines are given in Ronald M'Donald's Collection :—
Chi mi Loch Eilein nan craobh,
'S au caoran air lùbadh thar tuinn,

[2] The ancient spelling is *giús*. In the third line of this stanza, where the word is dissyllabic, we have given the modern orthography, *giubhas*, gen. *giubhais*.

[3] The correct form of the genitive is *darach*, nom. *dair* (oak), a *c*-stem ; but *daraich* is now more commonly used.

O! éirich thus' le t'òran ciùin,
'S cuir naidheachd bhochd do bhròin an céill;
'S glacadh Mac-talla gach ciùil
An guth tùrsa sin o d' bheul.

Tog do sgiath gu h-àrd thar chuan,
Glac do luath's o neart na gaoith;
Is éibhinn ann mo chluais an fhuaim,
O d' chridhe leòint'—an t'òran gaoil.

Innsibh, o'n thréig mo shùil a' ghaoth,
C'àit 'bh-'eil a' chuile a' gabhail tàmh,
Le glaodhan bròin, 's na bric r'a taobh,
Le sgiath gun deò a' cumail blàir.

'Togaibh 's càiribh mi le'r làimh,
'S cuiribh mo cheann fo bharrach ùr;
An uair 'dh'éireas a' ghrian gu h-àrd,
Biodh a sgiath uain' os ceann mo shùl.

An sin thig thusa, aisling chiùin,
'Tha 'g astar dlùth measg reul na h-oidhch';
Biodh gnìomh m' oidhche ann do cheòl,
Is thoir aimsir mo mhùirn gu m' chuimhn'.

O m'anam! faic an rìoghain òg
Fo sgéith an daraich, rìgh nam blàth,
'S a sneachd-làmh measg a ciabhan òir,
'S a meall-shùil chiùin air òg a gràidh.

Esan a' seinn r'a taobh 's i balbh,
Le 'cridhe leum, 's a' snàmh 'na cheòl,
An gaol o shùil gu sùil a' falbh,
Cur stad air féidh nan sléibhte mòr.

Nis thréig an fhuaim, 's tha 'cliabh mìn-gheal
Ri uchd 's ri crìdh' a gaoil a' fàs;
'S a bilibh ùr mar ròs gun smal,
Mu bheul a gaoil gu dlùth an sàs.

Sòlas gun chrìch do'n chomunn chaomh,
A dhùisg dhomh 'n t-aoibhneas ait nach pill;
'S beannachd do t'anam-sa, a rùin,
A nighean chiùin nan cuach-chiabh griun.

'N do thréig thu mi, aisling nam buadh?
Pill fathast, aon uair eile, pill;

Cha chluinn thu mi, Ochoin! 's mi truagh!
A bheannta uain' mo ghràidh, slàn leibh!

Slàn le comunn caomh na h-òige!
Is oigheanna bòidheach, slàn leibh!
Cha lèir dhomh sibh; dhuibhse ta sòlas
Sàmhraidh, ach dhomhs' ta geamhradh chaoidh.¹

O cuir mo chluas ri fuaim Eas-mòir,
Le 'chrònan a' teàrnadh o'n chraig;
. . . .
. . . .

Thig thus' le d' chàirdeas thar a chuan.
Osag mhìn, a ghluais gu mall;
T'og mo cheò air sgèith do luaith's,
Is imich grad gu eilean fhlaith's,

Far 'bh-'eil na laoich a dh' fhalbh o shean,
An codal trom, 'nan dol le ceòl—
. . . .
. . . .

Biodh cruit is slige làn ri m' thaobh
'S an sgiath a dhìon mo shinnsr' 'sa' chath:
Fosglaibhs'! thalla Oiscin 's Dhaoil!
Thig 'n oidhche 's cha bhi'm bard air bhrath.

Ach O! mu'n tig i, seal mu'n triall mo cheò
Gu teach nam bard air Àrd-bheinn as nach pill,
Thugaibh dhomh cruit 's mo shlige dh' ionnsuidh 'n ròid
An sin mo chruit 's mo shlige ghràidh, slàn leibh!

THE WISH OF THE AGED BARD.
Translated by the REV. DR. HUGH MACMILLAN.

Oh! bear me where the streamlets stray,
   With calm slow footsteps o'er the lea;
My head beneath the birch-shade lay,
   And thou, oh! sun, be kind to me!

---

¹ After this verse, the following is given in Ronald M'Donald's Collection:
    O! cuiribh mi ri gréin tràth-nòin,
    Fo'n bharrach aig siubhal an lòin;
    'S air an t-seamraig 's anns an neoinein
    'N tig aisling na h-òige a'm' chòir.

K

My side stretch gently on the bank,
  Which soft winds cool and flowers bestrew
My feet laved by the grasses rank,
  That bend beneath the noontide dew.

Let primrose pale with beauty dress
  My couch, through scent of waters green
My hand reclined the daisy press,
  And *ealvi*[1] at my ear be seen.

Let blossom-laden trees surround
  My glen's high overhanging brow;
And let the aged crags resound
  With songs of birds from every bough.

From cliffs with ivy mantled o'er,
  Let fountains pour their copious flood,
And echo multiply the roar
  Of waters through the solitude.

Let voice of hill to hill repeat
  The thousand lowings of the herd,
That by the rural cadence sweet,
  My heart's deep pulses may be stirred.

Let the soft wing of every gale
  The bleatings of the fold prolong,
The timid lambkin's lonely wail,
  The ewe's quick answer to her young.

Let frisking calves around me stray
  Along the stream, or upland high;
And let the kid, tired of its play,
  Upon my bosom fearless lie.

Oh! let me hear the hunter's tread
  And bay of dogs upon the heath;
Then youth shall crown my hoary head,
  And happy visions round me wreathe.

The marrow of my bones shall thrill,
  When the wild chase I hear again;
My feet leap swiftly up the hill
  At the glad shout, "The stag is slain!"

[1] St. John's Wort.

Methinks I see the faithful hound
    That followed me at eve and morn,
The moors o'er which I loved to bound,
    The rocks that echoed back my horn,

The cave where we reposed, when night
    O'ertook us in our wild employ,
Where by the wood-fire blazing bright,
    The hunter's cup inspired our joy.

The smoking deer, Treig's sounding wave,
    Gave food and music for our feast;
And in that cave, though ghosts should rave,
    And mountains roar, deep was our rest.

I see Ben-Ard's sky-piercing rocks
    Above a thousand mountains rise;
The dreams of stags are in his locks,
    The dark cloud on his summit lies.

Scur-Eilt's broad shoulders loom in view,
    And the green hill with fir trees crowned,
Where first is heard the lone cuckoo,
    And elk and roe unharmed abound.

A pine-fringed tarn lies in its cup,
    O'er which the wild ducks swiftly swim;
Beyond, a dark strath[1] opens up,
    With rowans dipping in its stream.

Oh! let the swan that left her home
    In that cold realm where tempests rave,
Where never sail can mock the foam,
    Or oaken prow divide the wave—

Glide graceful o'er the loch at rest,
    Or soar the summer clouds among,
And pour forth from her wounded breast
    The mournful music of her song!

I love to hear the plaintive wail,
    That tells the story of her woe,
Borne by the echoes on the gale,
    In soothing sadness round me flow.

---

[1] In the original the phrase means "strath of dark green firs," but, as the same epithet is used in the previous verse, I have altered it to avoid repetition.

From what land do the breezes stray
   On which thy sorrow's voice is borne,
Oh! youth that wandered far away,
   And left my hoary locks forlorn?

Do tears bedim thy modest eyes,
   Oh! maiden with the hand of snow?
Blest is the smooth young cheek that lies
   Within its narrow bed laid low!

Say, since my aged vision fails,
   Oh! wind, where is the reed's resort,
Through which an eerie music wails,
   And by whose side the fishes sport?

Oh! raise me with a tender hand,
   And place me 'neath the birken shade,
That when the sun at noon shall stand,
   Its green shield may be o'er my head.

Then shalt thou come, oh! starry dream,
   That glidest through the realms of night,
And bring to me a soothing gleam
   Of vanished days of joy and light!

My soul, the lovely maid behold,
   Within the shady oaken grove,
Her white hand 'mid her locks of gold,
   Her blue eye on her youthful love!

He sings most sweetly by her side,
   And scarce her lips draw in the breath;
Her heart swims in the music's tide,
   And deer stop listening on the heath.

'Tis hushed now, and her smooth white breast
   Heaves to her love's in rapturous bliss;
Her rosy lips are closely pressed
   To his in one long honied kiss.

Oh! be ye happy, lovely pair!
   Who've wakened in my soul a gleam
Of joy that I no more may share;
   May love forever round you beam!

Oh! pleasant dream! hast thou thus gone?
   Come back; let me but one glimpse hail!

The Wish of the Aged Bard.

Alas! thou wilt not hear my moan;
    Then oh! ye cherished hills, farewell!
I do not see you now, adieu!
    Thou comely youth, thou lovely maid!
A summer's joy was given to you,
    But ah! my winter ne'er can fade.

Oh! carry me where I can hear
    The cascade murmuring afar;
And let my harp and shell be near,
    And shield that saved my sires in war.

Then, gentle breeze, that lov'st to stray!
    Oh! come with kindness o'er the wave,
And swiftly bear my shade away,
    To the bright island of the brave;
Where those who long have left our arms,
    Whose absence we have sorely wept,
Are deaf to music's sweetest charms,
    And in soft chains of slumber kept.

Oh! open to my weary ghost
    The hall where Daol and Ossian dwell;
The night shall come, the bard be lost,
    And none his hiding place may tell.

But yet, before the hour is come,
    In which my spirit shall be borne
To Ardven, and the bard's bright home,
    From whence none ever may return,
Give me, to cheer the lonely way,
    My much-loved harp and soothing shell,
And ending thus my life's last day,
    I'll bid them both for aye farewell!

NOTES ON GAELIC GRAMMAR AND ORTHOGRAPHY.

(Continued from p. 79.)

The following notes apply more especially to the edition of the Gaelic Scriptures with marginal references, recently published by the National Bible Society of Scotland. We expect to be able, at another time, to notice more fully this last attempt to revise the Gaelic Scriptures; and, therefore, we confine our present remarks to some points suggested by a somewhat careful reading of the last two chapters of the New Testament. It is, perhaps, right to state that we take up these chapters, not because we consider them either better or worse than other chapters in the same edition, but simply because they happen to come first under our notice. To enable the reader to judge how far later revisers have improved upon the work of their predecessors, we print the successive verses of these chapters from the editions of 1690, 1767, 1796, 1826, 1860, and 1880 respectively. A few words about these editions may be interesting.

The edition of 1690 is O'Donnell's Irish Translation published in the Roman character, for the benefit of the Highlanders of Scotland, by Mr. Robert Kirke, minister of Balquidder. This edition is now very scarce. The edition of 1767 was the first published in Scottish Gaelic. It was prepared by Dr. James Stewart, minister of the parish of Killin, Perthshire, and may be regarded as a translation from the original, although the translator must have made use largely of O'Donnell's previous translation. The edition of 1796 was revised by Dr. James Stewart before his death; and it was, subsequently, prepared for publication by his son, Dr. John Stewart, minister of Luss, the translator of the 1st, 2nd, and 3rd parts (Genesis—Canticles) of the Gaelic Old Testament. The edition of 1826 was prepared by a committee of the General Assembly, and is the last edition which received the Assembly's sanction. The edition of 1860 was prepared by Drs. Maclauchlan, Edinburgh, and Clerk, Kilmallie, for the Edinburgh Bible Society, and now forms the 8vo edition sold, but with a different title-page, by the National Bible Society. Since this edition was first published in 1860, many corrections, several of which were suggested by the writer of these notes, have been introduced into it; but in consequence of the difficulty of making alterations in stereotype-plates, the attempts at correction have frequently resulted in other errors as awkward as those it was sought to remove. Altogether, this edition is extremely inaccurate; and now it stands practically condemned, as we shall have occasion by-and-bye to show, by its own editors! The edition of 1880, to which the following remarks chiefly refer, has been prepared by the editors of the edition of 1860:—

Rev. xxi. 1.—"Agus do chonnairc mé neamh núadh, agus talamh

nuadh: òir do chúaidh an céidneamh agus an céud thalamh thoruinn: agus ní raibh fairrge ann ní sa mhó." (Kirke, 1690).

"Agus chunnaire mi neamh nuadh, agus talamh nuadh: oir chuaidh an ceud neamh agus an ceud talamh thairis; agus cha raibh fairge ann ni's mò." (Stewart, 1767).

"Agus chunnaic mi nèamh nuadh, agus talamh nuadh: oir chaidh an ceud nèamh agus an ceud talamh thairis; agus cha robh fairge ann ni's mò." (Stewart, 1796.)

"Agus chunnaic mi nèamh nuadh, agus talamh nuadh: oir chaidh an ceud nèamh agus an ceud talamh thairis; agus cha robh fairge ann ni's mò." (Assembly's Edition, 1826).

"Agus chunnaic mi nèamh nuadh, agus talamh nuadh: oir chaidh an ceud nèamh agus an ceud talamh thairis; agus cha robh fairge ann ni's mò." (M'L. and C., 1860).

"Agus chunnaic mi nèamh nuadh, agus talamh nuadh: oir chaidh an ceud nèamh agus an ceud talamh thairis; agus cha robh fairge ann na's mò." (M'L. and C., 1880).

"An ceud talamh" means "the hundred earths," not "the first earth," which in Gaelic is "an ceud thalamh."

The well-known rule in Gaelic grammar according to which *ceud* (first) aspirates, whilst *ceud* (hundred) does not aspirate the word following, is easily explained. *Ceud* (first), in O. Gael. *cét*, is from a base with vocalic auslaut (cf. p. 39 and the Gaulish names *Cintu-genus*, *Cintu-gena* = O. Gael. *Cet-gen* = mod. *Ceudghin*, *Cintu-gnatus*, *Cintu-gnata* = O. Gael. *Cet-gnáth* = mod. *Ceudghnáth*); but *ceud* (hundred) in O. Gael. *cét*, W. *cant*, terminated originally with a consonant (cf. Lat. *centum*, Skr. *çatam*, Zend. *çatem*, Gr. 'ἑ-κατόν, all from a primitive base *kantum*). Kirke's edition, which follows O'Donnell's, has "an ceud thalamh" (the first earth) correctly. In all subsequent editions, a mistake, which originated probably from oversight, has been continued.

"An ceud nèamh," which, according to the present mode of printing Gaelic, may mean either "the first heaven" or "the hundred heavens," furnishes an example of the inconvenience of not having the aspiration of the liquids l, n, and r distinguished by appropriate signs. This serious defect in Gaelic typography might easily be remedied by marking, in future publications, the aspirated sound of l with a cross-bar, and of n and r with a dot placed over them, as in the 1826 edition of the Gaelic Scriptures and the Highland Society's Dictionary.

Chonnaire (saw), from *con-darc* (saw, have seen; root *dark*, to see, connected with Gr. δέρκ-ομαι, I see), is not now used in Scottish spoken Gaelic; but the *nn* of *chunnaic*, from *conacciu* = *con-ad-ciu*, from root *cas*, Skr. *caksh*, may, perhaps, be traced to its influence. It may be noticed that the sing. forms of the consuetudinal past tense, in O'Donovan's Gramm., are from the root *dark*, whilst the plur. forms are from the root *cas*. In Scottish Gaelic, *chunnaic*, 3rd pers. sing., is the common form for the three persons, sing. and plur. In *chonnairc*, *nn* = *nd*. Initial *c* is aspirated because *do*, or older *ro*, is understood before the preterite.

Na's has been substituted, very unnecessarily, for *ni's*, O. Gael. *indaas*, before the comparative *mò* in the edition of 1880. See O'Donovan's Gramm., p. 118, where the following quotation from a poem, attributed to St. Columba, is given in support of *nios* or *ni's*: "Gidh airchind shíres ní is mó" (though a prince should ask more). *Ni's* is the form hitherto used in the Gaelic Scriptures and in all other works written with any degree of accuracy; and, therefore, it should not have been displaced merely for reasons based upon erroneous views of Gaelic etymology. We have heard one of the editors of this edition urge as a reason for the adoption of *na's*, that it is connected with the comparative *neasa* (next)!

2. "Agus do chonnairc misi Eóin, an chathair náomhtha Ierusalem núadh, ag teachd o Dhia a núas ó neamh, ar na hullmhughadh, amhuil ghléusas bean núadhphósda i fein fá chomhair a fir" (Kirke, 1690).

"Agus chunnairc mise Eoin a' chaithir naomha, Ierusalem nuadh, ag teachd a nuas o Dhia a neamh, air a h ull'uchadh mar bhean-bainnse air a sgeadachadh gu maiseach fa chomhair a fir" (Stewart, 1767).

"Agus chunnaic mise Eoin a' chathair naomha, Ierusalem nuadh, a' teachd a nuas o Dhia a nèamh, air a h-ulluchadh mar bhean-bainnse air a sgeadachadh fa chomhair a fir" (Stewarts, 1796).

"Agus chunnaic mise Eoin am baile naomh, Ierusalem nuadh, a' teachd a nuas o Dhia á nèamh, air ulluchadh mar bhean-bainnse air a sgeadachadh fa chomhair a fir" (Assembly's Ed., 1826).

"Agus chunnaic mise Eoin am baile naomh, Ierusalem nuadh, a' teachd a nuas o Dhia á neamh, air ulluchadh mar bhean-bainnse air a sgeadachadh fa chomhair a fir" (M'L. and C., 1860).

"Agus chunnaic mise Eoin am baile naomh, Ierusalem nuadh,

a' teachd a nuas o Dhia á nèamh, air ullachadh mar bhean-bainnse air a sgeadachadh fa chomhair a fir" (M'L. and C., 1880).

In the edition of 1826, "am baile" (the town) was substituted for "a' chathair" (the city) and "air ulluchadh" (he was prepared) for "air a h-ulluchadh" (she was prepared). These changes appear awkward in Gaelic, chiefly on account of *Ierusalem* (fem.), which is represented as a "bride adorned or prepared for her husband," being followed by a masc. pronoun (he, i.e., the bride, was prepared). This awkwardness would be entirely removed by restoring *cathair* (fem.) and "air a h-ulluchadh," as in the edition of 1796.

In the edition of 1860, "neamh" has no accent; but this mistake has been corrected in the edition of 1880.

The apostrophe, which stands for the masc. poss. pronoun between an infinitive beginning with a vowel or *f* and the preceding preposition, was omitted before "ulluchadh" in the ed. of 1826, and has not been supplied in any subsequent edition. For "air ulluchadh," therefore, write "air 'ulluchadh" like "air 'aireamh" (Is. liii. 12).

In the ed. of 1880, *a* has been substituted for *u* in "ulluchadh," a word which has known many changes, and which, therefore, might have been spared one for which no good reason can be assigned. From the root *las* (= Lat. *las*, Skr. *lash*) came *air-lam* (ready, prepared) with its various forms *er-lam*, *ir-lam*, *aur-lam*, *ur-lam*. From *urlam* came, through assimilation and aspiration, *ullamh*, and from *ullamh* came *ullamhuchadh*, *ullmhuchadh*, *ull'uchadh* (1767), and *ulluchadh*. In Arran and some districts of the Highlands, *ullmhuchadh* is the form now in regular use. The pref. *air* = **pari*, is cognate with Eng. *for*. For the double suff. *ugad*, *ugud*, &c., cf. Z. 803.

3. "Agus do chúala mé guth mór ó neamh, ag rádh; Feuch, tabernacuil Dé ag daóinibh, agus do dhéunuidh seision comhnuidhe na bhfhochair: agus béid siadsan na bpubal aige, agus biáidh Día féin na bhfochairsion" (Kirke, 1690).

"Agus chuala mi guth mòr a neamh, ag radh, Feuch, ata pàilliun Dhe maille re daoinibh, agus ni è comhnuidh maille riu, agus bithidh iadsan 'n am pobull aige, agus bithidh Dia fein maille riu, agus 'n a Dhia dhoibh" (Stewart, 1767).

"Agus chuala mi guth mòr a nèamh, ag radh, Feuch, tha pailliun Dhé maille re daoinibh, agus ni esan comhnuidh maille riu, agus bithidh iadsan 'nan sluagh aige, agus bithidh Dia féin maille riu, agus 'na Dhia dhoibh" (Stewarts, 1796).

"Agus chuala mi guth mòr á nèamh ag ràdh, Feuch, *tha* pàilliun Dhé maille ri daoinibh, agus ni esan còmhnuidh maille riu, agus bithidh iadsan 'nan sluagh dha, agus bithidh Dia féin maille riu, agus 'na Dhia dhoibh" (Assembly's Ed., 1826).

"Agus chuala mi guth mòr á nèamh ag ràdh, Feuch, *tha* pàilliun Dhé maille ri daoinibh, agus ni esan còmhnuidh maille riu, agus bithidh iadsan 'n an sluagh dha, agus bithidh Dia féin maille riu, agus 'n a Dhia dhoibh" (M'L. and C., 1860).

"Agus chuala mi guth mòr á nèamh ag ràdh, Feuch, *tha* pàilliun Dhé maille ri daoinibh, agus ni esan còmhnuidh maille riu, agus bithidh iadsan 'n an sluagh dha, agus bithidh Dia féin maille riu, agus 'n a Dhia dhoibh" (M'L. and C., 1880).

In *agus* and *ag*, both from the same root *anc*=*nac* cognate with Eng. *nigh*, the tenuis has sunk into the medial in the modern language. It may be noticed here that the conjunction *is* (and) is not, of course, a contraction of *agus*, which is only a modern form, whilst *is* occurs frequently in ancient Gaelic—both prose and poetry. It occurs also side by side with *ocus*, the ancient form of *agus*, with which, according to the phonetic laws of Gaelic, it does not seem to have any connection. We regret to find this Gaelic word, which is still used in spoken Gaelic, banished from the last edition of the metrical psalms, and the contraction '*us* (pronounced like *oose* in *loose*, *goose*), which does not even represent the sound of *is*, substituted for it. This change has been introduced under the idea that *is* is a contracted form of *agus*.

Such of our readers as are not acquainted with Gaelic may form some idea of the value of this last attempt to improve the Gaelic language, by picturing to themselves two joint-editors of Virgil trying to improve the Aeneid by substituting for the conjunction *et* the second syllable of *atque* with an apostrophe before it to mark the elision of the first syllable, the editors having taken into their heads the idea that *et* is a contracted form of *atque*, and that '*que* would be a much better word—in short, that Virgil and all other Latin writers committed a mistake, or something akin to a mistake, when they did not use '*que* instead of *et!*

The aspiration of "chuala" is caused by the preceding particle *do* (understood) cognate with Eng. *to*, but in ancient Gaelic *ro* cognate with Lat. *pro*, Gr. πρό. *Ro* was prefixed to the preterite, with which it formed one word. It has disappeared from modern Gaelic except in a few petrified forms, but its influence remains in the regular aspiration of the preterite.

Chuala is a reduplicated preterite (*cochla) from root *clu* (to hear), cognate with Gr. κλύω, &c.

Ràdh (= O. Gael. *rád*; infin. of *rád-im* or *rád-iu*, I say, cognate with Goth. *rod-jan*, to speak, A. S. *ráed-an*, Eng. *rede*) occurs sometimes without an accent, but should always be accented. The practice of using the grave accent in the modern language where the acute is used in the old, is awkward. We know of no good reason for discontinuing the ancient mode of accentuation.

In *feuch* (behold), *eu = é*. Cf. O. Gael. *féchaim* = Mod. Ir. *féachaim*. No accent should be written over *eu*; for, (1) it is unnecessary as *eu* is always long, and (2) it is erroneous, for as *eu = é*, *éu* is equivalent to *e* with two accents! In the matter of accentuation, as well as in many other things, Mr. James Munro's Grammar is not a safe guide. The other modern diphthongs which are always long, and, therefore, require no accents, are *ao = ae*, *ia = é* (frequently), and *ua = ó*.

The attenuated or weakened form *tha* was substituted here in the edition of 1796 for *ata*, the form in the edition of 1767. On the frequent use of *tha*, Dr. A. Stewart has the following pertinent remark (cf. Gram. 2nd Ed. p. 75):—"The present affirmative 'ta' is often written 'tha.' This is one of many instances where there appears reason to complain of the propensity remarked in Part I. (of Grammar) in those who speak Gaelic, to attenuate its articulations by aspiration." The general rule of aspiration in Gaelic should be adhered to as closely as possible, except where invariable usage has sanctioned a departure from it, as in those cases in which it has become a regular mark of gender. When, however, two forms of the same word, a more organic and a more weakened or corrupt form, exist side by side in the living language, the former ought surely to be used in preference to the latter in a translation of the Scriptures.

We heartily concur in Dr. Stewart's emphatic disapproval of the introduction of corrupt provincialisms into the Gaelic Scriptures; but had he been acquainted with ancient Gaelic, he would have written differently in regard to the particular example of supposed corruption condemned in the following remarks: "Another corrupt way of writing 'ta,' which has become common is 'ata.' This has probably taken its rise from uniting the relative to the verb; as 'an uair *ata* mi,' instead of 'an uair *a ta*,' &c.; 'mar *a ta*,' &c. Or, it may, perhaps, have proceeded from a too compliant regard to a provincial pronunciation." These statements, however, are of great value, as showing the place which *ata*, correctly *atà* or *atá*, held, in Dr. Stewart's time, in the language of the people, a place which, indeed, notwithstanding the unfair treatment to which it has been subjected, this old and classical form still maintains. *A tá* (= *ad-tá*) is from *atáu* (I am) = *ad-táu* (= *ad-stau), agreeing both etymologically and as to meaning with Lat. *asto* (I stand, I exist) = *ad-sto* = *ad-stao*.

Towards this ancient but still healthy and vigorous form, the editors of the eds. of 1860 and 1880 have conceived an inveterate hostility which has moved them to do their utmost to destroy it. Accordingly, they have deliberately removed it from the numerous places in which it was retained, although with its prefix separated from it, in the edition of 1826 and its reprints, and have substituted for it, not *tá*, but the weakened form *tha*, of which Dr. Stewart disapproved. So great, indeed, has been their destructive zeal that, in numerous instances, they have cancelled the relative before *tá*, mistaking it for the prefix of *atá*. Of this mode of revising the Scriptures by cancelling words which hold an essential place in the construction of sentences, the following examples occur in the early chapters of John's Gospel (eds. 1860 and 1880,): (Ch. i. 22), "Ciod tha thu 'g ràdh mu do thimchioll féin" (the relative *a* cancelled before *tha*); (ch. i. 38) "Ciod tha sibh ag iarraidh" (the relative cancelled before *ta*, which is changed into *tha*); (ch. iii. 4) "'n uair tha e aosda" for "'nuair a ta e aosda" in edition 1826; (iv. 9) "Cionnus tha"? for "Cionnus a ta"? in edition 1826; (iv. 11) "Cia as tha"? for "Cia as a ta"? in edition 1826; (iv. 27) "Ciod tha thu 'g iarraidh"? for "Ciod a tha thu 'g iarraidh"? in 1826; (v. 7) "Ach am feadh tha" for "Ach am feadh a ta" in edition 1826; (v. 21) "Oir mar tha an t- Athair" for "Oir mar a ta an t-athair" in edition 1826; (v. 21) "Is amhuil sin tha am Mac" for "Is amhuil sin a ta am Mac" in edition 1826; (v. 26) "Oir mar tha aige an Athair" for "Oir mar a ta aig an Athair" in edition 1826; (vi. 57) "Mar tha 'n t-Athair beò" for "Mar a ta 'n t-Athair beò" in edition 1826.

These mistakes, for they cannot with propriety be called anything else, caused by not distinguishing the parts of speech, have produced, as we might expect, anomalous constructions without number, which must prove very perplexing to persons desirous of learning the grammar of the Gaelic language. For example, in John v., 57, the relative is cancelled before *tha* in the first clause of the verse, but is retained before it in the very next clause, the antecedent being the same in both cases! It is scarcely necessary to notice that, in the above examples, the relative is used as a conjunction. Cf. the last quotation from Stewart's Grammar, and also p. 94 of the same work.

"Esan." *S* before or after a slender vowel is pronounced in Gaelic like *sh* in *show*, but before or after a broad vowel like *s* in *sort*. It is irregular, therefore, in mod. Gaelic, to have *s*, in the same word, preceded by a slender and followed by a broad vowel, and *vice versa*. In "esan," therefore, the pronoun *e* should be separated by a hyphen from the emphatic particle -*san*. In accordance with the rule of pronunciation now referred to, the demonstrative pronouns *so* (this) and *sud* (yonder, that there) should be written *seo* and *siud* as the modern forms of *seo* and *siut*, which are found in the ancient language alongside of *so* and *sút*. In these pronouns, *s* is invariably pronounced like *sh* by Scottish Highlanders.

(*To be continued.*)

CUMHA MHIC-CRIOMTHAINN.
(MACRIMMON'S LAMENT.)

Bratach bhuadhail Mhic-Leòid o'n tùr mhòr a' lasadh,
'S luchd-iomramh nan ràmh greasadh bhàrc thar a' ghlas-chuan;
Bogha, sgiath, 's claidheamh mòr, 's tuagh gu leòn, àirm nan fleasgach,
'S Mac-Criomthainn cluich cuairt, " Soraidh bhuan do Dhun-Bheagain."

Slàn leis gach creig àrd ris 'bh-'eil ghìrich àrd-thonnon,
Slàn leis gach gleann fàs 'san dean cràc-dhaimh an langan;
Eilein Sgiathanaich àigh! slàn le d' bheanntaibh 's guirm' fir-ich,
Tillidh, dh'fheudtadh, Mac-Leòid, ach cha bheò do Mhac-Criomthainn.

Soraidh bhuan do'n gheal-cheò, a tha còmhdachadh Chuilinn!
Slàn leis gach blàth-shùil, 'th'air an Dun 's iad a' tuireadh!
Soraidh bhuan do'n luchd-ciùil, 's tric 'chuir sunnd orm is tioma—
Sheòl Mac-Criomthainn thar sàil, is gu bràth cha till tuilleadh.

Nuallan allt' na pìob-mhòir a' cluich marbh-rainn an fhilidh,
Agus dearbh-bhrat a' bhàis mar fhalluing aig' uime;

Ach cha mheataich mo chrìdh' is cha ragaich mo chuislean,
Ged dh' fhalbham le m' dheòin 's fios nach till mi chaoidh
    tuilleadh.

'S tric a chluinnear fuaim bhinn caoi thiom-chridh' Mhic-
    Criomthainn
'Nuair 'bhios Gàidheil a' falbh thar an fhairge 'gan iomain—
O! chaomh thir ar gràidh, o do thràigh 's rag ar n-imeachd ;
Och! cha till, cha till, cha till sinn tuilleadh!

MACRIMMON'S LAMENT.

(Translation by Sir Walter Scott).

Macleod's wizard flag from the grey castle sallies,
The rowers are seated, unmoored are the galleys ;
Gleam war-axe and broad-sword, clang target and quiver,
As Macrimmon plays "Farewell to Dunvegan for ever!"

"Farewell to each cliff, on which breakers are foaming ;
Farewell, each dark glen, in which red deer are roaming ;
Farewell, lonely Skye, to lake, mountain, and river ;
Macleod may return, but Macrimmon shall never!"

"Farewell the bright clouds that on Coolin are sleeping ;
Farewell the bright eyes in the fort that are weeping ;
To each minstrel delusion, farewell! and for ever—
Macrimmon departs, to return to you never!"

"The Banshee's wild voice sings the death-dirge before me,
And the pall of the dead for a mantle hangs o'er me ;
But my heart shall not flag, and my nerve shall not quiver,
Though devoted I go—to return again never!"

Too oft' shall the note of Macrimmon's bewailing
Be heard when the Gael on their exile are sailing :—
"Dear land! to the shores, whence unwilling we sever,
Return—return—return we shall never!"

    Cha till, cha till, cha till sinn tuilleadh,
    Cha till, cha till, cha till sinn tuilleadh,
    Cha till, cha till, cha till sinn tuilleadh,
    Ged thileas Mac-Leòid, cha till Macrimmon!

AN TUIREADH[1].

(THE DIRGE).

Dh'iadh ceò nan stùc mu eudan Chuiliun,
Is sheinn a' bhean-shìth a torman mulaid ;
Tha sùilean gorm ciùin 'san Dùn a' sileadh,
O'n thriall thu uainn 's nach till thu tuilleadh.

  Séisd.—Cha till, cha till, cha till Mac-Criomthainn,
   An cogadh no 'n sìth cha till e tuilleadh ;
   Le h-airgiod no nì cha till Mac-Criomthainn,
   Cha till gu bràth gu là na cruinne.

Tha osag nam beann gu fann ag imeachd,
Gach sruthan 's gach allt gu mall le bruthach ;
Tha ealta nan speur feadh gheugan dubhach,
A' caoi gu'n d'fhalbh 's nach till thu tuilleadh.

Tha'n fhairge fa dheòidh làn bròin is mulaid,
Tha'm bàta fo sheòl ach dhiùlt i siubhal,
Tha gàirich nan tonn le fuaim neo-shubhach,
Ag ràdh gu'n d'fhalbh 's nach till thu tuilleadh.

Cha chluinnear do cheòl 's an dùn mu fheasgar,
'S mac-talla nam mùr le mùirn 'ga fhreagairt,
Gach fleasgach is òigh gun cheòl gun bheadradh,
O'n thriall thu uainn 's nach till thu tuilleadh.

[1] The Dirge is said to have been the response of Macrimmon's sweetheart to the "Cumha" or Lament.

For the music of "Macrimmon's Lament," on next page, we are indebted to Mr. Colin Brown, editor of the *Thistle*. This air, one of the finest of our Highland melodies, is more accurate and natural as now noted than in the common sets. The change of Mode of the Scale between the first and second parts without any change of key is peculiarly striking and effective.

We gladly avail ourselves of this opportunity of calling the attention of our readers to the *Thistle*—a musical publication carefully edited, and in which are found many of our finest Scottish and Highland melodies admirably arranged.

MACRIMMON'S LAMENT.—"CHA TILL MI TUILLEADH."

VARIATION.

www.ingramcontent.com/pod-product-compliance
Lightning Source LLC
Chambersburg PA
CBHW020308170426
43202CB00008B/534